The Last Rising of
the Agricultural Labourers

*Rural Life and Protest in
Nineteenth-Century England*

BARRY REAY

CLARENDON PRESS · OXFORD
1990

Oxford University Press, Walton Street, Oxford OX2 6DP
Oxford New York Toronto
Delhi Bombay Calcutta Madras Karachi
Petaling Jaya Singapore Hong Kong Tokyo
Nairobi Dar es Salaam Cape Town
Melbourne Auckland
and associated companies in
Berlin Ibadan

Oxford is a trade mark of Oxford University Press

Published in the United States
by Oxford University Press, New York

© Barry Reay, 1990

All rights reserved. No part of this publication may be reproduced,
stored in a retrieval system, or transmitted, in any form or by any means,
electronic, mechanical, photocopying, recording or otherwise, without
the prior permission of Oxford University Press

British Library Cataloguing in Publication Data
Reay, Barry, 1950–
The last rising of the agricultural labourers: rural life
and protest in nineteenth-century England.
1. England. Rural regions. Agricultural industries.
Labourers. Riots, history
I. Title 331.7630942
ISBN 0-19-820187-7

Library of Congress Cataloging in Publication Data
Reay, Barry.
The last rising of the agricultural labourers: rural life and
protest in nineteenth-century England/Barry Reay.
p. cm.
Includes bibliographical references.
1. Hernhill (England)—History. 2. Agricultural laborers—
England—Kent—Political activity—History—19th century. 3. Poor
laws—England—Kent—History—19th century. 4. Villages—England—
Kent—History—19th century. 5. England—Rural conditions—19th
century. 6. Kent (England)—History. I. Title.
DA690.H55R43 1990
942.2'33—dc20
ISBN 0-19-820187-7

Typeset by Cambrian Typesetters, Frimley, Surrey
Printed and bound in
Great Britain by Biddles Ltd.
Guildford & King's Lynn

For Harold Kay

PREFACE

The year 1988 was one of celebration and commemoration: the millennium of the Russian Orthodox Church, the 400th anniversary of the defeat of the Spanish Armada, the tercentenary of the English 'Revolution' of 1688 (and the death of John Bunyan), Australia's bicentenary, the centenaries of Lawrence of Arabia and Jack the Ripper, the fortieth anniversary of the British national health service, the twenty-fifth anniversary of the death of J. F. Kennedy. I was in London for the whole of that year, completing a study of an event whose sesquicentenary (also in 1988) came and went with little impact, apart from some coverage in the Kent press, a few columns in the *Independent*, and an article (my own) in *History Workshop*. I refer to the Battle of Bosenden Wood (1838), the last rising of the agricultural labourers. While others were reliving the glories of 1968 (twenty years on), I was engrossed in another century and another year. I leave it to the reader to decide whether my self-denial has proved worth while.

As with the making of most books, the emotional, intellectual, and financial debts have piled up over the years. The greatest of all is to my own long-suffering family, Athina Tsoulis and our children Alexa and Kristina. Ignoring their grim protests that they do not want to be mentioned in my 'bloody book', I acknowledge their contribution first, for reasons that they will be painfully aware of. Friends too bear the brunt of a researcher's obsessions. I would particularly like to thank John Walsh (of Walthamstow, not Oxford) for reasons which again need not be listed in black-and-white. Typists are too often mentioned last in a book's preface. Let me flout convention and warmly thank Barbara Batt for struggling with the Reay manuscripts—even by post from the UK!

I was once accused of using acknowledgements as a kind of exorcism to ward off potential criticism; those mentioned in a preface are unlikely to turn against the person who is thanking them for their help or stimulus, and possible critics, so the logic goes, are disarmed accordingly. I must admit that this possibility had never occurred to me before, and I am sure that this is an instance where the review tells us more about the reviewer (in this case, Clive Holmes) than it does about the book or its author. How does one acknowledge debts? 'Thank you to all those unnamed people who have helped me in unmentionable ways'? I can only say that editors of journals of review, and potential reviewers, should not feel at all restricted by the totemistic ritual that I am about to observe. Indeed, my acknowledgements include many people who would relish the opportunity to defy exorcism.

As a seventeenth-century historian moving into a new topic in a new period—indeed, as something of an interloper—I have been struck by the generosity of those working on the nineteenth century. Alun Howkins, David Jones, John Stevenson, and David Vincent read what was to become Chapter 4 and were encouraging from an early stage. So too have Ian Carter and Mick Reed, who have been a constant source of stimulus and expertise. Other nineteenth-century specialists have provided me with references and specific information, or have listened to me tolerantly: Malcolm Chase, Jules Ginswick, Roger Kain, Rohan McWilliam, Jean Robin, Brian Short, W. B. Stephens, David Thomson, Richard Wall, Roger Wells. I owe a special debt to Keith Snell, who has patiently read and commented upon the whole manuscript, and whose enthusiastic and constructive response played an important role in the final shaping of the book.

I have drawn too upon the kindness of friends and colleagues working on other periods or countries. David Rollison was very helpful. Ken Lockridge and Maureen Molloy helped me get started on family reconstitution, while Vivien Brodsky spent many a long hour in Auckland and Adelaide checking my forms with me and answering what must have seemed intolerably inane questions. Michael Belgrave and Jack Vowles took time away from New Zealand topics to devise computer programs to answer the questions that I wanted to ask of the nineteenth-century census material. Hilary Haines very kindly found time to read my chapter on Courtenay's madness. As ever, Bridget and Christopher Hill have been a source of encouragement and advice: both have read the typescript, and their comments have been invaluable. Bob Bushaway, Terry Byres, Lyndal Roper, and Jim Sharpe arranged for captive audiences upon whom I could try out my ideas.

The University of Auckland has been generous in its responses to repeated demands for financial assistance, and I am grateful for the patience of successive research committees. A variety of libraries and other institutions have been helpful: the State Library of Tasmania, the Institute of Historical Research, the Institute of Agricultural History and Museum of English Rural Life (Reading), the John Rylands University Library of Manchester, Lambeth

Preface ix

Palace Library, Mary Evans Picture Library, the National Army Museum, the Bodleian Library, Oxford, the Postgraduate Medical Centre of the Kent and Canterbury Hospital, Somerset House, University College Library, and the University of London Library. Most of my research, however, was carried out either at, or with material provided by, the various branches of the British Library (particularly the Newspaper Library at Colindale), the Cathedral, City, and Diocesan Record Office at Canterbury, the Kent County Archives Office at Maidstone, and the Public Record Office (principally at Portugal Street and Kew), so I owe them a great debt. I am particularly grateful to the staff of the Kent Archives Office, who sometimes must have despaired of ever ridding themselves of their overseas visitor but who none the less were always cheerful, informative, and super-efficient. Individuals too have come to my assistance. J. W. Horsley kindly allowed me to consult family papers. Ian Knight put me on the track of some important illustrations in the *Weekly Chronicle*. Arthur Percival has been consistently helpful, providing me with, among other things, copies of material held by the Faversham Society. In Auckland, at the University Library Cathie Hutchinson and Rainer Wolcke have been especially tolerant of my continual requests; Brian Donovan and his colleagues in the University's photographic laboratory have done wonders with my feeble attempts with the camera; and Jan Kelly, of the Department of Geography, has provided technical expertise on map-making (though she should not be held responsible for the final products).

But this book would never have been written at all without the contribution of people living in Hernhill and Dunkirk. Graham Hudson has been extremely generous with his knowledge of the events of 1838, providing me also with copies of photographs, a rare print, and a valuable map of the battle. Tommy Boorman and Len Rooks have helped with visual material for the book. The Reverend E. A. Stacey very kindly arranged for the copying of local parish registers. Sandys and Lesley Dawes and Harold and Marian Kay provided a wonderful blend of hospitality and encouragement—how often does a historian get fed by the people who allow him access to their private papers, and who read and comment on his work-in-progress as well! Without Sandys's encouragement, the writing of this book undoubtedly would have been a more protracted and less enjoyable experience.

I owe most of all to the knowledge and enthusiasm of Harold

Kay, the great-great grandson of the bailiff William Kay (one of the cast in the pages that follow). Our walks (and drives) around the parish, armed with my annotated copy of the nineteenth-century Hernhill tithe survey, provided a feel for the place that can never come from archival work. Harold's collection of local postcards and photographs has also proved invaluable. On each visit there would be some new document, photograph, or piece of information. The dedication of this book is but small recompense for such kindness.

B.R.

Auckland
January 1989

CONTENTS

List of Plates	xii
List of Figures	xiv
List of Maps	xv
List of Tables	xvi
Abbreviations	xvii
Introduction	1

PART I   THE SETTING

1. Structures	7
2. Labouring Life	42
3. Conflict and Discontents	69

PART II   THE RISING

4. The Rising	85
5. Courtenay	110
6. The Rioters	130

PART III   THE AFTERMATH

7. Repercussions	151
8. Epilogue	165

PART IV   IMPLICATIONS

9. Rural Life and Protest in Nineteenth-Century England	175
Notes	191
Index	219

LIST OF PLATES

1. The area between Faversham and Canterbury
2. Hernhill: a view from the church tower, pre-1912
3. Mount Ephraim c.1838 (before the rebuilding)
4. Mount Emphraim today
5. Bessborough House (Bessborough Farm)
6. Lavender Farm
7. Waterham Farm
8. Dargate House
9. Barnfield Farm
10. Brook Farm
11. Cherry Orchard Farm (or Coleman's Land), early this century
12. An archetypal small farm: Forge Farmhouse, Staple Street, 1904
13. Bosenden Farm
14. The Spratts' cottage, Dargate
15. Fairbrook House
16. The Red Lion public house, Hernhill, pre-1912
17. The Dove beerhouse, Dargate, c.1870
18. Noah's Ark beerhouse, Bessborough, before its demolition this century
19. St Michael's church, Hernhill, c.1870
20. Courtenay
21. The march
22. Edward Curling on horseback
23. The murder of the 'constable', contemporary print
24. The death of Nicholas Mears: another version
25. The battle, from a contemporary drawing
26. The battle, from a contemporary print
27. The battle, from a contemporary print
28. The battle, from a contemporary print
29. The battle, from an original drawing
30. Map of the battle area, drawn in 1838
31. Plan of battle site, 1838
32. Courtenay campaigning in Canterbury in 1832
33. Contemporary oil portrait, believed to be of Courtenay
34. Courtenay—Knight of Malta
35. Courtenay—gentleman
36. Courtenay—Byronesque figure

37 Courtenay in Rookwood
38 The dead rioters
39 The dead rioters
40 Courtenay's corpse on display
41 Thomas Mears
42 William Price
43 The Dove, Dargate, in the process of refurbishment, c.1890

LIST OF FIGURES

1 Seasonality of Boughton, Dunkirk, and Hernhill marriages, 1813–1840
2 Seasonality of Boughton, Dunkirk, and Hernhill burials, 1813–1840

LIST OF MAPS

1. The hamlets and settlements of Hernhill and Dunkirk, c.1838
2. The recruitment march on 29 and 30 May 1838, starting from Courtenay's base at Bosenden Farm
3. The residences of the rioters: Dargate
4. The residences of the rioters: Bessborough

LIST OF TABLES

1 Some population figures, 1801–1841
2 Completed family size, Hernhill and Dunkirk, 1780–1850
3 Household structure, Hernhill and Dunkirk, 1851
4 Rural household sizes, 1851
5 Landownership and occupation in Hernhill, 1840, and Dunkirk, 1827–8
6 Male occupations, Hernhill and Dunkirk, 1841 and 1851
7 Female occupations, Hernhill and Dunkirk, 1851
8 The annual cycle and division of labour in the nineteenth century, by gender and age
9 Places of birth of Hernhill and Dunkirk inhabitants, 1851
10 Social structure of illiteracy in Hernhill and Dunkirk, 1800–1850
11 Occupations of the rioters
12 Age structure of the rioters
13 Dependency structure of the rioters
14 Social structure of the rioters: rental values

ABBREVIATIONS

CCDRO	Cathedral, City, and Diocesan Record Office, Canterbury
KAO	Kent Archives Office, Maidstone
PP	*Parliamentary Papers*
PRO	Public Record Office

Introduction

ON a warm May afternoon in 1838 (31 May, to be precise), two groups of men faced each other across a clearing in a wood in Kent, not far from Canterbury. A grossly outnumbered band of agricultural labourers confronted an armed detachment of the 45th Infantry Regiment, a number of the local landed élite (gentry and farmers), and a hastily commissioned group of constables. The labourers were led by a man known locally as 'Sir William Courtenay', but who was really one John Nicholls Tom, a former maltster from Cornwall. Within minutes of the confrontation, about twenty men, most of them the followers of Courtenay, lay dead, dying, or wounded. (Several, it would become clear from the coroner's inquest, had been both bayoneted and shot.) It was, as was observed at the time, 'a most desperate affray'; in the words of the historian E. P. Thompson, 'perhaps the most desperate on English soil since 1745'.[1]

There is already a book on the episode, by P. G. Rogers.[2] It is good on detail; there is little in the newspaper accounts that Rogers misses. But his *Battle in Bossenden Wood* is largely antiquarian in method and aim. Rogers's approach is poles apart from current historiography. The book was written over twenty-five years ago, before the impact of the now not-so-new social history and current interest in popular culture and popular protest. Rogers treated Courtenay as an early Victorian curiosity, concentrating on the man rather than on his social endorsement and the local context of his activity. However, even if his account is not likely to persuade readers to take the event seriously, Rogers did at least write a book on the Courtenay affair. For it would not be too much of a distortion to say that the battle—I will argue that it should be seen as an abortive rising—has become at best a mere footnote in British history. True, it gets a few paragraphs in J. F. C. Harrison's *Second Coming*, Thompson's *Making of the English Working Class*, and George Rudé's *Protest and Punishment*.[3] But it is in a *footnote* that it is mentioned in John Stevenson's valuable textbook *Popular Disturbances in England*;[4] and Sir William Courtenay does not rate an entry in the *Biographical Dictionary of Modern British Radicals*.[5]

I had several reasons for writing this book. The first, possibly the

2 Introduction

most compelling motive for writing anything, is that it is a fascinating story. An impostor, a man who has spent time in an asylum (the Courtenay affair touches too upon the issue of madness), becomes a messianic figure and heads a movement of popular protest. The ill-fated rising ends abortively, with a savage military massacre of civilians.

As will become clear, I see the battle as a manifestation of popular protest, and it may well be asked, Why yet another book on this subject? However, several years ago E. J. Hobsbawm and George Rudé bewailed the lack of scholarly work on *rural* protest. 'Indeed, of all the many gaps in our knowledge of the farm-labourers' world in the nineteenth century none is more shocking than our total ignorance of the forms of agrarian discontent between the rising of 1830 and the emergence of agricultural trade unionism in the early 1870s.'[6] This lacuna is less noticeable now because of the recent work of J. E. Archer, David Jones, John Knott, John Lowerson, and Roger Wells; but since the Bosenden Wood episode occurred in 1838, it should hold intrinsic interest as a way into the post-1830 period. In comparison to the attention that has been lavished upon Chartism, nineteenth-century agrarian protest remains a neglected area.[7]

Perhaps the main justification for my intervention relates to the wider field of what Charles Tilly has called 'popular contention'.[8] There has been a wealth of research on this topic—we are even aware of what hours of the day were most often chosen for demonstrations[9]—but we know surprisingly little about popular mobilization and motivation. The recent work of John Walter on an abortive rising in sixteenth-century Oxfordshire and David Jones's book on the Newport insurrection of 1839 highlight the sort of analysis that can be done.[10] We know when people protested, who protested, what people did when they protested—but little about *why* individuals participated (or did not participate). In spite of the good intentions of work, much of it Marxist-inspired, on what conservative historians used to dismiss as 'the mob', the collectivity prevails. We do not know enough about the faces in the crowd, their hopes, their fears, their often muddled aspirations. The Battle in Bosenden Wood provides a unique opportunity to anatomize the crowd, to produce a detailed case study of mobilization of a kind rarely provided in studies of popular protest.

However, the events in a wood in Kent provide more than just an intriguing story and an opportunity to anatomize the crowd. Although it is a single incident, the rising sheds light in many directions. It provides a unique entry—through historical research, and in the surveys carried out in the wake of the trouble—into the world of the village, a vivid portrait of cultural divisions and day-to-day existence, a sometimes startling picture of the rural underside of early to mid-nineteenth-century England. In short, this book represents an exercise in historical reclamation. I hope to convince my readers that the abortive insurrection of 1838, and not the Swing rising of 1830, deserves the appellation 'the last rising of the agricultural labourers'. The Kent rising should be taken seriously; it merits a more prominent place in history.

PART I
The Setting

1
Structures

WHEN William Cobbett left Canterbury in September 1823, on his famous 'rural rides', he stopped on the London road on Boughton Hill, four miles from the town. It was harvest time. You there look down, he wrote, on to 'one of the finest flats in England. . . . The land here is a deep loam upon chalk. . . . The orchards grow well upon this soil. The trees grow finely, the fruit is large and of fine flavour.'[1] This was the area which, in the following decade, was to become the scene of Courtenay's ill-fated rising. The barrister Frederick Liardet, who arrived in the district in the wake of the Courtenay troubles, was also struck by its beauty. He thought it peculiarly English. 'Fields of waving corn are interspersed with gardens, hop-grounds, and orchards.' Liardet considered it both ironic and tragic that 'the moral condition of the inhabitants of so fair a spot should stand . . . in such mournful contrast with its order and beauty'.[2]

Hernhill and the Ville of Dunkirk, the parishes from which Courtenay drew nearly all his support (Dunkirk was actually an extra-parochial area at this time), were part of what Kent's historian Alan Everitt has termed the 'foothills', the county's main grain district—with the highest yields per acre—and centre for hops and fruit.[3] There were substantial acreages of turnips and pulse crops (peas and beans). Sheep were kept too on the marshes. (In the 1860s there were about five sheep for every Hernhill inhabitant.) It was therefore a mixed economy, which (we will see) provided a variety of opportunities for employment. Although our two observers were impressed by the show of 'a minute and skilful husbandry', this was also a woodland district which had provided a level of subsistence for a squatting population and a rather more lucrative income for absentee landlords and their lessees. As late as 1866, only about one-fifth of the area of the Ville of Dunkirk was clear for crops or pasture.[4] It is worth emphasizing that in some respects the early nineteenth century was still an age of wood. It was an essential raw material for use in shipbuilding, houses, and farms, for the manufacture of furniture and farm equipment, for fuel and fencing, and, important in the local context, for the

8 The Setting

making of hop-poles.[5] Timber and underwood formed investments that landowners zealously protected against the depradations of local wood-stealers.

We should not present too rosy a picture of this area between Faversham and Canterbury. It bordered malaria country, the marshes, 'a most unpleasant and unhealthy country' according to Hasted's late eighteenth-century topographical survey.[6] It also contained some dry and sandy soil, hilly land covered by broom and furze. Nor did the outsiders (who came mainly in summer) comment on the poor quality of the roads, impassable for part of the year and a great handicap to efficient farming.[7] Cobbett and Liardet were transitory observers who, unlike the agricultural labourers who comprised the bulk of the local population, did not have to eke out a living on these 'gently rising hills, and picturesque vales'.[8]

The two settlements varied in character. Neither was a traditional English village in the sense of a single nucleated settlement.[9] Hernhill was (and is) almost a classic Kent settlement, a series of hamlets rather than a village, with dwelling houses and cottages erected around several long-established farms. Dunkirk was a late settlement by Kent standards, a product of the population boom of the long eighteenth century which, according to Everitt, saw greater changes to the rural landscape than any comparable time since colonization after the Conquest.[10] Although some of the cleared settlements in the mainly forest area of Dunkirk were described in an 1820s survey as 'ancient', the Ville was essentially a squatter community. There has been some debate over its origins. Oral tradition, recorded by the minister of Boughton in the eighteenth or nineteenth century, claimed that the forests of the Blean were settled by Protestant refugees after the revocation of the Edict of Nantes. Other early nineteenth-century sources said that the area was a notorious haunt for smugglers landing contraband goods from France—hence the name 'Dunkirk'. Hasted's *History of Kent* offered a French connection of a slighly different kind. Because it was an extra-parochial area, he wrote, the forest was a haven for 'low persons of suspicious characters' (sic), 'as in a free port, which receives all who enter it without distinction': thus, again, its name.[11]

Whatever the etymological niceties, it is clear that the bulk of settlement in Dunkirk occurred in the Napoleonic wars (1793–1815) when, throughout England, the impact of war put pressure

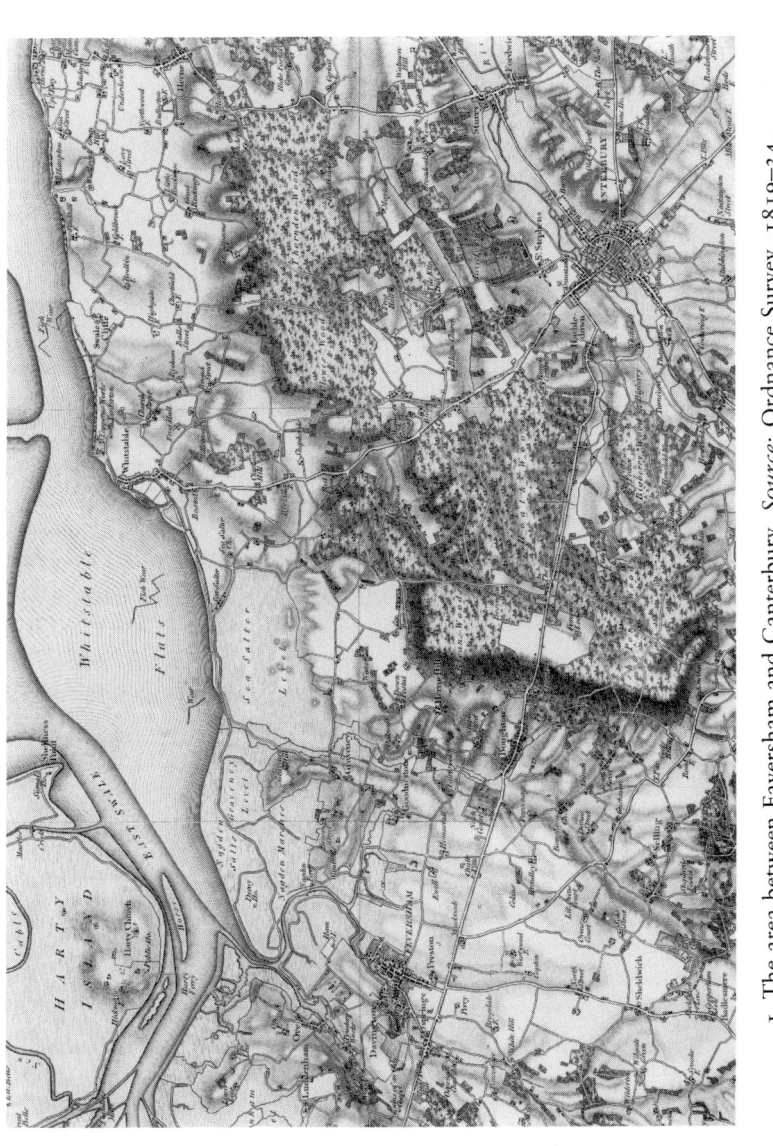

1 The area between Faversham and Canterbury. *Source:* Ordnance Survey, 1819–24.

on commons and wastes.[12] Kent was a county of long-established enclosures, and was, as the historical geographer Roger Kain has put it, 'singularly void of common';[13] Dunkirk must have been one of the few areas opened up at this time in that county. Denstrode and Dargate Commons were enclosed and their forest land was cleared.[14] A rather unique terrier, drawn up on the orders of the Commissioners of Woods, Forests, and Land Revenues, records the ages of the properties of 122 of the 132 owners of land and dwellings in Dunkirk in 1827–8. Nearly 70 per cent had been built, enclosed, or first settled in the thirty years before the survey was made: that is, since the 1790s. About 60 per cent of settlement took place in the period 1795–1815.[15] This in-migration is confirmed by the census, which records a 32 per cent increase in population in a mere ten years, 1801–11 (see Table 1).

Although they settled in Dunkirk in the 1780s rather than the 1790s, the story of the Ralphs, recorded in the settlement examinations, those 'annals of the labouring poor',[16] provides a brief sketch of what must have been the experience of many Dunkirk settlers. Thomas Ralph came from Kingsdown, near Sittingbourne—indeed, retained settlement there, for he and his wife Susanna 'frequently' received poor relief from that parish despite their links with Dunkirk. In the 1780s he obtained permission to enclose about an acre of wasteland in the manor of the hundred of Westgate (Dunkirk) at an annual quit rent of 5s. The land was in a bad state, Susanna Ralph recalled in 1817; Thomas grubbed it up and converted it to tillage. In the early 1800s they erected a small cottage which cost something between £10 and £20. (Susanna Ralph was vague about this.) Susanna remained in the cottage after the death of Thomas in 1809, although she had to send five of her seven children to Kingsdown because she could not provide for them. Her eldest son, Thomas, later appears in the settlement examinations after his discharge from the army in 1817 when he returned to Dunkirk to seek residence.[17]

Though the present number of people in Hernhill is almost identical to the number of inhabitants at the time of the Courtenay rising, the population structure of our two communities in the nineteenth century is very different from what we would expect to find today.[18] If a modern-day observer could be transported through time to Dunkirk or Hernhill in the late 1830s or early 1840s, he or she would be struck by the large numbers of young people in the lanes and around the cottages: 40 per cent of the

TABLE 1 Some population figures, 1801–1841

	1801 No.	1811 (% incr.)	1821 No.	1821 (% incr.)	1831 No.	1831 (% incr.)	1841 No.	1841 (% incr.)	1801–41 (% incr.)
England	8,350,859	(14)	9,553,021	(18)	11,281,883	(16)	13,090,523	(14)	14,997,427 (79.6)
Kent	308,667	(20)	371,701	(15)	427,224	(12)	479,558	(12)	549,353 (78.0)
Boughton	884	(13)	1,002	(23)	1,237	(5)	1,300	(6)	1,373 (55.3)
Dunkirk	338	(32)	446	(22)	543	(13)	613	(4)	638 (88.8)
Hernhill	359	(11)	398	(20)	477	(6)	507	(19)	603 (68.0)

Source: PP lxxxv (1852–3), 330–1.

population was under 15 years of age, compared with half that number today. There was also a lower proportion of elderly people. In 1851 only one in ten people was aged 60 or above: today there would be twice that number.[19] This was a period of rapid population growth, of natural increase in the national population in both town and country. As Table 1 shows, the population of Dunkirk and Hernhill rose substantially in the period 1801–41, the one just above, and the other just below, county and national averages.

People married young in this part of Kent, from 18 to 21 years of age for women and from 22 to 24 for men. In Hernhill over half the women who married between 1800 and 1851 were under 20 years old.[20] This meant that the average wife was faced with a long period of potential childbearing: it was not unusual for women to continue to have children into their late thirties or early forties, still bearing infants when their eldest began to produce their own. Consequently, families were large, bigger in fact than demographers have suggested.[21] The commonest family size was six or more children (compared with two today); 70 per cent of Hernhill and Dunkirk wives produced this number of children in the first half of the nineteenth century, and 40 per cent had from eight to ten children each (see Table 2).[22] Furthermore, their offsprings' chances of survival were good, much better than in the early modern period or in the nineteenth-century town. Though still five or six times higher than today, the infant mortality rate of 93.4 per 1,000 for Hernhill and Dunkirk was lower than the national average.[23] About one in seven children would be dead before they reached the age of 5, but most (five out of every six) would survive into their teens.[24]

It is also worth noting that these large families started early, before marriage in many cases. About 50 per cent of brides were pregnant when they stood before the altar in the first half of the nineteenth century (slightly more in Hernhill than in Dunkirk).[25] When the chances of fertilization and spontaneous miscarriage are taken into account, it is quite clear that sexual relations before marriage were commonplace in these rural communities. Indeed, first births conceived in wedlock were outnumbered by illegitimacies and premarital conceptions. As Jean Robin has pointed out (slightly tongue in cheek), the permissive society was alive in the early Victorian hamlet and village.[26]

It is a number of years since Peter Laslett established that the most common form of family structure in the England of the past

TABLE 2 Completed family size, Hernhill and Dunkirk, 1780–1850

No. of children	0	1	2	3	4	5	6	7	8	9	10	11	12	13	14	15	16	Total
No. of families	8	4	6	12	12	13	16	10	26	25	21	13	7	5	–	3	1	182
% of families	4.4	2.2	3.3	6.6	6.6	7.1	8.8	5.5	14.3	13.7	11.5	7.1	3.8	2.7	–	1.6	0.5	

No. of children	0–3	4–7	8–11	12–15	16+
No. of families	30	51	85	15	1
% of families	16.5	28.0	46.7	8.2	0.5

Mean completed family size: 7.3
Median: 8.0

TABLE 3 Household Structure, Hernhill and Dunkirk, 1851

Type	No. of households	%
Hernhill		
Solitaries	3	2.3
Simple family	104	80.6
of which:		
Married couples with children (nuclear)	(76)	(58.9)
Widowed with children	(5)	(3.9)
Married couples alone	(23)	(17.8)
Extended family	22	17.0
Multiple family	—	—
Co-resident siblings	—	—
TOTAL	129	
Dunkirk		
Solitaries	16	10.5
Simple family	112	73.2
of which:		
Married couples with children (nuclear)	(86)	(56.2)
Widowed with children	(6)	(3.9)
Married couples alone	(20)	(13.1)
Extended family	23	15.0
Multiple family	1	0.6
Co-resident siblings	1	0.6
TOTAL	153	

was the simple family household or nuclear family.[27] Few households contained kin other than husband and (or) wife and child (or children). Table 3 shows that Dunkirk and Hernhill conform to expectations. In both communities, well over half the households were nuclear in structure; only a minority (15 and 17 per cent) could be categorized as extended in form. The average household sizes (including servants) of 4.5 (Dunkirk) and 5.0 (Hernhill), and the mean nuclear family sizes of 4.0 (Dunkirk) and 4.3 (Hernhill), are close to those for other nineteenth-century rural communities (see Table 4). Just over 20 per cent of Hernhill households, mostly those of farmers, contained servants.[28]

TABLE 4 Rural household sizes, 1851

Mean no. per household of	Rural 1851*	Hernhill	Dunkirk
Heads	1.0	1.0	1.0
Wives	0.8	0.9	0.8
Children	2.5	2.4	2.2
All nuclear family	4.3	4.3	4.0
Kin	0.5	0.2	0.2
Lodgers	0.2	0.0	0.0
Servants	0.6	0.4	0.2
All	5.5	5.0	4.5

* *Source*: M. Anderson, 'Household Structure and the Industrial Revolution', in P. Laslett and R. Wall (eds.), *Household and Family in Past Time* (Cambridge, 1974), 235.

But the census-type listing (the above material was drawn from the Census of 1851) can be misleading. It provides a convenient snapshot at a given point, yet it fails to capture movement over time. When households in Hernhill and Dunkirk are traced through their *life-cycles* for three or more censuses, it emerges that from just under 50 to 60 per cent of families experienced an extended phase. If my findings are typical of the English rural experience, the hallowed nuclear family, though important, was not as normative as the Cambridge Group's studies have led us to assume.[29] Finally, while it is true that the mean household size was small, the *majority of people* (56 per cent in Hernhill and Dunkirk combined) lived in households of six or more members.

The main unit of community in both Hernhill and Dunkirk, beyond that of the household, was surely the hamlet, the equivalent of the 'neighbourhood' in urban settlements. Each hamlet would have its own well or pump, often a beershop or public house, perhaps its own common land, and usually a source of nearby employment in the form of a farm or farms. At this time Hernhill comprised four main hamlets: the area around the church (or 'Hernhill'), Staple Street, Dargate, and Bessborough (or Besborough) or the Fostall (or Forstal). There were also smaller groups of houses and cottages around farms such as Waterham and Way (Wey or Weigh) Street. Dunkirk was more untidy in its settlement pattern. There were hamlets at Denstrode, Winterbourne, and Boughton Hill, and cottages and houses were strung out along the London Road, from Boughton through to Harbledown. Hamlets did not necessarily recognize parish boundaries. Dargate, a settlement that

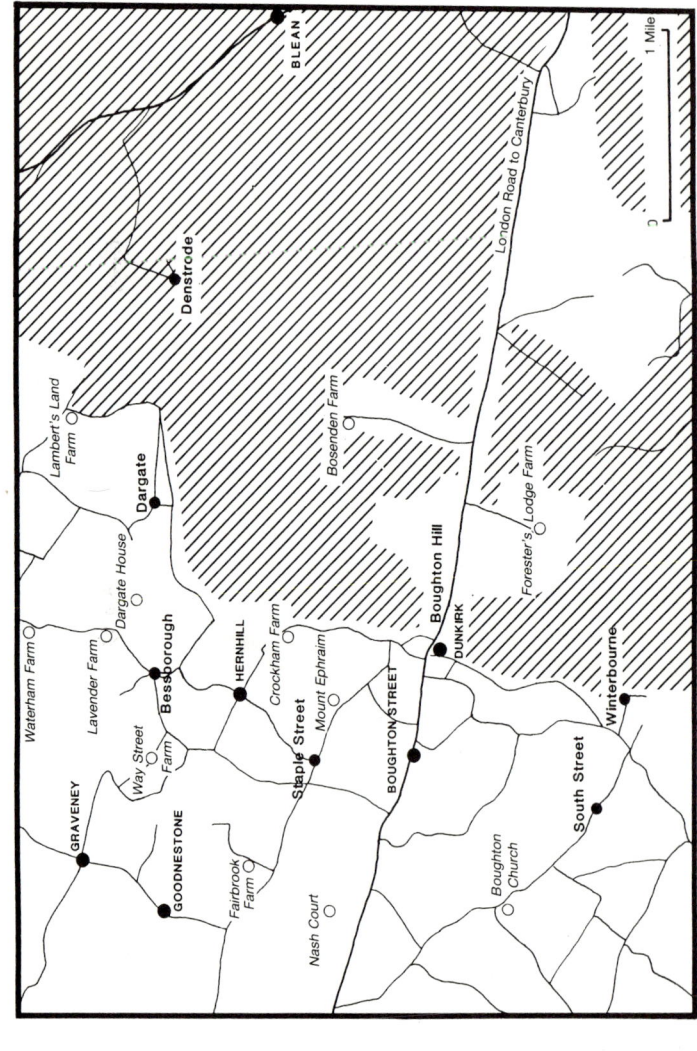

MAP 1 The hamlets and settlements of Hernhill and Dunkirk, c.1838.

2 Hernhill: a view from the church tower, pre-1912. *Source*: Len Rooks photography.

would supply much support for Courtenay, straddled the boundaries of Dunkirk and Hernhill. Denstrode was half in Dunkirk and half in Blean parish.[30] In a sense, then, Dunkirk was a fractured community looking in several directions. It merged in one corner with Boughton Street, and because it did not have a church its inhabitants turned to the churches of Boughton, Hernhill, Blean, and Harbledown.[31] When an excise officer called at a local beershop and asked for a drink, the proprietor was wary and said that she had not seen him in Dunkirk before; he was able to allay her fears by explaining that he had only been in the Ville for *two years*.[32] Dunkirk's coherence, its community identity, was something of an illusion imposed from outside. It was seen by outsiders as a settlement of lawbreakers;[33] insiders within the Ville probably identified with a particular wood or hamlet, or with a group of cottages in a bordering parish. In short, there was no single settlement that corresponded, respectively, to either the Ville of Dunkirk or the parish of Hernhill. Instead, there was a series of overlapping social arenas.[34] These 'communities' involved both self-definition and perception of the other—in a revealing phrase, the vicar of Boughton referred to his graveyard as being full of 'strangers' from Dunkirk.[35]

Agrarian historians are fond of using the categories 'open' and 'close' to describe parish structures in the nineteenth century. A close parish was in few hands, with most of the land owned by a single landlord or a few landlords who, particularly if resident in the parish, could exert a great deal of control over its inhabitants. An open parish, on the other hand, contained many estates, with a substantial number of smallholders, dispersed settlement, and less gentry control. These are what the sociologists call ideal types, helpful starting points for discussion rather than hard-and-fast lines of classification.[36]

Dunkirk and Hernhill contain elements of both categories. In Dunkirk, in classic close parish style, just over half the land was owned by two large proprietors: Sir Edward Dering, and the Dean and Chapter of Canterbury. Yet in every other respect the Ville was an archetypal open parish: a woodland, squatter area, extra-parochial, without resident squire or even a significant number of substantial farmers. It was a large parish (over 5,000 acres), a community of cottagers and small freeholders; at the end of the 1820s over 80 per cent of Dunkirk landowners had properties of less than 10 acres (see Table 5).[37]

TABLE 5 Landownership and occupation in Hernhill, 1840, and Dunkirk, 1827–8

Acres	Hernhill, 1840			Dunkirk, 1827–8		
	No.	%	% of land owned	No.	%	% of land owned
Ownership						
Under 1	16	20.0	0.2	49	37.1	0.4
1–3	3	3.7	0.2	33	25.0	1.3
3–10	16	20.0	3.2	29	22.0	2.9
10–25	14	17.5	8.2	3	2.3	0.8
25–50	10	12.5	12.8	5	3.8	2.7
50–100	12	15.0	23.2	4	3.0	5.5
100–150	6	7.5	23.6	3	2.3	6.2
150–200	—	—	—	1	0.8	3.7
200–300	2	2.5	18.2	—	—	—
300–400	1	1.2	10.2	2	1.5	13.8
400–500	—	—	—	—	—	—
500+	—	—	—	3	2.3	62.6
Occupation						
Under 1	22	27.2	0.2	66	40.7	0.5
1–3	3	3.7	0.2	30	18.5	1.1
3–10	14	17.3	2.7	35	21.6	3.5
10–25	9	11.1	4.9	10	6.2	3.2
25–50	12	14.8	12.9	5	3.1	3.4
50–100	10	12.3	21.1	4	2.5	5.5
100–150	6	7.4	23.2	4	2.5	8.8
150–200	2	2.5	11.5	2	1.2	7.2
200–300	3	3.7	23.2	1	0.6	5.0
300–400	—	—	—	2	1.2	13.4
400–500	—	—	—	—	—	—
500+	—	—	—	3	1.8	48.2

As one of the nineteenth-century gazetteers put it, the land in Hernhill was 'much subdivided'. But Hernhill had a lower percentage of smallholders than the Ville: 44 per cent compared with Dunkirk's 84 per cent. Half of the land here was in the hands of nine main landowners, although no one individual enjoyed a controlling interest. Most landownership was in the middle range of acreage (50–300 acres), reflecting an important middle range of landowners and occupiers, the farmers and the bailiffs.[38] What is most noticeable about the two parishes is the contrast in their situations, yet they both lean towards the 'open' category.

The gentry had a low profile in the immediate area. Large landowners were thickest on the ground in nearby Boughton, with John Price Lade at Wellbrook and Edward Jarman of Brenley House, both of whom had estates elsewhere in Kent. Colonel Percy Groves, a purely local figure, and one of the first to raise the alarm about Courtenay in 1838, made it into the Post Office Directory of 1845. But Nash Court, for many years the home of the most prominent landed family in the neighbourhood, and certainly the most cartographically imposing estate in the area, stood empty for the first part of the nineteenth century. (Owned by the Knatchbulls, its farm was run by a bailiff.)[39] At Hernhill, the Daweses of Mount Ephraim, who would re-establish themselves at the end of the century, were likewise absent in our period. The vicar of Hernhill, Charles Handley, occupied their then more modest residence on the hill (see Plate 3); though less grand than the late nineteenth-century Mount Ephraim (see Plate 4), the house's topography (its spacious gardens, its place on the hill) combined with Handley's life-style (his six servants and wife's fortune) to endow him with the status of *de facto* leading parish gentleman.[40] The only other gentleman in Hernhill in 1838 was Edward Stone, at the manor house near the church, but he seems to have been a very minor figure. He farmed a small piece of land and had only two servants compared with Handley's six.[41]

In Dunkirk, as Frederick Liardet complained in 1838, there was no one above the status of farmer, 'neither gentry, clergyman, surgeon, nor anybody above their own condition to connect them with the civilization of the higher classes'.[42] By 1841 there was Berkeley Lodge on Boughton Hill, home of the prosperous Liverpool mercer and haberdasher Henry Woolright, with its gazebo, 50-foot observatory, and 14 acres of terraced walks and grottoes—complete with model ships, telegraph, windmill, and lighthouse. ('Neither words nor painting can do it adequate justice', a sale catalogue coyly put it in 1845.) But Woolright would never really count: Dunkirk's first curate described the Lodge as 'a retired Cockney's residence'.[43] And, anyway, Berkeley Lodge and the Woolrights do not seem to have been in the Ville in 1838.

Almost 80 per cent of land in Hernhill and a staggering 98 per cent of land in Dunkirk was owned by outsiders, non-resident landowners.[44] Men such as Sir Edward Dering and Lord Sondes could, and did, intervene to protect their interests in the area; but they were among the largest landowners in Kent, with scores of

3 Mount Ephraim *c.*1838 (before the rebuilding), from a nineteenth-century watercolour. *Source*: Dawes collection.

4 Mount Ephraim today.

holdings in a great many parishes. They—and there were many others with Kent properties of over 1,000 acres who had investments in the Blean area, including the Hiltons, the Neames, the Knatchbulls, William Baldock, William Hyder, George Gipps, Thomas Ford, William Hammond, and Sir John Bridges—were able to exert influence, yet their hearts, their seats, and their purses were elsewhere.[45] They governed, as it were, by remote control, through their stewards or, at a more modest level, through their agents the bailiffs and woodreeves. Or they may have been content simply to receive their rents from the farmers. They would however appear on the scene readily enough during a time of crisis. When Courtenay led the rising of the agricultural labourers in 1838, Charles Neame, Baldock, and one of the Knatchbulls were there on horseback with the farmers and military. But the essential point is that they came from outside the immediate area and that Poore, the magistrate in charge, had to be called from Sittingbourne, ten miles away.

We need to look, then, below the level of the great landlords to those on the margins of the gentry, the substantial farmers who exercised local power as employers, members of the vestries, and Poor Law commissioners, a kind of pseudo-gentry of many a nineteenth-century rural community. It was this rural middle class which, James Obelkevich has argued, stood face to face with the labourers in the villages just as industrial capital confronted labour in the towns.[46] In a sense, the story of much nineteenth-century rural conflict is the story of a silent war between the agricultural labourers and the farmers. Although we will see that hostility to the gentry emerged in the drama of 1838, one is tempted to say that at the immediate level of conflict the great landlords were almost irrelevant.

Most of the farmland in Hernhill was owned, rented, or leased by outsiders, run either by bailiffs or as part of an agrarian capitalist's nearby estate: seven or eight farms, varying in size from 100 to 300 acres, large (though not huge) by Kent's standards.[47] Julius Shepherd, a Faversham lawyer, owned Bessborough Farm and held Lavender and Dargate Farms, all run through bailiffs (see Plates 5 and 6). The Lambert family owned Yocketts or Yorkletts Farm (290 acres), managed in the 1820s by the ubiquitous Edward Curling. John Wilks of Preston was the tenant of over 140 acres of arable land and pasture, including Way Street Farm. Thomas Murton of Bredgar farmed Waterham (see Plate 7), presumably by

5 Bessborough House (Bessborough Farm). The parish rented this house in the 1820s and 1830s and used it to accommodate some of the Hernhill poor.

6 Lavender Farm

7 Waterham Farm

8 Dargate House

agent, for he occupied over 1,400 acres in various parts of the county. We could also include Dargate House (see Plate 8) and its surrounding farmland (260 acres), owned and farmed by the Canterbury bankers the Snoultons before Osborne junior's bankruptcy in 1841. Snoulton senior was an alderman and former mayor of Canterbury. Snoulton junior spent part of the year in Hernhill, for his name crops up in the vestry minutes and he was assessed in the rates as an indweller. But the farming was carried out by their Scottish bailiff William Kay.

Although these men and their agents were obviously power brokers in the community in the sense that they were major employers of labour, they rarely attended vestry meetings. The day-to-day power was exercised by another group of farmers, those who actually lived in Hernhill. There were less than twenty such people in the late 1830s. Of them, eight were wealthy farmers by local standards. Their holdings varied. The brothers Stephen and John Butcher, for example, farmed 130 acres between them, including Barnfield Farm (see Plate 9), owner-occupied and divided into two. Edward Curling owned little land but was tenant of at least two properties, Crockham and another farm at Dargate. The James Wraights senior and junior farmed 200 acres, including Brook Farm (see Plate 10); Wraight senior owned just over 70 acres, mostly arable.

Although most of their holdings fell into the 100–300 acre category, our farming élite would also include one or two owners of smaller properties. Edward Browning of Cherry Orchard Farm (see Plate 11) is a good example. He farmed 46 acres but he owned it all, and most of it was hop ground and orchard; by 1851 (when the Census was taken) he was running 140 acres and employing ten labourers. It was this group, together with the wheelwright-farmer John Foreman, that dominated the parish, serving year after year (in rotation) as the parish surveyors, church wardens, and overseers and who attended the vestry meetings concerned with the day-to-day running of the parish.[48] These men hired the labour for work on their farms as well as organizing it (through the vestry) for work on the roads. They also owned what could be called the community's plant: they were the people with the carts, ploughs, horses, and hop oasts, the agricultural equipment needed by the smaller farmers at crucial times of the year. Together with the outside rural bourgeoisie and their agents, they formed what Obelkevich has termed the 'true farming class'.[49]

9 Barnfield Farm

10 Brook Farm

11 Cherry Orchard Farm (or Coleman's Land), early this century. *Source*: Harold Kay collection.

They included women as well as men—though always in the absence of their menfolk. Sophia Curling ran Crockham Farm with her sons for a number of years after Edward's death in 1841. Stephen Butcher's wife, Jemima, was left the estate so that, as his will stated, she could continue 'my business . . . for her support and maintenance and for that of my six children'.[50] A recently widowed Mary Wraight, whose husband Edward was killed in the battle of Bosenden Wood, was still renting 33 acres of arable land at Dargate when the tithe survey appeared in 1840.

This leaves the small farmer, the real peasantry of the nineteenth century.[51] Farm sizes are notoriously difficult to gauge, and it is foolhardy to try to map rates of wealth and status, or even to establish subsistence levels, from bare acreages. National averages rarely make sense at a county level; county levels do not necessarily tally with local criteria. It is probably impossible to be precise, for much depended on the nature of the holding and type of cultivation; but in Hernhill the thin red line seems to have been somewhere between 20 and 30 acres.[52] Even here there were exceptions. James Pell had a holding of about 30 acres, employed several labourers, and owned several cottages. He was a cattle salesman who would have seen himself, and have been perceived, as part of the farming class proper. (His house, which still stands, proclaims as much.) The élite of the small farmers included the farmer/publican Noah Miles, who owned a 14 acre farm and rented an equivalent amount of land. He was not a wealthy man, but neither was he poor. Those holding below 20 acres, unless they also had a trade or craft, and always depending on the type of agriculture, were on or below subsistence level, relying heavily on family labour, probably having to sell their own labour to survive or as payment or exchange for specialist help on their farms. Seven of Hernhill's farms fit into this category, though the number would swell to ten if we include the carpenter Thomas Adams, the blacksmith John Curling, and the shoemaker Richard Eldridge, who also farmed smallholdings. Hernhill's small farmers included Alex Foad, who farmed 8 acres of his own land at Dargate (arable and hops); Edward Wills, member of an old but declining farmer family, who rented 20 acres; John Hadlow, who was also a tenant (of a mere 4 acres) and who worked as a bailiff for Julius Shepherd; and William Curling, tenant of 10 acres, a diker who worked regularly for the farmer Edward Curling, and who was described by the latter as a 'capital labourer'.[53]

12 An archetypal small farm: Forge Farmhouse, Staple Street, 1904. *Source*: Harold Kay collection.

As was hinted earlier, the relationship between the large and small farmers was one of unequal dependency. The small farmers needed the equipment and, it seems, the organized labour of the larger farms. A recently discovered account book from Crockham Farm shows that the Curlings frequently dried hops, threshed wheat, ploughed, harrowed, and carted for smaller farms in the areas. They ploughed land for Alex Foad, for example 8 acres at 15s. an acre, a total of £6. They fetched fish for manure and hop-poles for William Curling's small hop ground—clearly, he did not own a horse and cart.[54]

As might be anticipated from the structure of landownership in Dunkirk, the small farmer predominated in that parish. And they were *small* farmers. In the Censuses of 1841 and 1851, those described as farmers occupied or owned properties as small as 2 or 3 acres. There were about fifteen farms in Dunkirk in the late 1830s, most of which were less than 10 acres. The two largest farms were Lambert's Land Farm and Forester's Lodge. Lambert's Land (190 acres) was part of the estate of the family who owned Yorkletts in Hernhill; it was run by a bailiff, John Curling (son of Edward). Forester's Lodge (186 acres) was farmed by tenants. The only other farms of any size were those of Thomas Berry, also a tenant (107 acres), and William Culver, who occupied a medium-sized holding at Bosenden (60 acres) (see Plate 13).[55] Divisions were therefore sharper in Dunkirk than in Hernhill: farmers were either large or barely distinguishable from the many cottagers and agricultural labourers who also inhabited the Ville. The advantage enjoyed by these smallholders was that most of them owned their small patches of ground. However, many must have been heavily mortgaged by the time they had erected their cottages on their newly acquired land.[56] It would have been precarious living on these tiny plots, with perhaps an acre of hops, an acre of arable, a few pigs, possibly some woodland.[57] Some sought extra work in the surrounding woods.

We should however be wary of overemphasizing the poverty of the small farmers. When she died in 1876, Olive Hadlow, a small farmer's widow, left household furniture, plate, linen, china, glass, books, trinkets, and wearing apparel to the value of £300.[58] Dunkirk men could own small parcels of land in other parishes. Yet what they had was soon dissipated, for inheritance customs in this part of the country encouraged equal distribution among their often large families. It is therefore not surprising that most of the

13 Bosenden Farm

sons of small farmers were unable to follow the occupations of their fathers, and instead became labourers.[59]

Unlike most nineteenth-century rural communities, few Hernhill and Dunkirk people were employed in the crafts and trades. Craftsmen and tradesmen made up a small fraction of male occupations in the Censuses of 1841 and 1851: 3–7 per cent each (see Table 6). Liardet observed that neither community contained a shop of any description. In Hernhill in 1841 there was a wheelwright two blacksmiths, two shoemakers, a tilemaker, two higglers, two publicans, and two beerhouse-keepers. Dunkirk had four beerhouse-keepers or publicans, a butcher, a blacksmith, and three potters and tilemakers. This was in total contrast to Boughton, where in 1851 over a quarter of the working male population was employed in a trade or craft. The vast range of services available in nearby Boughton presumably explains their paucity in Hernhill and Dunkirk. There, within walking distance, were carpenters, butchers, wheelwrights, blacksmiths, shoemakers, bakers, bricklayers, plumbers and glaziers, builders, grocers, millers, tailors and a tailoress, drapers, milliners, dressmakers, a watchmaker, a chemist, even a hairdresser and perfumer.[60] The church wardens' accounts for Hernhill show that it was often Boughton craftsmen who were employed to refurbish and repair the church.[61]

TABLE 6 Male occupations, Hernhill and Dunkirk, 1841 and 1851

Occupation	Hernhill 1841 No.	Hernhill 1841 %	Hernhill 1851 No.	Hernhill 1851 %	Dunkirk 1841 No.	Dunkirk 1841 %	Dunkirk 1851 No.	Dunkirk 1851 %
Gentry	1	0.7	3	1.4	—	—	—	—
Clergy/professional	1	0.7	2	0.9	—	—	2	0.9
Farmers (incl. bailiff)	22	14.6	31	14.6	19	9.2	28	12.3
Trades (incl. apprentices)	6	4.0	12	5.7	6	2.9	13	5.7
Crafts (incl. apprentices)	11	7.3	15	7.1	8	3.9	15	6.6
Agr. labourers	83	55.0	87	41.0	149	72.3	123	53.9
Labourers	—	—	30	14.1	5	2.4	18	7.9
Farm servants	21	13.9	23	10.8	13	6.3	16	7.2
Servants	3	2.0	4	1.9	4	1.9	2	0.9
Others	3	2.0	2	0.9	2	1.0	5	2.2
Paupers	—	—	3	1.4	—	—	6	2.6

One hesitates to say that the crafts formed a closed group, but they certainly had a degree of corporate identity. In 1841 Sarah Anslow, a blacksmith's daughter, married the Dunkirk tilemaker, John Standen. By 1842 she was a widow, carrying on her husband's craft, but shortly afterwards she fell pregnant to another tilemaker, George Howland, whom she married in 1845. Two of their children followed their parents' craft. In the hamlet of Staple Street at the same time, there were other Howlands and Standens: William Standen, a shoemaker, and his wife Jane Howland. William's father, who lived with them in 1851, was a carpenter and builder. One of the couple's daughters became a shoebinder; the other married a carpenter. Sons of craftsmen tended to become craftsmen themselves, and several, as the example above suggests, married women from a craft family. Their daughters, too, married into this group. They were also far more literate than the general population: all the Hernhill craftsmen were able to write their names.[62]

Then there were farm servants. Like the rest of the south-eastern and southern countries, rural Kent was in process of transformation, from a traditional agrarian society, with the decline of farm service and its fixed-term employment and residency, and the banishment of the labourer from the home of the farmer, to a 'free' agricultural proletariat, with the division of rural society into landlord, farmer, and labourer.[63] Few Dunkirk males were employed as farm servants: 6 and 7 per cent of male occupations in the Censuses of 1841 and 1851 (see Table 6). The figures were higher for Hernhill (14 and 11 per cent, respectively), although as in Dunkirk the majority of work in agriculture was performed by day labour. Yet we should not exaggerate the decline of the farm servant. Just as the Census fails to represent household change over time, it misses the life-cycle of employment. Many men still spent part of their lives as farm servants, usually in a parish other than that of their place of birth.

In Dunkirk and Hernhill the bulk of the employable population, male and female, young and old, were agricultural labourers or labourers: 55 per cent of the working male population in Hernhill in 1841 and in 1851 were so described; 75 and 60 per cent in Dunkirk (see Table 6). They ranged in age from 10–14-year-olds to the over-85s, for the nineteenth-century work-force lacked the tidy specificity of modern times—people started work and stopped work at widely differing ages. (The modern meaning of retirement, as Michael Anderson has pointed out, is an alien notion in this world.[64]) All were involved in farm work of some sort or found employment in the vast tracts of woodland. Because of the agricultural diversity of the area, there was, as we shall see, a variety of different work available; but seasonal employment predominated, and consequently required a reserve army of labour—male and female, adult and child—for harvesting. Work was irregular; many would be laid off in the winter months, and so weekly rates of pay give little indication of annual income. The situation of labourers differed somewhat in the two parishes, although it was essentially a case of roundabouts and swings. In Hernhill, agricultural labourers formed a rural proletariat in the classic sense of the term. Of 65 agricultural labourers who were heads of households in 1841, only one owned any farmland (6 acres, which he let!). Two (one was William Curling, described as a farmer in 1851) rented 10 acres. And George Epps owned a cottage and garden and rented 1 acre. The rest, for whom there is information, rented cottages or parts of houses, usually with gardens.[65]

When Liardet visited the parish he surveyed fifty-one labouring families, although one gets the impression that his sample also may have included some small farmers. Of this sample, seventeen kept pigs, five kept a horse and cart, but none of them owned a cow. 'Few, indeed, of the cottagers aspire so high as to the possession of a cow.' He found that local farmers were opposed to their labourers holding land or livestock; there was 'a lurking apprehension that the labourer would become more independent and less manageable'.[66] Such misgivings were realized in adjoining Dunkirk, for here about twenty of those described as agricultural labourers or labourers in the Census of 1841 (104 heads of household in all) were owner-occupiers of cottages and gardens and, in eleven cases, of small parcels of land ranging from $3/4$ of an acre to $5½$ acres. A further three rented 2–3 acres of land a piece, and Edward Carr farmed just over 16 acres. (He was indeed being described as a farmer by 1851.)[67] The 1827–8 survey of landholding in Dunkirk, plotted against my work on family reconstitution, shows that, of forty-eight cottagers actually living in the Ville at that time and with holdings of less than 1 acre, twenty-one (44 per cent) were owner-occupiers.[68] Liardet noted the presence of freehold cottages but commented that most of them were 'mortgaged nearly to their full value'. Of fifty Dunkirk cottager families interviewed by the solicitor, nineteen kept pigs, two a cow, and six a cart and horse or donkeys.[69] But in Dunkirk there was less farm work available than in Hernhill, so the cottagers were more dependent upon their tiny holdings. In short, while there was a substantial minority of landowning labourers in Dunkirk, the majority, in both communities, had only their labour to sell.

They were essentially a socially static group, with little prospect of material or social improvement. Some would marry into the crafts or local farming families, but most were condemned to the same life as their parents. Of 162 sons of labourers listed in the Census of 1851 for Hernhill and Dunkirk, 129 (80 per cent) became labourers themselves. Nearly 80 per cent of labourers who married between 1800 and 1850 had fathers who were labourers. And two-thirds of the daughters of labourers listed in the 1851 Census (for whom we have information on marriage) married men who had the same occupation as the bride's father.[70] Some would acquire possessions and some wealth, either by inheritance or through their own efforts—life-cycle prosperity was as real as life-cycle poverty. The labourer John Spratt, follower of Courtenay, was on poor relief in the 1830s, but when his wife Sarah died in 1849 she left £200 worth of material possessions and cash.[71] (For their rented cottage—which still stands—see Plate 14.) Over the years, a few Dunkirk labourers were to acquire not one but several cottages on their small parcels of enclosed common and waste. Yet they were a minority. Most labourers did not even bother to make a will—they had little to leave but their clothing and perhaps a bed.

I hinted earlier at a tripartite structure in rural society, but for the residents of Dunkirk and Hernhill a duality would be a more appropriate description. Despite the occupational nuances in each community, in the line-up of substantial farmers, bailiffs, small farmers, craftsmen, tradesmen, and agricultural labourers, the main division was between the parish élite—the farmers—and the farm and other labourers. Most small farmers were more socially aligned with labourers—in terms of literacy levels and life-styles—than with large farmers. Those in the crafts and trades varied. Some were landlords, owners of the cottages of the agricultural labourers, and employers of labour; others existed closer to subsistence level. Even the more modestly exclusive and highly literate craft families married labourers as well as the sons and daughters of craftsmen and farmers. To employ the imagery of Eric Hobsbawm and George Rudé, each parish contained two parishes: that of those

14 The Spratts' cottage, Dargate (now a post office).

who counted, i.e. the men (and they were usually *men*) whose names were recorded in the county gazetteers, and the 'dark village' of the labouring poor.[72]

The rural élite included the gentry-aspiring George Francis of Fairbrook Farm in Boughton (see Plate 15), who like many a social-climbing farmer acquired the obligatory 'esquire' after his name, was, for a while, a member of the socially exclusive Faversham Farmers' Club, and was to be flattered by the attention of the bogus Sir William Courtenay.[73] But it also included Edward Curling, 'cock of the village' in Hernhill, described in 1838 as a self-made man who had 'raised himself from the condition of a labouring man to his present respectable position', culturally closer, in education and demeanour, to the farmworkers than the rural squirearchy.[74] From what we can gather, life at Crockham Farm was a far cry from the genteel lot of the wealthy Essex farmers portrayed so marvellously in the recent work of Leonore Davidoff and Catherine Hall.[75]

Farmers enjoyed a more comfortable life-style than the bulk of the population. Their households, complete with servants, were larger than those of agricultural labourers, as were their houses. Their wills mention feather-bed mattresses, bolsters, pillows, blankets, sheets, linen, bedsteads, hangings, chests and other furniture, plate, china, glass, pictures, prints and books, wines and liquors, jewellery, trinkets, watches and clocks—hardly luxuries by today's materialistic standards, but few labourers' cottages would have held such contents.

The farmers, along with the craftsmen, a banker, and Hernhill's vicar, had the formal political voice in Hernhill and Dunkirk in an electorate with an effective male franchise of 16 and 12 per cent. (Only eight out of several hundred labourers in the two parishes were able to vote in the 1837 election.[76]) Farmers were more likely to send their children to school, sometimes in another parish, and thus their literacy levels were high.[77] A Hernhill 5–14-year-old was most likely to be at school if she was the daughter of a farmer, least likely if he was the son of an agricultural labourer.[78]

This rural élite was also bound together by a bewilderingly complex skein of kin networks. Edward Curling was the nephew of Edward Rigden, a large property-owner in the parish in the first part of the century.[79] Curling's sister, Ann Ward, ran Lavender Farm at one stage, and his brothers were John Curling the Staple Street blacksmith and George Curling a Hernhill farmer. William

15 Fairbrook House

Curling (the blacksmith), John's son and Edward's nephew, was married to Harriett Miles, daughter of the farmer/publican Noah Miles and Mary Wraight. Mary Wraight, in turn, belonged to a farming family, that of William Wraight senior and Susanna Wraight. One of the Wraights' other daughters, Hannah, married into yet another farming family, the Butchers. Hannah Wraight's brother-in-law, Stephen Butcher, also a farmer, left a widow, Jemima, when he died in 1834 (we encountered her earlier in the chapter); eight months later she remarried—her choice, the farmer James Wraight junior![80] Yet it was not a closed caste. While in a better position to pass on their wealth, their estates were frequently sold off to ensure equal distribution among their offspring—they too were victims of the population revolution and the Kent inheritance system. Of thirty-seven sons of farmers listed in the Census of 1851, less than 40 per cent were to follow in their fathers' occupational footsteps. Nor was endogamy a strict rule when it came to marriage: farmers' daughters frequently married agricultural labourers.[81]

Although such class ascendancy was not always expressed in cultural terms, the social tensions were no less real. Whether of the Francis or the Curling stamp, such farmers were the 'little kings' of nineteenth-century rural society.[82] Courtenay was able to establish a base in Hernhill and Dunkirk because of the initial hospitality of Francis and the shelter of the bailiff John Hadlow and the farmer William Culver. He was able to enrol a following because of labouring antipathy (and the hostility of some small farmers) towards the farming élite. It is impossible to understand the abortive rising of 1838 without understanding this social context.

2
Labouring Life

AGRICULTURAL work had a rhythm. The high point of the year, the labourer's 'jubilee', was harvest time. August and September were the months of peak activity and maximum earning power, followed by the bustle of post-harvest October—when people were most likely to get married (see Figure 1), when farm and domestic servants left their employ, and when pockets were full after harvest work. This contrasted with the low point of the year, the torpor of the winter months from November to February—one of the peak periods for burial (see Figure 2), a time of idleness and, for many,

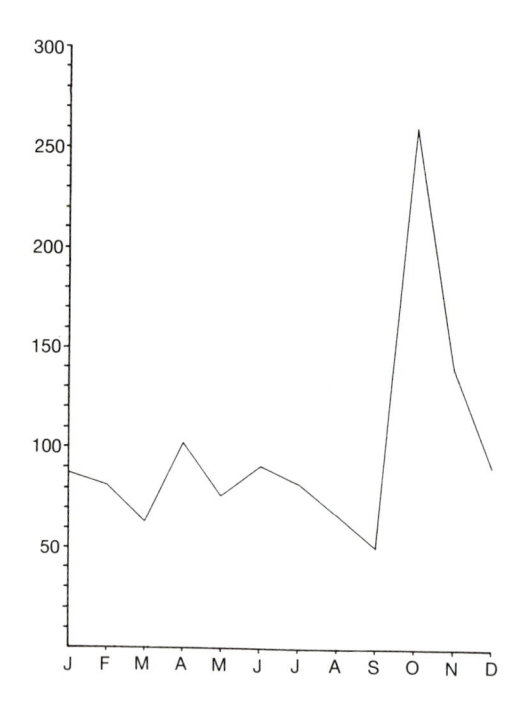

FIG. 1 Seasonality of Boughton, Dunkirk, and Hernhill marriages, 1813–1840 (standardized)

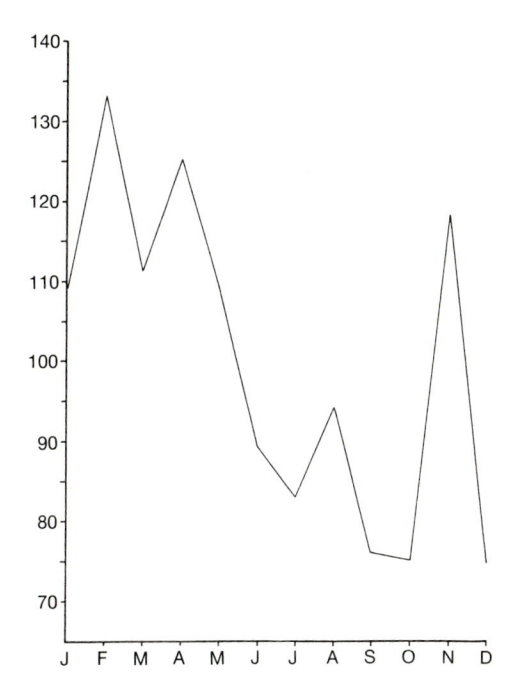

FIG. 2 Seasonality of Boughton, Dunkirk, and Hernhill burials, 1813–1840 (standardized)

winter desperation. During this season, 60–70 per cent of male agricultural labourers could receive some kind of poor relief.[1]

From my account in the previous chapter, it would be easy to come away with the impression that work was a male prerogative. Nothing could be more misleading. From the level of the farming class down, all women worked in the early nineteenth century, regardless of their invisibility in the notoriously gender-biased censuses. The same was true of most children. As more sensitive social analysts have pointed out, we should think of two economies: the formal market, the capitalist economy, with the wage as its totem, and the informal economy, non-wage-based, located in the family and dominated by the labour of women and children just as the other was ruled by men.[2] Indeed, our economic *primum mobile* should be the household economy. Whether it was a girl looking after younger children while her mother earned some money weeding or tying hops, children gleaning with their mother, a boy

TABLE 7 Female occupations, Hernhill and Dunkirk, 1851

Occupation	Hernhill No.	%	Dunkirk No.	%
Gentry	—	—	—	—
Clergy/professional	—	—	1	2.8
Farmers	1	2.4	1	2.8
Trades	—	—	2	5.6
Crafts	2	4.8	2	5.6
Agr. labourers	—	—	—	—
Labourers	3	7.1	4	11.1
Farm servants	—	—	—	—
Servants	32	76.2	11	30.6
Others	4	9.5	1	2.8
Paupers	—	—	14	38.9

stealing wood for the family fire, or a wife keeping rabbits or poultry, all were making a contribution to the family economy just as legitimately as the male householder who earned 2s. 3d. a day when he could and who was recorded in the Census of 1841 or 1851 as an 'agricultural labourer'.

In the 'formal' economy, most women in Hernhill and Dunkirk earned their living as servants (see Table 7). With its more substantial farming population and gentry vicar, Hernhill provided greater employment opportunity in this sector than the relatively impoverished Ville. Of the female occupations listed in the 1851 Census returns for the former, 76 per cent were employed as servants. The percentage was smaller for Dunkirk (30 per cent), but it was still the largest single female occupation. Those who were single female emigrants from Hernhill and Dunkirk, picked up in the Census in surrounding parishes, were all house servants, maids, housekeepers, and general servants.[3]

However, the Census does not get us very far with women's work. The gap between census and reality can be demonstrated in several ways. Beerhouses and public houses were nearly always listed under the occupation of the man. And yet we know from incidental information in some of the Quarter Sessions and Petty Sessions records that the women in the family (wife and daughter) served in the tap room during the day and of course baked the bread that would be sold with the beer. The men served in the evenings.[4] Or there is the case of Olive Butcher, the daughter of a

Hernhill farmer, who had no occupation according to the Census of 1851; however, a Quarter Sessions deposition tells us that she kept fowls, and the Hernhill church wardens' accounts list payment to her for hemming and marking the church's communion cloth and napkin.[5] Eliza Packman, from Dunkirk, was another who did not work according to the Census. But we know she helped her stepfather in the woods, dragging the poles that he had cut, for it was there that he raped her in 1848.[6]

Female employment in agriculture was an area spectacularly understated by a census taken in March or April.[7] As with the men, the majority of women were employed as farmworkers. Keith Snell has argued for a declining participation of women in the agricultural work-force in nineteenth-century eastern England.[8] This may have been true of the pure corn lands, but in our area the presence of hops and fruit ensured an important role for women in the cycle of employment, as Table 8 shows. Labour by the task was common in East Kent, and so it was often the man of the labouring household who 'employed' his wife and children to help him fill his contract. He might agree to thresh by the quarter, assisted by his son in the barn. Or he might contract to reap by the acre, and husband and wife would work together using the sickle, or he would use a bagging hook and she would tie the sheaves after him. Working like this, they could, for a brief period, earn together between 16s. and 36s. a week. In hop-picking the whole family would take part; with payment by the bushel, all hands counted. A good picker could pick about 20 bushels in a day; a child of 12 years, about 12 or 13 bushels. Women were considered better pickers than men. Hop-poling was done by men with help from women and boys who positioned the poles. But women also did piece work on their own account: hop-tying was done by the acre, exclusively by women.[9] In hops, then, as one commentator somewhat romantically put it, 'the soil is handled and subdued by the man; the plant is tended and trained by the woman; in the gathering are united all,—man, woman, and child.'[10] The diversification of this part of Kent offered other opportunities for female labour. Women were employed in weeding the corn, stone-picking, turnip and pea-pulling, and potato-gathering. There was orchard work too in a variety of fruit harvests.[11]

Child labour was an established cog in the rural economy. Girls do not seem to have been as much employed in farmwork, apart from the harvests, although they contributed in other ways to the

TABLE 8 The annual cycle and division of labour in the nineteenth century, by gender and age

Month	Women	Girls	Men	Boys
January	Pole shaving	Same as women	Threshing Hop and orchard digging Ploughing Woodcutting	Same as men *plus* pole shaving and bird scaring
February	Pole shaving	Same as women	Hop and orchard digging and planting Ploughing Woodcutting Opening of hills for hops Drilling and planting	Same as men *plus* pole shaving and bird scaring
March	Hop poling		Drilling and planting Opening of hills for hops Ploughing Woodcutting Hop poling Bark stripping	Same as men *plus* bird scaring
April	Hop poling		Drilling/planting Hop poling Woodcutting	Same as men
May	Hop tying Weeding	Same as women		Weeding
June	Hop tying Fruit picking (berries)	Fruit picking	Weeding	Weeding Fruit picking

	Women	Men	Children
July	Fruit picking (cherries) Hay making Pea pulling	Hay harvest	Same as men Fruit picking
August	Fruit picking (plums)	Grain harvest	Same as women
September	Grain harvest Hop picking Fruit picking (apples and pears) Gleaning	Grain harvest Hop picking Fruit picking Bean cutting	Same as men
October	Potato picking Mangold pulling	Ploughing Drilling/planting Threshing Ploughing/digging potatoes	Same as men
November	Turnip pulling	Ploughing Drilling/planting Woodcutting Threshing Hop digging (pulling up poles)	Same as men *plus* bird scaring
December	Turnip pulling	Wood cutting Hop digging Threshing Drilling/planting	Same as men *plus* bird scaring

N.B. Men, women, and children would be involved, in varying degrees, with the care of livestock—poultry, milk cows, cattle, sheep, and pigs.

household economy and must have spent time with their mothers in the fields and hop grounds in order to pick up the skills that they would require when it was their turn to do similar work.[12] Boys, however, were doing many of the tasks of the men, from a very early age. They either assisted their fathers—' "At eight years old", says a farmer in East Kent, "a boy is fit to help his father in the barn a little at threshing" '[13]—or were hired at 3*d.* or 4*d.* or 6*d.* a day, depending on the age. Boys worked in the hop fields, weeded and picked up stones, and were used to lead horses at the plough on the corn lands and at the hoe in the hop gardens. They were employed to keep birds off the corn, to harrow and drill wheat, to plant potatoes, and to top turnips. Of course, they also assisted with the various harvests, and in the woodland areas found winter employment cutting faggots and stacking and shaving hop-poles.[14] In fact, apart from the constraints of skill and physical strength, there was little a boy could not undertake or assist with. The danger was that at 6*d.* a day child labour could undermine that of the adults.[15]

Life was hard in the rural communities of nineteenth-century England. Water had to be carried, sanitation was primitive, effective lighting did not exist. It seems trite to talk of an age before electricity and piped water, but the implications of such absences were real enough. We know notoriously little about the actual living conditions of the nineteenth-century agricultural labourer.[16] Liardet's statistical and ethnographical survey pronounced the condition of the villagers of Hernhill as 'superior to that of many rural populations in the country, and scarcely inferior to any'. 'They are nearly all lodged in separate cottages, the generality of which exhibit both externally and internally unquestionable signs of neatness and comfort.' Nearly all were close to wells. He was struck by the presence in many of a 'sufficiency of well-made chairs', polished tables, shelves and crockery, even clocks. Just over 40 per cent of his sample lived in cottages with three rooms or less, but the majority (nearly 60 per cent) had three or four rooms.[17] A few of the labourers had brick and tile cottages, which are still standing, but most of their dwellings, long since pulled down, were no doubt stud and plaster with thatched roofs, a pantry and sitting room on the ground floor, and a bedroom or two upstairs.

Liardet's verdict of comfort is undermined somewhat when we recall that it was not unusual for the wives of agricultural labourers to have from eight to ten children. (Over 40 per cent of the wives of labourers in Dunkirk and Hernhill in the first half of the nineteenth century produced families of this size.) The mean completed family size (number of children) for this social group was 7.0 (the median was 8).[18] Some children died, and not all lived in the cottage at the same time, of course; but the decline of farm service, with its practice of living-in—aptly described by the historian Anne Kussmaul as a form of *ex post facto* family planning—meant that increased pressure was put on the small homes of the labouring population.[19] In 1851 there were, on average, 4.5 persons per house in the homes of the agricultural labourers and labourers. Averages, however, can be misleading. A third of the households of agricultural labourers contained six or more people.[20] It is unlikely that life in the Hernhill proletariat's cottages was comfortable. In Dunkirk, over 60 per cent of Liardet's sample of cottages had three rooms or less; nearly 70 per cent had three or four rooms. The residences in the Ville were not so close to wells, and thirteen of his sample of fifty dwellings were described as 'dirty and uncomfortable'.[21]

The *Morning Chronicle*'s study of labouring life in 1850 noted that the women of rural Kent were particularly 'deficient in knowledge of cookery'. The staple diet in Kent was bread, butter, and cheese for most meals. There was little in the way of actual cooking. Something like 60 per cent of the agricultural labourer's budget went on bread or flour, by far the greatest single item of expenditure. Liardet found that about a quarter of the Hernhill women he talked to and about a half of the women in Dunkirk could not bake, so presumably they purchased their bread from one of the beershops or had it brought in from nearby Boughton.[22] (As far as we know there were no professional bakers in Hernhill until the later 1840s, and none in Dunkirk even then.) Others must have baked their own bread, perhaps in communal ovens. Hernhill and Dunkirk people may have supplemented their diet with pork and potatoes: the farmer Curling did a brisk trade in these items. They may have eaten fish from the nearby fishing villages.[23] They drank tea and also quite a quantity of beer. Children would go to the public houses to buy jugs of beer to take home for their parents; men would be in the beerhouses early in the mornings to drink beer and buy bread. Some of the people in our parishes kept rabbits, and had gardens attached to their cottages which could be used to grow vegetables. Some poached in the woods and stole crops from field and barn. They were as likely to sell these items as they were to eat them; survival was a fine art. Alan Armstrong has suggested that the calorific intake of the nineteenth-century farmworker would have been similar to that of the underdeveloped world in the 1960s.[24]

We know relatively little about health in this part of Kent. Hernhill was on the edge of a malaria area, but there is no evidence from mortality patterns that the disease affected the parish.[25] People died from measles, smallpox, scarlatina, croup, typhus, hydrocephalus, pneumonia, cancer, and consumption. By national standards, it was not a dangerous area to live in; as we saw in Chapter 1 the infant and child mortality rates for both parishes were considerably lower than the national average. But of course, mortality patterns should not be equated with general conditions of health. Rheumatism, fever, asthma, thrush, inflammation of the lungs, and work-related illnesses such as rupture and leg injuries were commonplace.[26] Doctors working in the Kent and County Hospital at Canterbury who treated outpatients from this area in the late 1830s noted that the field labourers' 'constant exposure to cold and wet' determined the nature of their ailments. Thus they encountered, 'in abundance', inflammation of the lungs and the air passages, 'obstinate rheumatisms of muscular parts', and 'neuralgic affections from cold, sometimes amounting to complete paralysis'.[27] Life may not have been as short as in some parts of the country, but for many it was accompanied by discomfort and pain. Large numbers of people did not have access to a doctor. The closest was in Boughton—but costs were high. (I know of medical bills of 10s. 6d. and £1. 6s., about half a year's rent for a cottage.) Medical care in Hernhill seems to have been the responsibility of the women: the overseer's accounts record payments to midwives and to women who nursed the sick poor.[28] One of the doctors at the Kent Hospital complained that the poorer people were more likely to visit popular healers, 'wisewomen' and 'knowing men' (white witches), than they were to consult 'educated practitioners'. He was aghast at some of the local remedies.[29]

Can we comment on the standards of living of farmworkers in Hernhill and Dunkirk? Farm servants in this part of the country contracted by the year, on or about Michaelmas (late September—early October). As elsewhere in England, employers would sometimes employ them for slightly less than a year to avoid settlement obligations. There was a finely graded hierarchy, a pecking order among farm servants: waggoner, waggoner's mate, second man, third man, second boy, third boy. The head waggoner at Lambert's

Land in the 1820s received 13s. a week, rent-free, and he was also paid for boarding the farm servants.[30] This £30 a year plus was at the top end of the scale. Male servants in husbandry recalled in settlement examinations that at the beginning of the nineteenth century they were earning £7–£10 a year. By the 1830s and 1840s the rates were much lower: £5–£6 for a waggoner's mate, £10 for a waggoner. Women employed on farms as servants generally received half the income of the men.[31]

The theme of the decline of farm service in the eighteenth and nineteenth centuries often implies the erosion of an organic relationship between master and man, 'the progressive distancing of the farmer from his labourer'. Yet as Mick Reed has argued, there was always a degree of distance in what was an inherently unequal relationship.[32] Disputes between farmers and servants over the care of animals and the pilfering of grain (usually to provide extra feed for their horses), and arguments over hours worked and the time servants should be in bed, demonstrate that conditions were far from idyllic.[33] The hours were long and living conditions sometimes cramped, several men sharing a chamber and 'in most cases' a bed, according to an address to the Sittingbourne Agricultural Association in the 1850s. In winter the sleeping quarters were cold, damp, and smelly. The waggoner's day started at 3.30 a.m. in East Kent and finished at about 6 p.m. His mate began work at 5 a.m. but would work into the evening, and it would be as late as 10 p.m. before the horses were fed and locked up. There was Sunday work too, for the animals had to be fed: as the same Kent reported noted, 'the hours of divine service are wantonly selected for "baiting" [feeding]'.[34]

As far as the majority of workers—the day labourers—were concerned, we need to distinguish between the few 'constant men' and the vast bulk of casual labour. The 'constant man', employed by the same farmer over a number of years on a regular basis, could live comfortably. The account book of Crockham Farm shows that there was a wide range of regular work for a few skilled men: harrowing potatoes, beans, and wheat and shimming hops in April, carrying out hop-poles in May, shimming peas, potatoes, and beans in June, carrying hay in July, carrying and threshing wheat in August and September, ploughing up potatoes and carrying potatoes and beans and drying hops in October, ploughing and threshing in November, work on hops from December to March.[35] Those who, along with their families, worked more or less permanently for Curling earned £35–£57 in day work plus £4–£14 extra for the harvest and hopping. James Adlow, his wife, two boys, and one girl were able to earn a total of £65. 5s. 2d. in one year; James Hawkins, his wife, and one boy brought in a total of £41. 2s. 8d.[36] Yet these were the labouring élite; the experience of the majority was radically different.

Perhaps the best way of demonstrating the lot of the agricultural labourer is to try to draw up a budget. The *Parliamentary Papers* for 1837 contain an interview with a 47-year-old Sussex labourer. He had a 40-year-old wife and seven children. (Two were 16 and 12 years old, the rest were younger.) Four of his children depended on him for support; two had been put into the poor house. His average wage was 9s. 6d. a week. He said that 10s. was enough to support three children provided that no one was ill. His wife could not work in the fields because she had a child at the breast, but she was normally able to glean a few bushels of wheat at harvest. The gleaning was important for the family economy, because when there were six children in the house they spent 9s. a week on flour. There was seasonal work which boosted his earnings. The bark harvest for two or three weeks earned him £2–£3; and hay-making and the corn harvest brought in about the same amount, although he pointed out that the upkeep of tools cost about 6s. a year. His eldest daughter earned £2 a year, but that was barely enough to keep her in clothing. His small garden, in which he worked evenings after a day's labour, produced vegetables for four months of the year; the family were out of greens all winter. Nearly the whole of the wage went on flour. When asked what he did about tea, cheese, butter, soap, firing, candles, clothes, beer, his answer was 'nothing'. They had picked up some wood from waste ground, and a friend had given them 6d. to buy candles and sugar for the child. Apart from that, they had not spent anything on such necessities for three months, not to mention the rent of 1s. 8d. a week (£4. 6s. 8d. a year) which was 'lying back'. Clothing consisted of the cast-offs of other people. The man did not want a lot from life. He had no extravagant ambitions: 'If I could get my living by my labour, I should be satisfied.'[37]

In the aftermath of the Courtenay rising, farmers in Hernhill and Dunkirk were either reluctant or unable to provide figures for regular employment of farm labour. Curling claimed that there was no hardship in his area. His rates were 2s. 2d. or 2s. 3d. a day for men (casual labour), 1s. for women, and 6d. for boys or girls.

Osborne Snoulton paid 2s. 6d. a day, which was considered a top rate. Curling claimed that his wages had been constant since the introduction of the New Poor Law in 1834, but he also said that other farmers in the parish had been forced by the collective action of their labourers to raise their wages in 1835. They had since returned them to their original level.[38] In 1838, then, the general rate for men's wages was about 13s. 6d. a week, which was roughly what rioters in 1830 and 1835 had said was a subsistence wage.[39]

In 1837 the Poor Law Commissioner for Kent drew up a table of the expenditure of a man, wife, and four children on a wage of 13s. a week. The items were as follows: 5 gallons of flour at 1s. 1/4d. a gallon: 5s. 6 1/4d.; 2 lb of butter at 10d.: 1s. 8d.; 1/2 lb of candles: 3 1/2d.; 3 lb of cheese: 1s. 6d.; meat: 2s.; 1 1/2 lb of sugar: 10 1/2d.; 2 oz tea: 7 1/2 d; 1/2 lb soap: 3d.; pepper and salt: 2d.; 1 oz tobacco: 3 1/2d. That is a total of 13s. 2 1/4d., just under the weekly income of our hypothetical Hernhill or Dunkirk family earning 2s. 3d. a day or 13s. 6d. a week.[40] The budget does not include rent (anything from £2 to £3 a year in Hernhill) or yeast (3d. a week), so let us substitute these two items for meat (an unnecessary extravagance—tobacco can at least be smoked to combat greenfly). There are no vegetables on the list, but let us assume that if they were eaten they were grown in the garden (for part of the year at least).

But there is another major flaw with the Poor Law Commissioner's budget: the wage rate of 13s. assumes regular employment. In the 1870s Alfred Simmons, a Kent union activist, asked some agricultural labourers to keep a tally of the days lost on account of inclement weather. Their replies showed an average loss of 85 days (not including Sundays).[41] Winter, we have already noted, was a slack season for employment: in Hernhill in January 1830 over 60 per cent of agricultural labourers and small farmers were on poor relief.[42] If we take away 85 days for wet or frosty weather or illness, this reduces the weekly wage over the year to 9s. 9d., slightly more than the 9s. average suggested by the *Morning Chronicle*'s survey in 1850.[43]

If the Poor Law Commissioner overestimated incomes, his account also underestimated them. Let us assume that our labourer's wife was able to bring in an income and that he received some help from the parish overseers during the winter months, and add an extra £10 a year or 4s. a week, including the man's harvest earnings or extra income from wood-cutting. This brings the total average weekly earnings back to 13s. 6d. a week. It is just over the weekly expenditure, but there are other large items not on the list: clothing and fuel. Fuel was plentiful in the area, but because most of the common land had fallen to enclosure and woodreeves guarded the investments of absentee landlords, wood had to be either stolen or bought. Curling, the farmer, sold a lot of wood locally, so we should probably add firewood to the budget—from 1s. 6d. to 2s. a week according to some nineteenth-century accounts.[44] Clothing was costly too: shoes or boots cost 4s. or 5s., shirts 3s., bonnets 3s., coats 10s., blankets 4s.[45] Then there was the price of tools. And all this assumes that our labouring family did not send their children to school or seek medical attention.

It is difficult, then, to generalize about the condition of the agricultural labourer. However, several things are clear. There was a thin line between survival and destitution. It really was an economy of makeshifts.[46] The problem with average weekly calculations is that real life was not like that: there was no planning for the whole year, no weekly rationalization. There were simply slack periods and periods of tolerable comfort. The harvest wages were not saved to top up meagre weeks but went to clear the year's debts, to buy some shoes or tools, to pay the rent. As one labouring woman put it, life was a continual contrivance; 'it's one struggle from morning till night, and from one week's end to another. I hope I'm prepared for a better, but there's nothing now in this world that I care living for, except to see my poor children doing for themselves.'[47] Letters home from New Zealand and Australia in the 1830s and 1870s provide a stark contrast between the old and new worlds. Dogs got more to eat in Queensland and Otago than labourers did in Kent. We 'don't get cold out here'; 'I go out to the back door and cut down a tree when I want it.' There was plenty of game to shoot; 'the police [don't] stop you when coming into town if your pockets are a bit bulky or you have a bag on your back'.[48]

Given the social conditions in the rural communities of nineteenth-century England, it is not surprising that many resorted to the pub and the beerhouse. Richard Jefferies waxed large on the role of the drinking establishment in the life of the rural male: 'It is at once his stock exchange, his reading room, his club, and his assembly room . . . Here he learns the news of the day . . . and if he cannot read himself he hears the news from those who can'; 'it is his theatre, his music hall, picture gallery, and Crystal Palace'.[49]

Jefferies exaggerated, but there is little doubting the importance of the public house in many an agricultural community. Although they did visit one another in their own homes, the cottages of the agricultural population must have been joyless places. Cramped, with little room to entertain friends, dark at night because of expensive or inadequate lighting, it was natural for people to gravitate towards such centres of warmth, light, and conviviality.

The drinking houses varied from the grander inn and public house to the humbler beerhouse-dwelling of a labourer. There were two public houses in Hernhill, both of them run by farmers: Edward Butcher's Red Lion, opposite the church (Plate 16), and the Three Horse Shoes at Staple Street, rented by Noah Miles. Hernhill also had two beerhouses: Noah's Ark at Bessborough (Plate 18), kept by Miles's son James, and the Dove (Plate 17), run for many years at Dargate by James Goodwin and his descendants. (The Mileses and Goodwin would all become supporters of Courtenay.) Dunkirk had Woodman's Hall, the Red Lion, and the Gate Inn, run for many years by the widow Mary Wildish, all situated along the London Road, and a couple of beershops, including the Church and State at Denstrode. People from Dunkirk and Hernhill also frequented the six public houses and three beershops in Boughton and others in Harbledown and Blean.

The public house was one of the few places where people could actually meet and talk and where political reticence was overcome by drink. There were good reasons for the authorities' condemnation of the beerhouses for their role in the Swing troubles of 1830. It was in such places that the Blean incendiarists discussed their grievances against a local wood-dealer in 1830, and where the rioters of 1838 talked about Sir William Courtenay.[50] As James Obelkevich has observed, the working-class beerhouse provided a rare escape from the surveillance of farmer and landlord.[51] The Dunkirk labourer, Henry Branchett, was in a Harbledown beershop when he showed a sack to a drinking companion and observed that 'it would do very well for him to put a sheep in'. His companion's response that he 'considered it mere talk' suggests that such banter was common.[52] people went to the public house after funerals. They went there to play cards (for beer or money), to toss for beer, or to play bowls for beer. Liardet complained that it was a general rule that no 'dry games' could be played at such establishments.[53] There was dancing, too—we know this because a woman was assaulted when she went into a room in the Ship Public House in Boughton where

16 The Red Lion public house, Hernhill (opposite the church), pre-1912. *Source*: Len Rooks photography.

17 The Dove beerhouse, Dargate, *c*.1870. *Source*: Harold Kay collection.

18 Noah's Ark beerhouse, Bessborough, before its demolition this century. *Source*: Harold Kay collection.

people were dancing.[54] There was music; Charles Tappenden, who was hired to play the violin at the White Horse in Boughton, lost three teeth when he attempted to break up a fight.[55]

Whatever the legal drinking hours, people started early and finished late. Drinking began at 8 a.m. or earlier in the Dove at Dargate and the Church and State at Denstrode.[56] There are references to men drinking to 2 or 3 in the morning at the King's Arms in South Street.[57] When a Hernhill woman, Susannah Butcher, went to look for her husband at the Squirrels Public House in Boughton Street at 2.30 a.m. she found the door locked and her husband and some others, including the constable John Mears, still sitting in the bar.[58] When some Dunkirk labourers were accused of stealing dogwood belonging to Lord Sondes, their alibi was that they had been at the public house all day, from 9 a.m. to 7 or 8 p.m., except when they had gone home for dinner.[59]

One should not over-romanticize these citadels of the poor. Interaction could be threatening and violent. The woman who was assaulted at the Ship in Boughton had her skirts pulled up as a group of men tried to kiss her.[60] Accepting a drink from a man could be interpreted as consent for sex. A man bought gins for a young woman at St Dunstan's and Harbledown and then attempted to rape her. The woman's response—'I said, if he insulted me because of my drinking his gin, I would pay him for it'—suggests such an unwritten code for some men.[61] It is not that women did not accompany friends or husbands to public houses or beershops, or that they were an exclusive male preserve—indeed, we have seen that women ran such places or served in them during the day when their husbands worked. But they were *male-dominated* domains, then as now, and could be dangerous haunts for women. Women's socialization was accordingly centred in the street and in one another's homes rather than in the pub and beershop.

Historians have long abandoned the myth of the static, isolated rural English settlement of the past, of families working the same land generation after generation. Communities were not static but highly geographically mobile. Over a given ten years, 40–50 per cent of the inhabitants of Hernhill and Dunkirk would have left their parishes (and only a small percentage of those would have travelled in coffins).[67] Nor were these populations cut off from wider influences, for the church provided a link with the outside world. Royal proclamations were read from the Hernhill pulpit; the monarch's arms were emblazoned inside the church. Bells rung out on his birthday or coronation, or tolled for his death. They would have been heard for miles around, a six-hour reminder of the area's connection with a central political stage. The recognition of Oak Apple Day and the fifth of November in the church calendar yet again indicated recognition of a broader political sphere.[63] News could reach the humblest of people, as a Boughton woman found out when she refused aid to three beggars and was threatened with 'the Bristol Business again'—that is, the Bristol Reform Act riots of 1831.[64]

And yet there were very definite boundaries to the cultural horizons of the majority of those living in these rural populations. Farmers might deal with markets in London or keep an eye on trade policies at a national level. A constable might apprehend suspects as far away as Gravesend or Maidstone. A church warden might be sent to the nation's capital to represent the parish at the coronation. But the bulk of social interaction went on at a far more circumscribed level. Hernhill and Dunkirk inhabitants patronized fairs, markets, and services at Ospringe, Faversham, Canterbury, and Boughton. If poor, they might end up in the workhouse at Harbledown (before 1834) or Faversham (after 1834); if they misbehaved, they might be called before a justice at Faversham or Sittingbourne. Hernhill and Dunkirk labourers drank at Boughton pubs; Dunkirk men frequented Harbledown drinking establishments. Whether we look at settlement examinations (which give the origins of those seeking settlement), at a farmer's dealings with corn factors and other farmers, or at the poaching patterns of Dunkirk labourers and the pawning practices of local thieves, the picture is the same. Most interaction and socialization occurred within a five-mile radius—in an arc from Whitstable to Chartham to Ospringe. Of several hundred emigrants from Hernhill and Dunkirk located in the Census of 1851, 80–90 per cent were in places less than five miles away. The social arena weakens as we travel out beyond the five-mile radius. The Census of 1851 shows that in both our parishes about 80 per cent of the inhabitants were living less than five miles from their place of birth. (Only about 10 per cent came from between ten and twenty miles away, and even less from over twenty miles' distance: see Table 9). Localism was still strong in this part of rural Kent.[65]

Walking distance determined the geographical horizons of the bulk of the local population, but their cultural vistas were governed by other factors. A handful of the children of farmers and craftsmen

TABLE 9 Places of birth of Hernhill and Dunkirk inhabitants, 1851

	No.	%	Cumulative %
Hernhill inhabitants: born			
in Hernhill	343	52.2	52.2
Less than 5 miles	179	27.2	79.4
5–10 miles	32	4.9	84.3
10–20 miles	42	6.4	90.7
Greater than 20 miles	46	7.0	97.7
Undetermined	15	2.3	100.0
Dunkirk inhabitants: born			
in Dunkirk	297	43.4	43.4
Less than 5 miles	275	40.1	83.5
5–10 miles	39	5.7	89.2
10–20 miles	36	5.2	94.4
Greater than 20 miles	30	4.4	98.8
Undetermined	8	1.2	100.0

attended Hernhill's lone high school, where, for 13s. 5d. a quarter, they could learn reading, writing, and arithmetic. One or two went as boarders to schools in neighbouring parishes. But the majority of the 30–40 per cent of children who were students in the first half of the nineteenth century attended one of the local day or dame schools, two in Hernhill and one in Dunkirk. Here they learned 'nothing but sewing and reading', the latter taught almost exclusively from the Testament.[66] Even when children did go to school, their attendance was erratic. Boys would be taken from the classroom to earn money, girls to attend to domestic chores. The school fees of 3d. or 6d. a week may seem trifling to us, but as Liardet pointed out, a boy's wage, 6d. a day, could cover the weekly rent. So there were lost earnings to take into account quite apart from the matter of fees. Not surprisingly, Liardet found that the child was 'removed whenever a job of work can be found for him'.[67] Parliamentary enquiries during the 1840s and 1860s noted the erratic attendance of Kent village children. Few went to school beyond the age of 9 or 10, and those who did were withdrawn quite regularly during the period March–October, that is, for the vast bulk of the year. One Kentish school register showed that not a single child had attended school for more than a half of the available school days in the year. When the various harvests did not interfere with school attendance, bad weather and lack of suitable clothing helped to keep the numbers down.[68]

There was a feeling that school education, book learning, did little to mould a potential agricultural labourer. School might be a budding agriculturalist's 'general education', but labour was his 'special education'. 'The spade, the scythe, the hoe, the axe, the sickle, the flail, the beck, the bagging-hook, and the other implements of husbandry,—all require a cunning and handicraft of their own.'[69] This skill was acquired at his father's side and not in a school room. Presumably this explains why only 13 per cent of agricultural labourers' sons aged 5–14 were at school when the Hernhill Census was taken in 1851.

Horrified commentators predictably encountered what they described as gross ignorance. 'It is quite common to meet with boys engaged in farms who cannot read or write', one man reported in 1843. 'The unity of God, a future state, the number of months in the year, are matters not universally known.' Another complained in 1838 that he had been unable to find a waggoner able to read the directions on parcels to be sent to London.[70] Liardet came across pupils in Hernhill who could not read even though they had been attending school for two or three years.[71]

Seventy per cent of those who married in Dunkirk in the first half of the nineteenth century, and 58 per cent of brides and grooms in Hernhill, were unable to write their own names in the register.[72] In only 10 per cent of households in Dunkirk and Hernhill in 1851 could both parents, and all children (if they had them), sign their names. This predominant illiteracy—higher than both county and national figures[73]—suggests that the skill of writing was not highly prized in these communities.[74] This was particularly true at the labouring level, where only one-fifth to one-quarter of Hernhill and Dunkirk labourers and their wives were literate according to this gauge (see Table 10). The children of Hernhill labourers were twice as illiterate as those of farmers. When Boughton labourers wanted to subscribe to the local coal club which provided fuel for its members in the winter season, the treasurer (the landlord of a pub) signed for them. Writing was not essential for the day-to-day existence of the agricultural workers who comprised the bulk of the population in both parishes. Labourers relied on their skill and strength to function in their world. Of what use was a pen? Writing was a skill beyond their realm of expectation. 'Master . . . if I could do that [meaning write], I would not use the flail and the shovel.'[75]

The presence or absence of a signature gives what Roger Schofield has called a 'middle range' measurement of 'literacy', a

62 The Setting

TABLE 10 Social structure of illiteracy in Hernhill and Dunkirk, 1800–1850

Social group	Male No. sampled	Male No. mark*	Male % mark	Female No. sampled	Female No. mark*	Female % mark
Hernhill						
Farmers	34	11	32.3	34	17	50.0
Crafts	21	0	0	21	9	42.9
Trades	12	6	50.0	12	7	58.3
Agr. labourers	75	58	77.3	75	59	78.7
Labourers	50	36	72.0	50	42	84.0
Dunkirk						
Farmers	28	18	64.3	28	15	53.6
Crafts	16	4	25.0	16	5	31.2
Trades	9	3	33.3	9	5	55.5
Agr. labourers	70	61	87.1	70	58	82.9
Labourers	75	54	72.0	75	57	76.0

* Number of those sampled who could not sign their name, but had to make the mark of a cross instead.

rough indication of the ability to write. The main problem is that it will underestimate those able to read, a skill taught before writing. It is difficult actually to measure the extent of this group of hidden readers, but nineteenth-century studies suggest that the numbers able to read but not write were one-and-a-half to two times the proportion able to sign.[76] In his survey of young people over the age of 14 in Hernhill, Dunkirk, and Boughton, Liardet found that only one-quarter could read and write but over a half could read. If the ability to sign had been used as the criterion for literacy, 75 per cent of his young sample would have been classified as illiterate when in fact only 45 per cent could not read *or* write.[77] Although the historian's measurement of 'literacy' underestimates those able to read, it has been suggested that it is quite a good indication of those able to read *fluently*. As Liardet put it, 'Whenever a poor man is in the habit of reading, you can be sure he can write.'[78] Using all these guides, we could estimate that about a half of the labourers in Hernhill and slightly less in Dunkirk would have been able to read but that less than a quarter of them would have been able to read with facility. The reading ability of the female half of the population may have been higher than this, but we will return to this question in a later chapter.

When the middle-class urban observers came to Hernhill, Dunkirk, and Boughton in the wake of the abortive rising of 1838, they were struck by the literary deprivation of the agricultural labourer. The habit of reading, the culture of the printed word, was relatively undeveloped in this part of Kent—and, I suspect, in most nineteenth-century rural villages and hamlets. Liardet visited 150 labouring homes in the Ville, Hernhill, and Boughton and found that in less than 10 per cent of them did parents claim to open a book in the evening. To the enquiry as to how they passed this time, most replied, 'About home, doing sometimes one thing sometimes another; but, most times, going early to bed for want of something to do.' Over 40 per cent of those interviewed possessed absolutely no reading material whatsoever. The lawyer was astonished by the lack of literature other than the Bible, Testament, and prayer or hymn books. 'Not a Penny Magazine, nor any of the other cheap publications of the day, which convey so much useful instruction and amusement to the working classes in the towns, was to be seen.'[79] Rural dwellers lacked the 'constant collision of mind' which was to be found in the towns, wrote the lawyer. Mere religious instruction did not equip 'men for discharging their duties to society'. They needed 'short histories of distinguished men, especially of such as have risen by their own merits from obscurity', 'a useful every-day kind of literature'.

> If, when the out-door work was over, the cottage family, sitting by a cheerful fire, and engaged in some light and profitable handicraft, could be entertained by a member of it reading some interesting particulars respecting the labours in which they are ordinarily engaged, or the natural objects with which they are conversant, their curiosity could not fail of being excited. In the same manner, tales of the lives of persons in their own sphere, showing the results of the prudential virtues and their opposites, could not but have the happiest effects.[80]

Liardet advocated that each family should have a small book explaining 'the legal rights and *duties* [my emphasis] of persons as members of society'.

Liardet's survey tells us as much about his own cultural prejudices and class assumptions as it does about the reading inadequacies of the rural poor. Light and heat were expensive, and fatigue was not conducive to intellectual or spiritual pursuit. Rural England was still partly an oral society, not fully literate.[81] When the village censuses were taken in 1841, the variety of spelling, the phonetics of naming, suggests that people were used to hearing and saying their personal names and place-names rather than having them written down. Literacy and illiteracy mixed in families. As we saw earlier, there were few households in Hernhill and Dunkirk where all members of the family could sign their names. Most of the totally literate families were to be found among the farmers and those employed in the crafts, but even here they were a minority. Most households contained a combination of those who signed and those who made a mark.[82] Yet despite Liardet's mental blinkers, the really striking finding of his survey is unassailable: the one book that a majority of labourers' cottages contained was the Bible or Testament.

There is little doubting the importance of the church in the life of the rural community of Hernhill. It supervised the rites of passage of all the inhabitants, including those of many Methodists. There is no indication that the population (as many demographers have assumed) forsook the church after civil registration was introduced in 1837: marriages, births, and deaths were still recorded in the parish registers. The church, and the Sunday school run by Cassandra Handley, the minister's wife, were resorted to by large numbers of the population. From a third to a half of the total population or one-half to three-quarters of the adult inhabitants were at church on any given Sunday; one-third of children aged 5–14 attended Sunday school, where their teacher attempted to acquaint them 'with moral and religious truths'.[83] Few received communion.[84] The type of worship favoured in Hernhill was the same as in James Obelkevich's rural Lincolnshire parishes: 'Holy Communion was for the élite; for the ordinary churchgoer, Morning and Evening Prayer were the standard services.'[85]

Of course, these bare facts of village Anglicanism tell us nothing of what the service meant to those who attended; what they thought, say, in 1811 as they gazed at the newly painted commandments or listened to the sermon.[86] Perhaps one of the attractions was the church music provided by the singers and the band who, led by the future rioter William Wills, performed in the church gallery.[87] (St Michael's still has the remnants of graffiti, scratched perhaps by one of the gallery minstrels.) Ministers throughout England bewailed this lay participation, complaining of sawing and jarring instruments and of the 'nasal twangs of ... untrained rustics', and they replaced them, eventually, with the

19 St Michael's church, Hernhill, c.1870. *Source*: Len Rooks photography.

organ and youthful choirs.[88] But the bands (Hernhill's had a flute, a bassoon, and a bass viol) were community institutions in the first part of the century.

Religious life in Dunkirk is more of a mystery than that in Hernhill. The Ville ranked high in the index of Anglican attendance in the Census of 1851.[89] But this was after the short and enthusiastic impact of Dunkirk's first curate. The first church in Dunkirk was established in *1841*, in response to the Courtenay trouble. Before that the Ville was extra-parochial. Its people, if they went to church, attended the parish churches at Boughton, Hernhill, Harbledown, and Blean; baptisms, burials, and marriages from Dunkirk are recorded in their parish registers. Children from the Ville were enrolled at the Hernhill Sunday School.[90]

Of course, there were alternatives to Anglicanism. Boughton had an established Wesleyan population in the 1830s, largely made up of farmers and trades and craftspeople; they ran a Methodist Sunday school.[91] The Wesleyan Methodist circuit plans, and surviving registers and certificates of dissenting churches, reveal that preachers were active in the Hernhill area from at least 1816 onwards, with ministers calling at Dargate and Staple Street during the 1820s. A chapel was established at Dargate in 1840.[92] Although there was a number of illiterate agricultural labourers among them, the Hernhill Methodists were disproportionately drawn from the farming class. They included Elizabeth Foreman, the widowed mother of John Foreman, who owned Dargate Farm, the Brownings at Cherry Orchard, and Edward Rigden, who, before his death in 1831, owned Lavender Farm and other property in the area.[93] The Wesleyans were also represented in Dunkirk. Dunkirk people attended meetings for worship in Boughton, but houses in the Ville itself were registered as meeting places from 1817 onwards, so ministers were presumably calling there too.[94] The Dunkirk Wesleyans included the farmers Thomas and William Berry and Thomas Bodle, some labourers, and a basket-maker.[95] There were over 300 Wesleyans in Canterbury in 1839, 170 in Faversham, 72 in Whitstable, 70 in Boughton. These were the main areas of strength, but their other branches in the Faversham circuit (which covered this part of Kent) included Doddington, Greenstreet, Throwley, Blean, Chilham, Chartham, and Luddenham.[96]

This milder and respectable brand of Methodism seems to have predominated in this part of Kent. The more plebeian and enthusiastic Primitive Methodists and Bible Christians never captured this part of the country. The Primitives had a base in Boughton in 1851, where they later built a chapel, as well as in Canterbury, but before that they had little impact.[97] The court records contain a reference to a Primitive Methodist woman preaching in Faversham market-place in 1836. We know of revivalist meetings in Sheerness and Sittingbourne in 1838, and of missions to 'country villages'.[98] And yet the weakness of Primitive Methodism in the area is underlined by the numbers in its Sunday schools in 1837: eighteen teachers and ninety-five children in the Sheerness *and London* districts combined.[99]

The desultory performance of the early Primitive Methodists was due in part to the dominance of Wesleyanism. But they had also to compete with a type of Christianity not dissimilar to their own, that of the Bible Christians. In the 1820s, in a burst of missionary zeal, a Bible Christian minister claimed that they had four or five hundred followers in Kent: 'Instead of drinking, swearing, and fighting husbands and wives, they are now sober, praying, meek husbands and wives.'[100] James Thorne was over-optimistic. The Sheerness Circuit Quarterly Meeting Minute Book shows that there was less than half this number in that part of Kent. What they lacked in numbers, however, the Bible Christians made up for in terms of geographical spread. They were in Teynham, Bapchild, Swalecliffe, Newnham, Preston, Kingsdown, Throwley, Sittingbourne, Rodmersham, Canterbury, and Faversham—all within walking distance of Hernhill and Dunkirk.[101] More important, we can actually place them in Hernhill, briefly, from 1826–7: in June 1826 there were three people on trial membership in Dargate; by March 1827 there were nine full members and one on trial; by early 1828 the Dargate membership had disappeared.[102] We have no idea who those Hernhill Bible Christians were. They may have been Wesleyans, flirting briefly with enthusiasm; they may just have left the parish. We will probably never know. Although Faversham remained a relative stronghold for the Bible Christians, with thirty to forty members throughout the 1820s and 1830s (and twice that number attending meetings) and a persistent presence in 1851, one gets the impression that the sect was in decline before the late 1830s.[103] Their Canterbury preaching house had to be abandoned in 1829 because the meeting was down to ten people.[104]

Whatever the original sources—and most of them seem to have been Anglican—the minds of at least a substantial minority of the population, including those at the labouring level, were fashioned by religious influences. If they attended Sunday school—and many did—they were catechized and read the Bible. If they attended school, they were taught to read the Testament and would consequently flounder when forced to read out of context, that is, when confronted with another book. If they owned reading matter—and the majority of the labouring homes visited by Liardet did contain books—it was nearly always religious in nature. Even the prints on the walls of their cottages were 'usually of a religious kind'.[105] This religious mind-set helps to explain the millenarian dimension of the rising of 1838.

3
Conflict and Discontents

THERE is a tendency in some studies of rural life in the past to gloss over tensions and conflict and to emphasize social harmony. One can search in vain through this rural nostalgia for any information on crime and violence, apart from the predictable page on a colourful poaching character. And yet conflict and violence was (and is) endemic in rural society: disorder is not the prerogative of the towns. There is little support in the pages that follow for those who look back to the past as some kind of rural Arcadia.

In fact, there is evidence of a level of casual violence in the Hernhill and Dunkirk area in the nineteenth century. Life was a struggle; it would have been surprising if there had not been an accompanying degree of habitual aggression. Tempers were short; people were ready to resort to verbal or physical force to resolve arguments. Both women and men were under threat. The modern observer is immediately struck by the nineteenth-century male's readiness openly to employ violence against women. There were no paternalistic or protective qualms about hitting the 'weaker sex'. James Adley quarrelled with Mary Wraight in the street in Boughton. He spat in her face, hit her, and kicked her in the stomach before he was pulled away by other women.[1] A woman passed a couple on the turnpike road at Boughton; the man had his companion on the ground and was kicking and punching her ('she appeared much hurt and begged for mercy').[2] These were not isolated examples. It is worth pointing out that, as is the case today, women had more to fear from relatives and neighbours than they did from total strangers. Several women took their husbands to court for domestic violence. George Howland was arrested for threatening to cut his wife's head off. William Burford, a future rioter, was detained for assaulting his wife.[3] The various cases of wife beating which appear in the court records show that battered wives had some protection, yet they also indicate the real presence of domestic violence. Much of it must have gone undetected. Nicholas Mears, the assistant constable killed by Courtenay in 1838, was said to have treated his wife like a dog, but he was never brought to court for such mistreatment.[4] Reported cases of sexual violence were rare, but they may also have concealed wider practice. Christopher Tong (also known as Pegden) sexually violated his stepdaughter for a year before he was caught, and was found out only because the girl's sister reported him to a constable.[5] Solitary women were particularly vulnerable to sexual violence. Nine-year-old Ann Milgate was alone in the house while her parents were out working when two Dunkirk youths attempted to rape her. Lydia Exton was tying hops in an isolated field when she was assaulted by Richard Culver.[6]

Male-against-male aggression took place within carefully defined limits. Extreme violence was rare—I do not know of any murders in Hernhill or Dunkirk other than those of 1838, which helps to explain the horror of the Courtenay killings. Though people possessed guns, knives, and axes, they seldom used them against one another. They might threaten to chop each other up or to cut off one another's ears, but such verbal violence was rarely converted into action. It is true that sticks or cudgels were used. Nicholas Mears was fined in 1831 for assaulting a Dunkirk labourer with a stick. Adman Packman attacked John Mears with a hop-pole in 1837 when the constable was searching his house for some stolen sheep. Two Dunkirk sheep-stealers used cudgels to intimidate a hostile witness.[7] However, the most commonly used weapons were fists and feet. Although the fact that some Dunkirk labourers concealed stones in their fists when they attacked a local farmer suggests an element of practised aggression (the rural form of street-fighting), most of the violence was in the heat of the moment, and often fuelled by drink.[8]

Dunkirk, we have seen, had a reputation as an unruly, lawless parish. The court records reinforce the stereotype. Over a hundred Dunkirk and Hernhill people appeared before the Petty and Quarter Sessions in the period between 1833 and 1845, an average of eight or nine people a year. Of this approximate hundred, only about twenty came from Hernhill. All of the seven men transported for theft during these years came from the Ville of Dunkirk. Other than the rioters of 1838, who are not included in these figures, few appeared before the Court of Assizes which dealt with the most serious offences.

The vast majority of offences were those against property, and mostly what one historian has termed 'crimes of survival': thefts of peas, grain, beans, rabbits, fowls, fruit, potatoes, turnips.[9] Mary James, a 16-year-old woman from Dunkirk, stole a pound of cheese from a Boughton shop. John Dalton, an 18-year-old labourer, took a loaf of bread and a piece of pork from a beershop while the woman serving there was washing dishes in an adjoining room. Edward Curling caught Mary and Susan Johncock in the field of another Hernhill farmer busily pulling up potatoes and putting them in a basket.[10] Not all of the stolen items were consumed or used. Goods were pawned in Canterbury or sold in nearby beershops. A man who stole a woodman's bill-hook from a house in Dunkirk sold it in Boughton Street for 1s. (about half a day's wage). Rabbits taken from hutches in the Ville were sold to a Whitstable beer retailer for 2s. 6d. each.[11] Some of the thefts were on a larger scale. Dunkirk sheep- and pig-stealers, transported for their offences, clearly knew what they were doing. They worked at night or in the early hours of the morning, slaughtering animals in the woods and hiding their carcasses. On his way home at 2 a.m., one of the men encountered a constable so he promptly began to stagger, pretending that he was returning home after a night of hard drinking.[12] The crimes reflected the nature of the local economy. In 1833 Richard Culver, a woodman from Dunkirk, was alleged to have stolen a packet of hops worth £14 from an oast in Boughton. They were first sold to a middleman for £3 and a £3 barrel of beer, but finally ended up with a Canterbury brewer.[13]

We can assume that those caught represented merely the tip of a larger undeclared 'dark figure of crime'. One of the insurrectionaries of 1838 was a reputed sheep-stealer, even though he was never actually prosecuted for the offence.[14] Some Blean protesters admitted to earlier undetected thefts of fowls when faced in 1830 with the far more serious charge of incendiarism.[15] The notebook of the constable of Boughton shows that, although his raids did not always result in prosecutions, he knew which premises to search or watch for stolen goods.[16]

Wood-stealing was one of the most common offences in the area. Wood, like hops, had a ready market, and there is evidence that some of the thefts were on an organized scale. Bundles of wood, ready-cut by some unsuspecting woodman, could be spirited away in the early hours of the morning and sold to dealers or to the powder works several miles away. Three Dunkirk men who were charged with wood theft in 1836 seem to have mixed stolen bundles with legitimate sales—the suspect wood was recovered in the yard of a Davington gentleman.[17] Another gang of wood-stealers, based in Boughton, plundered the Dunkirk woods of absentee landlords under cover of dark, conveying cartloads down Boughton Hill before morning to their base.[18] But the majority of thefts were small-scale, crimes of subsistence like the food thefts, commonest during the pressures of winter. They were cases like that of Arthur Lee, caught in February 1843, breaking down a hedge belonging to a Hernhill farmer; when brought before the magistrate, Lee said in his defence that he was only getting wood 'to make a light for his wife'. (He could not pay the 12s. 6d. fine imposed by the magistrate so was sentenced to 14 days in prison.)[19] All the posts of the pound on Dargate Common were stolen in the early nineteenth century, taken away by the poor for firewood during the winter.[20]

Poaching was rife too. But here there is no evidence of organized crime on a large scale. Those apprehended were not large professional poaching gangs but woodmen and labourers operating alone or in small groups to supplement their diet or their meagre incomes. Two Dunkirk men were caught, gun in hand, in the snow in Hurst Wood, tracing the bloodied tracks of a wounded hare.[21] Dunkirk men hunted for partridges in the fields, with dogs and guns, and pheasants in the woods, with wires.[22] Several ranged further afield. John Brunger was caught in Badlesmere in the early evening with a tell-tale stump in his hand and a wire around his hat (the basic material for a snare). John Branchett was apprehended with snares in Giles Hilton's rabbit warren at Selling; Christopher Pegden, with dog and gun, in Lord Sondes's wood in Sheldwich.[23] Liardet claimed in his 1838 report that Hernhill had 'formerly a character for poaching', but that the practice was 'much lessened'.[24] His claims seem to be borne out by the evidence of the courts; few Hernhill men were prosecuted for game offences.

Finally, there was smuggling. The north coast of Kent was notorious for its illicit trading during the eighteenth and early nineteenth centuries. The fisherfolk of Whitstable and Seasalter knew the coast well, and goods landed there could be hidden inland in the Blean woods or in isolated farmhouses. They were secluded spots but close to the sea and near to the market centres of Faversham and Canterbury. Some respectable families founded their fortunes on trade in contraband. There were elaborate methods of communication. Honey Hill Farm, in the Blean, was used as a signal point to warn traders of the authorities' movements in Canterbury. Contraband was hidden in Ellenden Wood.[25] There were organized gangs, but also the small-scale entrepreneur. As

Liardet put it, 'Many of the small farmers, who prospered so surprisingly on lands out of which their fathers could barely eke sufficient to pay their rent and support their families, had found out the secret, that ploughing the sea was a much more gainful trade than ploughing the land.'[26]

In the 1820s drink and tobacco were seized in Sheppey, foreign silks in Ospringe, handkerchiefs and silk in Greenstreet. The excise men located brandy in a cart in Bobbing, French gin in a Dunkirk beershop, and tobacco in a Boughton victualler's stable.[27] Some of the goods were shifted quite openly. An Upchurch man was caught loading contraband green tea into a wheelbarrow in broad daylight.[28] Prosecutions faded after the 1820s, possibly because of the efficiency of the excise men, probably because the reduction in tariffs made smuggling a less profitable business.

As far as the community was concerned, some of the 'crimes' that we have been discussing would not have been 'crimes' at all. A man who admitted stealing some chickens added, 'Those are the only acts of dishonesty (except shooting of a Sunday poaching) that I have ever been guilty of.'[29] Poaching was not quite an act of dishonesty. Liardet talked to a man in Dunkirk in 1838 who thought hares were common property and condemned a system that imprisoned a man and beggared his family because he had killed a bit of game.[30] Poaching, and probably small-scale smuggling and wood-stealing too, were what are now called 'social crimes', enjoying the sympathy, if not the open sanction, of large sections of the labouring population.[31]

Our area experienced—indeed, participated in—two spectacular examples of nineteenth-century protest: the Swing rising of 1830 and the Anti-Poor Law riots of 1835. The Swing rising is best seen as a series of sporadic, locally based riots rather than a nationally co-ordinated rising. True, the example of insubordination was contagious, relayed dramatically by the incendiarists' fires. (It is no accident that many were lit on the tops of hills.) Labourers and craftsmen protested over agricultural machinery, low wages, and high rents, as what Eric Hobsbawm and George Rudé have termed the 'multiformity' of their protest was replicated in neighbourhood after neighbourhood.[32] What superficially appeared as a nationally co-ordinated movement was in reality a series of local phenomena linked by common causes.

Possibly because of its commanding location, Boughton Hill witnessed some of the first outbreaks of the Swing rising in Kent, with fires there in early and late October and others in November.[33] The victims included Price Lade, Esq. at Boughton, Thomas Berry of Dunkirk, and Edward Rigden, a wealthy Hernhill farmer with properties in that parish and in Dunkirk and Harbledown, notably the Red Lion and Plough Inns. Lade and Rigden lost furze stacks, which must have provided tempting targets for their enemies.[34] A barn full of corn was fired at Selling Court, residence of Lord Sondes's steward, John Neame, who also owned land in Hernhill. *The Times* reported that labourers looked 'coolly' on as the fire blazed; someone attempted to cut the pipes of one of the fire engines. Neame lost £727 in fire damage according to the records of the Kent Fire Insurance Company.[35] There were two fires at Blean, one in a clover stack and another in a barn belonging to the Hernhill farmer William Wraight. He lost 20 tons of wheat, straw, beans, and hay, and two ploughs: £300 of uninsured property.[36] This intimidating behaviour provided the backdrop for collective action. In early November a band of labourers went from parish to parish in the area around Faversham and Boughton Street, reputedly numbering four hundred at one stage, pressing for an increase in wages to 2s. 6d. a day. Machine-breakers were active in Ospringe.[37]

It is difficult to convey the mixture of fear and anticipation in the minds of those who lived through 1830. As early as 28 September, farmers met at the Rose Inn, Canterbury, on a Saturday to discuss appropriate measures to protect themselves from those who were combining to destroy threshing machines. (One of those present was Hernhill's Edward Curling.[38]) The Kent Fire Insurance Company, whose directors included men with landed investments in the Hernhill–Dunkirk area—Thomas Ford, Osborne Snoulton, William Hyder, Giles Hilton, and John Neame—on 27 October requested their chairman to communicate to the Lord Lieutenant 'the alarming state in which the Agricultural Interest of the County is placed from the frequent and destructive Fires which have lately happened and it is feared are likely further to happen to Property occasioned by the Malice of Incendiaries'. By 24 November, the directors were informing farmers that the company was offering a £100 reward for the detection of incendiarists. The company was also worried by the number of false alarms 'in consequence of the great excitement', and urged those in charge of fire engines to assess the reliability of reported blazes.[39]

This excitement can be detected in places other than the minutes of the Kent Fire Insurance Company. In early November, special constables were sworn in in Faversham and watches were placed on farms in the neighbourhood. Men stood on the church tower to look out for fires. News of a fire at Doddington caused panic in the midst of the Mayor of Faversham's inauguration.[40] The Home Office's correspondent in Faversham reported almost nightly on the state of the surrounding countryside. 'I have been on the top of my House,' he reported of one fire, 'and it appears to be about 5 or 6 miles distant in a strait line between here [Faversham] and Lenham, perhaps in Throwley, Eastling, Stalisfield or Newnham.' In an age before electricity, the impact of a well-placed fire could be quite spectacular. The Home Office's man watched the fire at Wraight's barn in Blean, which, although six miles away, 'had the appearance of being very near the town'. So great was the light 'that, altho the Fire was at the back of the Church, yet the face of the Clock which is on the front was seen as at noon day'.[41] Even if the observer exaggerated the physical reality, his description speaks volumes for the psychological effects of incendiarism.

The fires bred suspicion. The Packman brothers, executed for firing Wraight's barn in Blean, were suspected because they arrived late on the scene to assist with putting it out. People who attended the fire discussed likely culprits. They remembered that the Packmans had been out and about on the night of the fire after they had left a local public house. A labourer recalled that he 'thought it looked very badly for the 2 Packmans to run away from their own home at that time of night'. 'You know what it is to do such a thing', a thatcher told one of the incendiarists as they both stood watching the fire. 'If any of you split you must be hung.' 'You give different stories: if you don't make up a goodish story than that I am sure you will be took up from what I heard the Gentlemen say.'[42]

There was a mood of anticipation in the neighbourhood. When George Bishop, one of the incendiarists, returned home late at night and left again, his father became uneasy and asked his housekeeper to check to see if their tinder box was still there. When his son returned and went up to bed, his father said he 'thought it would be the last time he would ever go up there'. On the night of the fire there had been talk in the pub about arson. The 'general conversation in the room' was about a local wood-dealer. It was said that 'Mr Parren had been buying wood and had done so many poor people out of their money that we should not wonder if his

Stacks were set on fire.' William Packman had said that it 'would serve him right'. Bishop and the Packmans had intended to fire Parren's property but had decided on Wraight's barn when they went to his yard to get some straw.[43]

One should not underestimate the impact of Swing on the local community. In the short term, the labourers gained a great deal. Farmers in the Faversham area, intimidated by the collective action and the spectre of incendiarism, did indeed raise wages for a while. Those with threshing machines stopped using them. Some lowered their rents.[44] According to a Kentish curate in 1834, the farm-workers had discovered that 'agitation and burning' did for them that 'which remonstration never could'; 'even now they commonly say "Ah them there riots and burnings did the poor a terrible deal of good." '[45]

Yet the lessons for the labourers were two-edged, for the costs had been high. The fires in 1830 may have shown the vulnerability of the farmers, but they also demonstrated the invincibility of the British state. The Packmans were executed on Penenden Heath on the 24 December 1830. (Bishop had cheated death by turning King's evidence.) They arrived in a wagon surrounded by javelin men and attended by four armed guards. The Governor of Maidstone gaol and the sheriff's officers rode on horseback carrying black wands, accompanied by a troop of Scots Greys. As the wagon reached the platform, the prison chaplain joined them and 'engaged in prayer with the condemned'. Their father, sister, and brother embraced them before they mounted the steps of the scaffold to join a third incendiarist who had been sentenced for a separate offence. Before the execution the men denounced those who had informed against them. The Packmans then embraced. The caps were pulled over their faces, but before the bolt was drawn William Packman raised the cover from his face, saying that he 'wanted to see the people'. He was persuaded to pull it down again. The platform fell. 'The two brothers seemed to suffer very little', but the other man, John Dyke, 'struggled much'. Minutes before the execution, William Packman had remarked to the chaplain that 'the greatest consolation he had, was that his friends had brought a horse and cart to carry away his body, and that he should be decently buried'. (The chaplain had replied that he should turn his mind to more important things; 'what would become of his body was quite of minor importance, compared with the infinitely more weighty concerns of the soul.'[48]) Presumably the

Packmans' friends did take their bodies away for they were buried in the Blean churchyard: the Blean register records their interment four days later, 'executed on Penenden Heath for arson'.[47]

The Packmans lived at Denstrode, right on the border of Dunkirk. Bishop lived a mile away at Honey Hill. There were Bishops and Packmans in Dunkirk and Hernhill who may well have been related to the Blean families. In any case, the events at Blean and Penenden Heath could hardly have failed to make their mark on our communities. Ironically, William Wraight, the Hernhill farmer whose barn was destroyed, was related to six future followers of Courtenay, one of whom, James Goodwin, had witnessed the fire first hand.[48]

The next wave of protest to affect the area was the anti-Poor Law movement of 1835, like Swing a series of locally based protests, in this case against the provisions of the New Poor Law. In 1835 bands of labourers, some with faces blackened and carrying sticks, protested over the replacement of money relief by a system that issued bread and tickets and only partial payment in cash. The magistrates addressed the crowd, explaining that they were merely carrying out the law. The protesters replied that 'they knew better, the justices had made the law themselves'. Those who accepted tokens were searched by protesters and sent back to demand cash. They forced the relieving officers to pay recipients according to the old method, and in at least one case intimidated them so much they increased the rates of relief. One man carried an ash stick on which was carved the words 'Plenty or this'. Another had a card in his hat with the caption 'we want no tickets, no bread'. The mob used a horn.[49] Over forty men were arrested, half of whom had been involved in disturbances in three or more separate villages, and tried before a special sessions in June 1835. We have details for thirty-six of them, a baker and thirty-five labourers. Twenty were illiterate, able neither to read nor write; ten could read only; and six could read and write. The average age was 29: just over half were in their teens and twenties, most of the remainder in their thirties and forties.[50] Most of this unrest occurred west and south west of our parishes, in Bapchild, Rodmersham, Lynsted, Teynham, Doddington, Newnham, and Throwley. But it was all within a ten-mile radius of Hernhill—indeed, almost the very area traversed by Courtenay in his recruitment march of 1838.[51]

In Hernhill itself in 1835 a group of men and women marched behind a flag attached to a hop-pole. They attempted to upset a baker's cart carrying bread for poor relief. They dragged people from their work and out of their yards and forced them to join the protest.[52] One of the leaders of the 1838 Courtenay rising, Thomas Mears Tyler, was to serve time in prison for his role in the Hernhill anti-Poor Law troubles of 1835, so there is at least one instance of individual continuity between 1835 and 1838.[53]

We need not assume that resentment faded with overt protest; in fact, it is likely that discontent intensified as the implications of reform began to bite. Before the New Poor Law provisions of 1834, the parish Poor Law system (known as the Old Poor Law) provided a wide-ranging system of social welfare. The rates were on a sliding scale with larger payments to those families with more mouths to feed. During the winter months, a large proportion of the male labouring population in Hernhill received poor relief or were employed in work relief either on the properties of farmers or on the roads. The highway accounts show payments during the 1810s and 1820s ranging from 1s. 6d. to 2s. 6d. a day, that is as much as 13s. 6d. for a six-day week. Sometimes they were paid per load of gravel, which worked out to between 1s. 8d. and 2s. a day. It was rare for individuals to work a six-day week (between one and five days was more common), but this kind of directed labour meant an important income for many in the winter months: it could mean £6–£10 a year for the family economy.[54] Combined together, relief payments under the Old Poor Law could involve substantial sums by farm labourers' standards. Some of the future rioters of 1838 were at times receiving poor relief payments of up to 14s. or 15s. a week. William Rye was paid an average of £4. 16s. a year in poor relief over the seven-year period 1824–30; Charles Hadlow received £8. 4s. per annum during the same number of years.[55]

The overseers' day book shows a whole range of welfare payments for a miscellany of items: food, tobacco, tools, clothing, fuel. The occasional doctor's bill was covered; women were hired to nurse, care, and wash for the elderly, the infirm, or the heavily pregnant. The parish paid for funeral costs, including payments for beer. We should not be too uncritical of the Old Poor Law system: in January 1830 men were being paid a derisory 1s. 6d. a day for directed labour on the farm of a local landholder.[56] But the old regime did provide a much-needed cushion. The vast majority of agricultural labourers and several petty traders and small farmers would receive poor relief at some stage of their lives—this is clear from my file of people in Hernhill who remained in the parish over an extended period. The only people who seemed exempt from life-cycle poverty, who did not call upon parochial or Poor Law assistance, were the farmers and the majority of those employed in the crafts. This has important attitudinal implications, for it is inconceivable that any real stigma was attached to a system from which the majority of the population were beneficiaries. As David Thomson has put it, 'paupers were ... no deprived minority, no subclass of society, but "everyone", except the very rich and the very fortunate'.[57]

It is difficult to chart the impact of the New Poor Law of 1834. The highway accounts do not survive for this period, but presumably men still laboured on the roads. Elsewhere it seems that there was a new rigour. Funeral payments remained. People received outdoor relief for illness; and the union would sometimes pay for a midwife. But the union records show less generosity in welfare payments, at least in the period up to 1840.[58] The new Act's ban on outdoor relief was unworkable from the start. Almost immediately, outdoor relief was a feature of the administration of the Poor Law in this part of Kent. In the first winter quarter under the new Act (i.e. up to March 1836), Dunkirk had 13 indoor and 93 outdoor paupers, Hernhill 1 indoor and 101 outdoor: the ratio of indoor to outdoor paupers in the Faversham Union, the local administrative district, was 1: 11.[59] But the actual *rates* of relief were very low. George James was a 41-year-old woodman with a wife and six children. When he and his eldest son were in employ, they could earn as much as 16s. a week. But James fell ill in 1840 and asked for help to support his family. He was awarded 6s. a week, *half* as much as he would have received under the pre-1835 system.[60] As we will see in a later chapter, there were other similar cases.

The spirit of the new regime can be traced in the first volume of the minutes of the Board of the Faversham Union. In May 1835, relieving officers were given guidelines for the weekly rate for able-bodied persons employed in parish work (half in bread and half in money): 7s. 6d. for a man and wife; 9s. for a man, wife, and child; and 1s. for each additional child up to a maximum of 12s. In July, Sir Francis Head, the assistant poor law commissioner, met with the chairman and vice-chairman of the Union of East Kent and told them that a fixed scale of relief was 'directly hostile to the principle of the poor Law Amendment Act'. Relief had to be decided according to the applicant's earnings, reasons for loss of employment, character, and conduct; 'the Pauper should never be able to calculate for himself with any degree of security on the relief which should be awarded to him—on the contrary, by its constant and to him incomprehensible fluctuation, he would eventually learn that he had a certain support—nothing on which he could safely rest, but *his own industry* and *his own providence.*' The cushion was to be removed with a vengeance in a way that would have gladdened the heart of many a 1980s Thatcherite. After 'several hours' of discussion, it was agreed that relief would not *exceed* 5s. a week for a man and wife, and 10s. for a man and wife and six children.[61] The New Poor Law provided the landlords and farmers—for it was they who were the guardians—with a potent weapon of social control. In the aftermath of the rising of 1838, ten wives and widows of rioters applied for poor relief: six were ordered into the workhouse 'on the ground of bad character'.[62] There is a lot to be said for Keith Snell's description of the New Poor Law as having had 'the most harmful and socially damaging effect on rural class relations in the south of any nineteenth-century legislation'.[63]

For those who went into the workhouse—the old, the chronically sick, the mentally unstable, the destitute, and the orphaned—life may have been easier than on the outside. Breakfast and supper were the same every day: bread and cheese (or butter). Dinner varied: bread and cheese most days, but on some days meat or suet pudding and vegetables.[64] The diet was simple, but it was probably more regular than the meals provided in many labouring cottages. In the winter of 1838, the Poor Law commissioners in Faversham anticipated that those forced into the workhouse would be pleasantly surprised by the clothing, diet, and shelter provided. However, the guardians also noted 'the prejudice against the place'.[65] Men and women were separated. Those who entered the institution had to abide by the rules of the house; if they wanted to leave, permission had to be obtained. When some boys absconded in 1838, they were punished with a whipping and twenty-four hours' solitary confinement. It is little wonder that there were problems with abusive language, absconding, theft, and cases of men being found in the female side of the house.[66]

The 1830s were a bad time for the agricultural labourer, apart from the rigours of the New Poor Law. As we saw in an earlier chapter, population had increased substantially in the rural areas, putting pressure on available jobs. E. A. Wrigley has demonstrated that in the nation at large male employment in agriculture was almost at a standstill in the first half of the nineteenth century. Some of the rise in the employable population was absorbed by expansion in the traditional trades and crafts, but it was not enough to match the population boom. There was, in short, a labour surplus.[67] Wage rates in Kent were higher than in many English counties, but T. L. Richardson's careful work, plotting wages against food prices, shows that in Kent, for those unemployed for three months of the year (a not uncommon occurrence), real wages were depressed for most of the period 1790–1840. For all farmworkers, including those in regular employment, there was a short-term fall in real wages over 1835–40.[68] Although it is invisible on the wage graphs, the 1820s and 1830s also saw a time of high unemployment. One agrarian historian has described this as 'a time when the condition of the majority of farmworkers sank to a depth unparalleled in modern times'.[69]

The immediate backdrop to 1838 was a disastrous winter. Its severity is reflected in the Poor Law Union papers. The Faversham Union, the catchment area for Hernhill and Dunkirk, ran out of places in December 1837 and had to order new beds and blankets. The number of people in the workhouse jumped dramatically in one week in January 1838, from 210 to 302. Hundreds more, labourers and their families, were given outdoor relief.[70] It was calculated from the Poor Law records that at the peak of unemployment in Hernhill about one in eight persons were in receipt of poor relief, but this was an underestimation, for we know that the farmers of Hernhill had *unofficially* relieved labourers, presumably to avoid a further increase in the poor rates. In Dunkirk one-third of the population sought help in the form of either indoor or outdoor relief.[71] The Faversham guardians wrote to London, explaining their departure from official policy prohibiting outdoor relief for the able-bodied: 'There is scarcely a Parish in the Union but the labourers in which have suffered exceedingly, having been prevented from working in consequence of the Frost and Fall of Snow.' The letter explained that there was a 'prejudice in the minds of many against receiving Relief in the Workhouse, but as many have been compelled to accept it from utter destitution, and others on the same ground must inevitably follow unless temporary Out Door Relief be offered'.[72] The *Kentish Observer* reported that the River Medway had frozen over. In Maidstone the outside temperatures dropped to a reputed 3°F (29 degrees below freezing).[73]

The crime rate increased too, a reflection of hardship, as the Poor Law commissioner for Kent and Sussex admitted.[74]

The severe winter had arrived on top of a bad harvest, a decay in the hop trade, and a fall in fruit prices owing to the removal of protective tariffs. Grain prices were healthy, but in the immediate short term they benefited only the middleman and were hardly helpful for a labouring population which spent most of its budget on bread or flour. Kent was experiencing a short-term depression, and the Poor Law commissioner for the county was advising restraint and stringency in the administering of poor relief.[75] Moreover, the rate book and the church warden's accounts indicate that Hernhill rents had jumped dramatically in 1837. The situation of the labourers in this part of Kent certainly was not as cosy as some nineteenth-century commentators pretended in the aftermath of the rising of 1838.

PART II
The Rising

4
The Rising

WHERE we begin our story depends ultimately upon whether we want to concentrate on the leader of the agricultural labourers, Courtenay, or on the labourers themselves. Rogers's *Bossenden Wood* emphasizes the individual rather than the movement, but I want to shift the focus. We will discuss Courtenay's earlier activity and life in the next chapter. All we need to note for the moment is that the man was an impostor whose real name was John Tom. He turned up in Canterbury in the early 1830s, dressed in oriental clothing and claiming to be Sir William Courtenay. (The real one was living in France.) He rapidly became embroiled in local politics, standing as a candidate in the national election of 1832 and indeed polling quite well. His political career was cut short in 1833 when he was imprisoned for perjury and then transferred to the Kent County Lunatic Asylum. When he was released in 1837, Tom, still calling himself Sir William, went to live not far from Canterbury in the region comprising the parishes Hernhill, the Ville of Dunkirk (which, as we have seen, was extra-parochial at this time), and Boughton-under-Blean.

It was here that he began in 1838 to agitate among the farm labourers, injecting a brand of millenarian fervour into an area that had already experienced agrarian discontent and protest in 1830 and against the New Poor Law of 1834. According to the vicar of Hernhill, the Revd. Charles Handley, Courtenay visited small farmers and labouring women and men 'at their own cottages'. He organized a meeting on Boughton Hill, attended by an estimated two hundred people, at which 'the subject of his address [was] the wrongs supposed to be inflicted by the rich on the poor, taking for his text the first of the fifth chapter of the general epistle of St James. Go to now ye rich men, weep & howl for your miseries that shall come upon you.'[1]

Then, on 29 May, Oak Apple Day (the commemoration of the restoration of Charles II), Courtenay and a small band began to traverse the village lanes of the area, marching in pseudo-military fashion under a flag, and carrying that traditional icon of popular protest, a loaf of bread on a pole. We can trace the group's

20 Courtenay. *Source*: *Penny Satirist*, 9 June 1838.

movements with some precision (Map 2). They were operating in a face-to-face society: little went unnoticed. In the trial of those who were later to be called 'the rioters', there was no shortage of woodcutters and labourers who had observed things over a hedge or had dropped in to hear Courtenay or to cadge some beer, bread, or cheese. The governing class of the area was also keeping an eye on the labourers' activities. Courtenay's band was shadowed. Norton Knatchbull, a Justice of the Peace, was later able to relate the number of the retinue with some accuracy: 48 on the twenty-ninth of May; 36 on the thirty-first, just before the encounter with

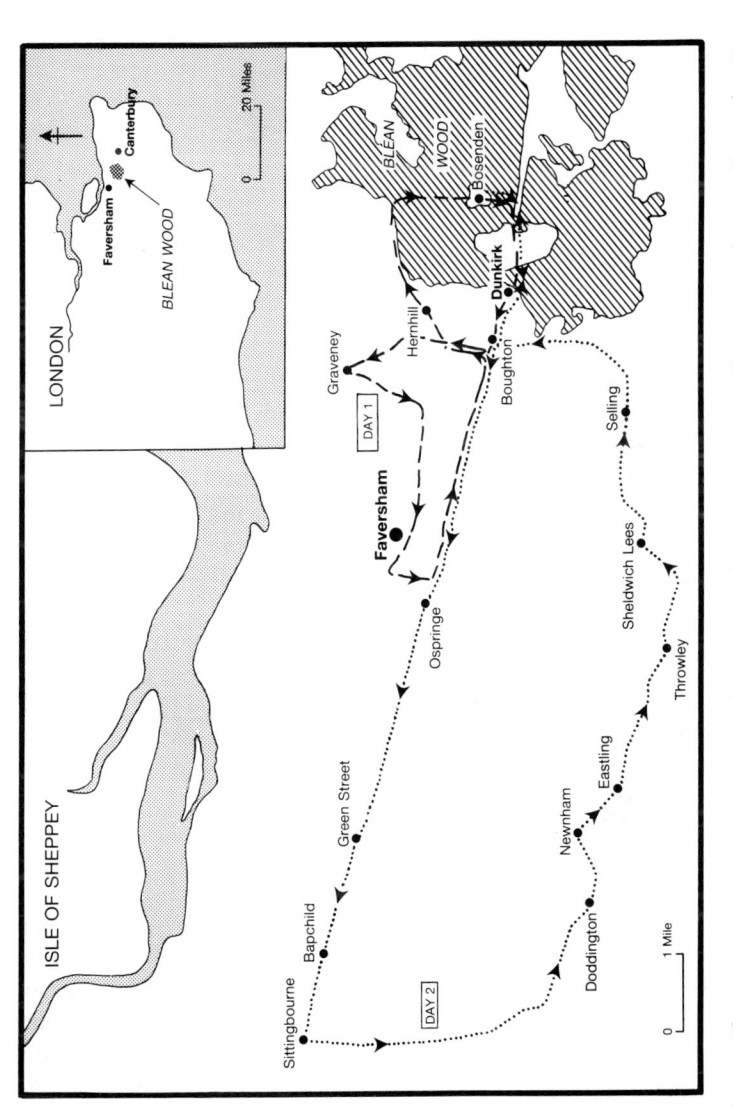

MAP 2 The recruitment march on 29 and 30 May 1838, starting from Courtenay's base at Bosenden Farm.

the military.[2] The group covered something like forty miles in two days, moving from village to village, hamlet to hamlet: from Dunkirk to Graveney to Davington and back by Hernhill on the Tuesday, from Dunkirk to Sittingbourne—through Boughton, Ospringe, and Bapchild—on the Wednesday, returning again via Newnham, Doddington, Eastling, Throwley, Sheldwich, and Selling 'through Lord Sondes's park'.[3] It could not have been mere coincidence that the area from which they were attempting to recruit support, the rural communities near and between Faversham and Sittingbourne, had been the site of protest in 1835 against the rigours of the New Poor Law.[4]

The marchers caused 'the greatest excitement', Courtenay 'asking the labourers as they passed to join his ranks,—as he would provide them with provisions and money', and telling them 'that there was great oppression in the land, and indeed throughout the world, but that if they would follow him, he would lead them on to glory'.[5] The marchers were men, although women gathered along the way to listen, and were later blamed, as readers of scripture, for having filled the men's minds with silly ideas. Some men joined the marchers for a while and then left; at times the party swelled to nearly one hundred strong. But as Knatchbull was aware, the central core was half that number.

The gentry and farmers began to complain that Courtenay was 'exciting the people by stating the Hardship the poor were under from the New Poor Laws' and that unless he was stopped, to quote one early complainant (Colonel Groves of Boughton), 'neither persons or property would be safe'.[6] Mr Edward Curling, a farmer of substance in Hernhill and Dunkirk, attempted to invoke the informal sanctions of paternalism, informing 'his' labourers that they would not be employed again unless they left Courtenay.[7] The Revd. John Poore, JP, was convinced that the troublemakers 'should not be allowed to go on', so he issued warrants for the arrest of Courtenay and two of his followers.[8]

The band had meanwhile returned to their base at Dunkirk, on the edge of Blean Forest, to Bosenden Farm, the home of the farmer William Culver whose wife and daughter, Sarah, had befriended Courtenay. In the early hours of Thursday morning, the constable of Boughton, John Mears, a plumber by trade, was dispatched to execute a warrant upon Courtenay and his companions William Wills and Edward Newman. Mears was accompanied by his brother Nicholas, a gardener, and also by an assistant constable.

21 The march. *Source*: From a drawing in the *Weekly Chronicle*, 10 June 1838.

22 Edward Curling on horseback, 'in disguise' in a workman's smock, at the time of the rising. *Source*: from an original oil painting in the possession of Hugh Curling, Faversham.

When the three arrived at Bosenden, Courtenay shot and stabbed Nicholas Mears, whose body was thrown into a ditch, thus sealing the fate of the agricultural labourers. Although it never came out at the trial, it was alleged later that the victim had accompanied the protesters several days before, so it is at least possible that Courtenay acted from a sense of betrayal.[9] One can only surmise what must have been in the minds of the agricultural labourers after the killing. Shortly before the man's death, Courtenay had told them that it was 'the first day of the Millenium—and this day I will put the crown upon my own head'.[10] Some were undoubtedly swept along by similar chiliastic fervour, but others were merely frightened and would attempt to slip away when the opportunity arose.

The justices sent for the military. Courtenay and his followers went first to Lavender Farm at Waterham, the property of Julius Shepherd, where John Hadlow was bailiff. Lydia Hadlow provided breakfast. Ninety-six-year-old Elizabeth Arnold, a waggoner's wife, and a friend of Lydia Hadlow, recalled in 1910 that she had seen the men 'seated beside the granary, eating bread and cheese, and drinking beer. They were bringing the beer out of the cellar in pailfuls.'[11] During the following hours they moved around the Hernhill area, followed by a force of constables and gentry and

23 The murder of the 'constable', from a contemporary print. *Source*: Dawes collection.

24 The death of Nicholas Mears: another version. *Source: Wilson's Wonderful Characters* (no date), Bodleian Library, Oxford.

farmer volunteers who had converged on the area from all the surrounding villages. The correspondence of Knatchbull, who trailed Courtenay during those final hours, provides a nice image of the class nature of the conflict: farmers and landowners sat on horseback on the crest of a hill; their quarry, the labourers, were in a willow-bed below, on foot. His pursuers attempted to snipe at Courtenay—a fact not mentioned at the trial—before the party retreated into Bosenden Wood. Knatchbull left them to rendezvous with the military but sent scouts to report on the labourers' movements.[12]

When the 45th Infantry—about 150 men strong according to Knatchbull—arrived from Canterbury, they split into two groups to intercept the agricultural labourers in the woods in a pincer manoeuvre, with each detachment accompanied by two magistrates and a commanding officer. One of the groups, led by Captain Reid and the magistrates Knatchbull and William Baldock, divided yet again. It was this small group, commanded by Lt. Bennett, that first encountered the labourers in the woods close to where the other detachment, under its officer Armstrong and the magistrate Poore, had circled round on the far side of Bosenden. Details of the actual engagement vary; reports are confused. Courtenay and Bennett fell upon one another; both were dead within seconds. Pandemonium ensued. Armstrong's men, who had only just finished loading their muskets, fired. The agricultural labourers turned on them, and Armstrong ordered his force to charge with bayonets.[13]

Officers and magistrates were later keen to emphasize the orderly, controlled way in which the 'riot' was suppressed; that 'the military, in self defence'—the words are those of Poore, the JP in charge—'were obliged to fire'. Knatchbull said much the same at the inquest on the dead rioters.[14] Others were more sceptical. The *Penny Satirist* printed a poem which summed up the doubts rather neatly:

> The parsons were in such a fright,
> They shot the trees 'dead'! Oh yes!! quite!!!
> .   .   .   .   .   .
> Coursing hares is less exciting
> Killing peasants! so inviting!![15]

Radical critics of the government were to refer to the 'magisterial murders' in Bosenden Wood. Bronterre O'Brien wrote in the *Northern Star*: 'nine of our countrymen have been assassinated, basely and cruelly assassinated'; 'will it be believed that 100 soldiers, besides officers, all well armed and assisted by at least as many more civilians equally well armed, could have any real ground of apprehension from less than forty unarmed labourers, most of them above 40 years old, and some of them boys and aged men?'[16]

The Chartist press exaggerated, but surely had a point. At least fifty loaded muskets and many more bayonets, plus reserves of gentry on horseback and constables, faced a force of thirty-six men, two of whom carried pistols, the rest cudgels. Armstrong said in his deposition that he 'never saw men more furious or madly determined in their attack',[17] but the labourers could be no match for the military. The casualty levels speak volumes. On one side, there were two dead (Bennett and the special constable) and one wounded (Lt. Prendergast, who was badly bludgeoned); Armstrong had had his legs 'severely bruised' while on his horse![18] On the other side, there were eight dead 'rioters' and others wounded (one of whom would die later of his injuries). William Coachworth had been hit in the neck by a ricocheting bullet; the ball had ended up in

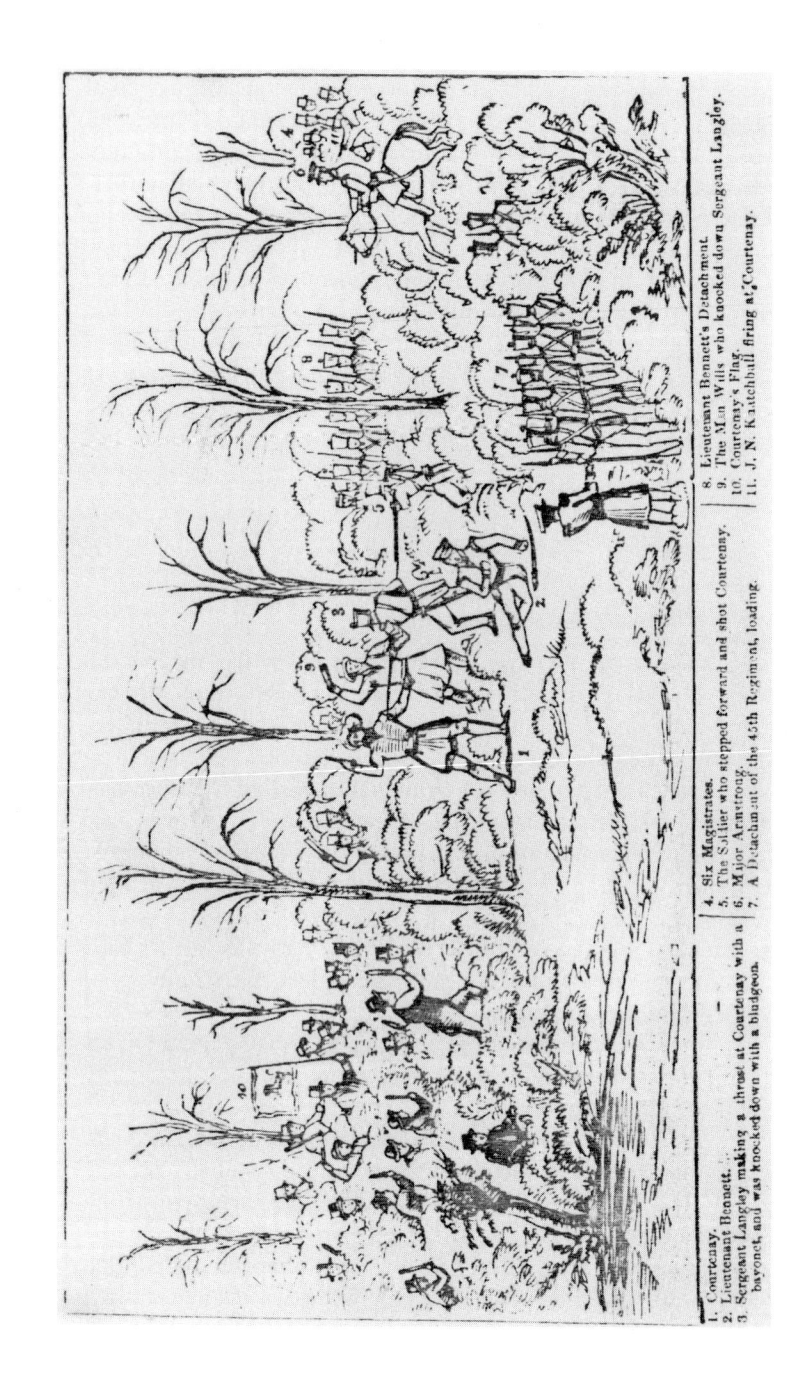

1. Courtenay.
2. Lieutenant Bennett.
3. Sergeant Langley making a thrust at Courtenay with a bayonet, and was knocked down with a bludgeon.
4. Six Magistrates.
5. The Soldier who stepped forward and shot Courtenay.
6. Major Armstrong.
7. A Detachment of the 45th Regiment, loading.
8. Lieutenant Bennett's Detachment.
9. The Man Wills who knocked down Sergeant Langley.
10. Courtenay's Flag.
11. J. N. Knatchbull firing at Courtenay.

25 The battle, from a contemporary drawing. *Source: Weekly Chronicle*, 10 June 1838.

26 The battle, from a contemporary print. *Source: Penny Satirist*, 9 June 1838.

27 The battle, from a contemporary print. *Source*: Courtesy of the Director, National Army Museum, London.

28 The battle, from a contemporary print. *Source*: Courtesy of the Trustees of the British Museum.

29 The battle, from an original drawing, 1838. *Source*: Mary Evans Picture Library.

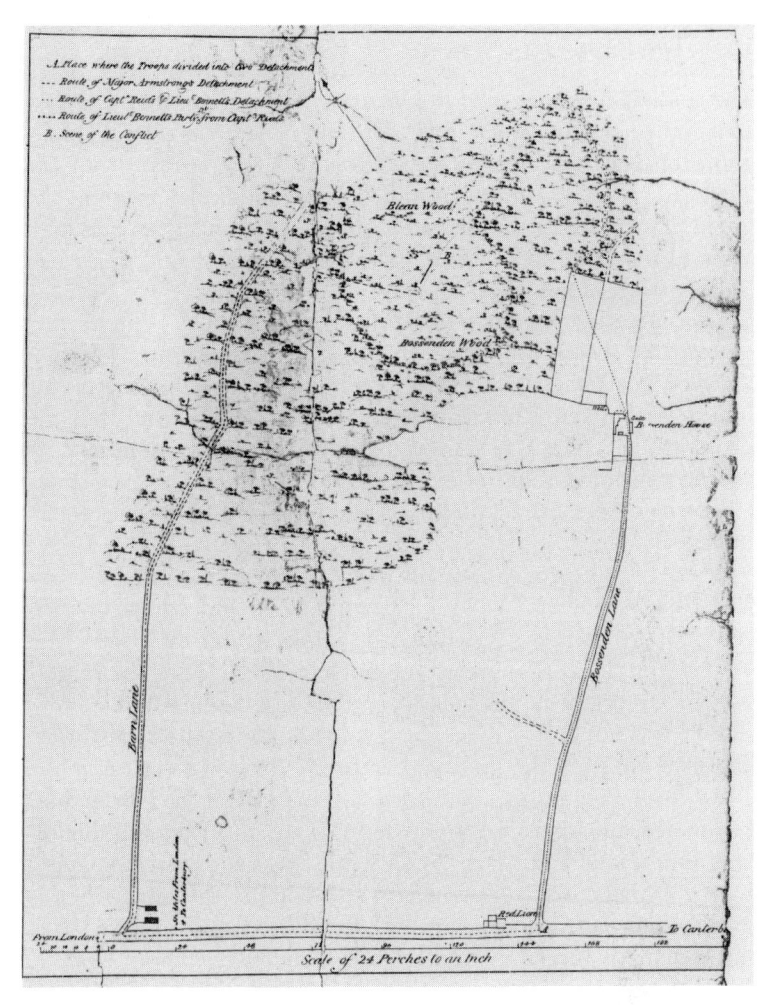

30 Map of the battle area, drawn in 1838. *Source*: Dawes collection.

his mouth.[19] A young agricultural worker, George Griggs, had crawled into a ditch, trying desperately to hold in his seeping intestines; he died shortly afterwards. His brother, Thomas, had been shot in the lungs. Another, the smallholder Alex Foad, had been either bayoneted or shot in the face—part of his jaw was missing and his smock was covered in gore.[20] It is a sobering thought that the number of deaths was the same as that at the better known Peterloo massacre of 1819. The 45th Regiment was to kill twenty Chartists a year later, during the Newport rising of 1839.[21]

The soldiers had been able to line up and shoot the rioters as they attempted to cross a small ditch. The wounded lay in a small circle, while the dead were quickly set in a row. When a reporter from *The Times* examined the battleground early on the Friday morning, he noted that the undergrowth had been trampled underfoot and that, 'notwithstanding some heavy rain', the ground still remained 'stained with blood'.[22]

The intention of the magistrates seemed clear. Before they entered the wood, the infantrymen were told to 'take Courtenay alive or dead and as many as possible of those that were with him'.[23] In private correspondence, Knatchbull referred to men dropping all around as musket balls whistled past his head.[24] A special constable, said to be eager to claim a £5 reward for taking Courtenay, was caught in the crossfire and died by a soldier's bullet.

There are also suggestions of panic on the part of the military. The officers had just returned from duty in India (one of them referred to Bosenden Wood as 'the jungle'), and their men were young and inexperienced. Armstrong referred to 'a scream of horror' coming from his men when they saw Bennett fall, so loud that he was not able to hear whether or not Poore, the magistrate in charge, had given the go-ahead to fire.[25] As noted earlier, it was clear from the inquest that some of the rioters had been both bayoneted and shot.[26] A companion of the dead 'bounty-hunter' was almost shot as a rioter. 'Several muskets were presented at him by the soldiers, who supposed him to belong to the gang, when he in an agony of fear threw himself on his knees and implored them not to kill him, declaring he was not a rioter.' This report, from the *Maidstone Journal*, suggests that the 45th was not exactly fussy about taking prisoners.[27]

Let us return to the marches around the Kentish villages in the days before the massacre in Bosenden Wood. One can assume that Courtenay and his lieutenants (the military metaphor is appropriate) were carrying out some kind of mobilization. The perambulations look like a recruitment march. As was noted earlier, the style was pseudo-military: Courtenay was on horseback, armed, the men carried sticks; there was a bugler; they had a flag—white, with a red lion painted in the centre; and, at one stage, they carried a loaf of bread on a pole. George Branchett, a Dunkirk labourer, one of those killed by the infantry, had served as a private in the East Kent militia. One of their number was styled 'the general'. When a

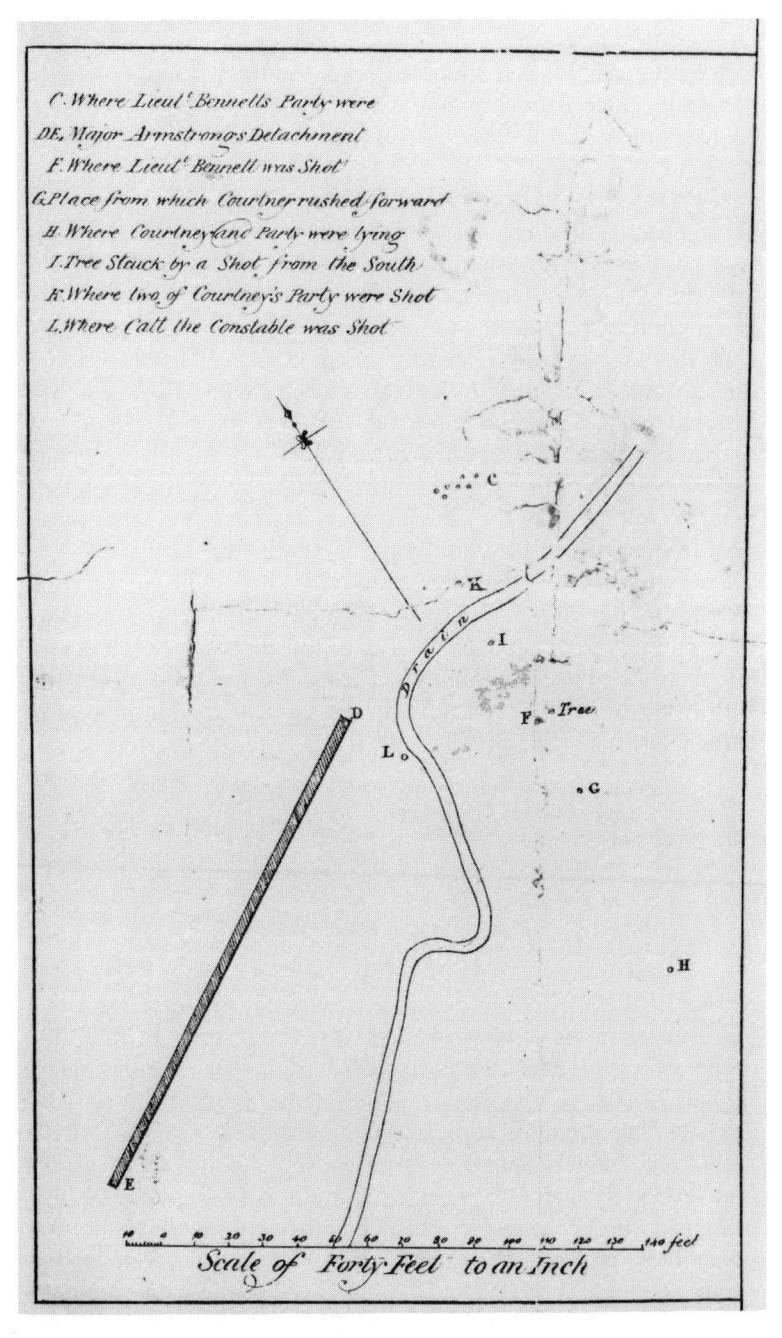

C. Where Lieut. Bennetts Party were
DE. Major Armstrongs Detachment
F. Where Lieut. Bennell was Shot
G. Place from which Courtner rushed forward
H. Where Courtney and Party were lying
I. Tree Stuck by a Shot from the South
K. Where two of Courtney's Party were Shot
L. Where Catt the Constable was Shot

Scale of Forty Feet to an Inch

31 Plan of battle site, 1838. *Source*: Dawes collection.

woodcutter and his son stumbled upon the small band, resting in the woods the evening before the death of the constable's brother, he took them for a force of some sort: 'What be ye here—a regiment of soldiers?'[28]

The party stopped from time to time at the homes of well-wishers or at inns. Courtenay spoke to them on social, political, and religious matters and either paid for or distributed food, drink, and tobacco. They also sang songs. While marching, the small band exhorted those they passed to join them. When they saw some men working in a hop field, Courtenay pointed to the loaf of bread on the pole and said, 'the loaf, the loaf, my boys; come on, or you will be sorry for it.' They said that Courtenay was going to 'put an end to the oppression of the poor by the rich'.[29] The fact that the men did not blacken their faces and moved around in daylight suggests that they felt they had the sanction of the community; there was no need to operate conspiratorially or clandestinely.

Courtenay and his followers employed a variety of mobilization techniques, drawn from a rich tradition of popular protest. Their quasi-military behaviour has already been mentioned. We noted, too, their use of songs and hymns. There is even evidence of graffiti, with a message written in lime on the door of the Hernhill tithe barn:

> If you new ho was on earth your harts Wod turn
> But don't Wate to late
> They how R
> O that great day of gudgement is close at hand
> it now peps in the dor
> every man according to his woks
> Our rites and liberties We Will have[30]

At one stage, in a dramatic gesture, Courtenay attempted to fire a bean-stack—in an area that had witnessed some of the first outbreaks of incendiarism and agitation during the famous Swing riots of 1830.[31]

The timing of mobilization is also interesting, as regards both the month and the day. That it occurred in May ties in with a seasonal cycle of popular activity: peaks during lulls in work (such as May), troughs during the extremes of full employment (harvest time) and winter desperation.[32] More specifically, recruitment began on Oak Apple Day: 29 May. In fact, the march may well have originally been part of Oak Apple Day celebration. The history of protest shows that it frequently coincided with holidays, the traditional time for ritual and festivity, when recreation could be given a nudge in the direction of riot. As Courtenay told his followers, they would have more to celebrate than the restoration of Charles II.[33] It was said after the riot that real mobilization had been scheduled for Whitsun, the following week.[34] Familiar, too, is the group's reported decision to travel to the Ospringe Fair to proselytize. The Oxfordshire rebels of 1596, so ably studied by John Walter, used the market and fair as a recruiting ground.[35]

One of the greatest puzzles about the events of 1838 is what Courtenay and his followers hoped to achieve. Was the episode a 'riot', as most contemporaries described it, or an attempted rebellion or insurrection? There are several possibilities, and the issue is further complicated by the fact that we need not assume that the aims of the leaders and rank-and-file were exactly the same, or, for that matter, that there was any unanimity in the motivations of either.

Some nineteenth-century commentators claimed that Courtenay was initiating a servile war, 'a revolution on behalf of the labouring classes', as the *Morning Chronicle* put it.[36] The vicar of Hernhill, who knew many of the rioters personally, and who wrote a private account of Courtenay's activities, was convinced that the real purpose of the 'riot' was 'an insurrection of the labouring classes':

To the small farmer, to the cottager with a little land, to the labourer aspiring to become an occupier; to all these the division of the land was the bait held out. He represented it as a system of monstrous injustice, that one person should possess so much land & have such luxuries & such advantages while they had so little, promising that if they would follow him & be faithful to him, all their supposed grievances should be redressed & every one of them should soon become possessed of a house & land of his own; for which neither rent nor taxes should hereafter be paid or required.[37]

Statements by witnesses at the trial of the rioters and by inhabitants of the area, interviewed after the troubles, provide further clues. An old woodcutter told a reporter that Courtenay had told his followers that the gentry were 'great oppressors' but that he would 'deprive them of their estates, and talked of partitioning them into farms of 40 or 50 acres among those who followed him'. Alfred Payne, a harness-maker from Boughton, deposed that he had heard Courtenay say to a group of people that 'this is the 29th May, and a glorious 29th of May it shall be for the poor who stick by me. They have been long enough imposed on, both for truth and liberty, and I will head them through it.' He proposed a toast of 'health to the poor, and may they gain independence'.[38] The discovery of a cache of bullets, and matches—the weapons of the incendiary—convinced many that Courtenay had a sinister purpose, although, as we shall see, the judge at the trial of the rioters admitted that the 'mischief' was not 'carefully defined'.[39]

There was disagreement at the time over the role of opposition to the New Poor Law in mobilizing support for Courtenay. The *Northern Liberator*, a Chartist paper, described the affray as a 'New Poor Law Battle'. The more mainstream Kent newspapers carried allegations that Courtenay and his men planned to raze the union workhouses and that Courtenay had spoken out against the oppressive nature of the New Poor Law.[40] *The Times* followed up one of these claims only to find that, while Courtenay had indeed condemned the injustice of the new system, he had not actually advocated a march on the Milton workhouse (the incident under investigation).[41] As we will see, Lord Chief Justice Denman, the judge at the rioters' trial, denied that anti-Poor Law feeling had anything to do with the affair. Lord John Russell said in the House of Commons on 1 June that 'the New Poor Law was one employed by the person in question to excite those who followed and listened to him. But he did not attach any great importance to that.'[42] Yet the government's understandable minimization of opposition to its policies is undermined somewhat by the early reports of the magistrates on the spot. Poore wrote to the Home Office that Courtenay had promised to redress grievances, 'particularly' that of the New Poor Law. He also justified his decision to use the military for fear that 'the scenes of 1835 would be repeated & probably to greater extent': i.e. the anti-Poor Law riots of 1835, which he had witnessed first hand. Some of Poore's correspondence was printed in the *Parliamentary Papers*: it is interesting that this passage does not appear.[43] We will see later that hostility to the New Poor Law was indeed an important factor in 1838.

What further emerges from the various reports and from statements by witnesses is a general tension between the haves and the have-nots—between the social stratum of the farming élite and that of their labourers. When he attempted to fire the stack, Courtenay warned that 'the streets that have heretofore flowed with water shall flow with blood for the rights of the poor'.[44] In the days before the 'riot', William Wills, a leading follower of

Courtenay, told his brother-in-law Mr John Foreman, wheelwright, carpenter, undertaker, and small farmer, that he should be preparing his own coffin 'instead of making those of his neighbours'. It was said that Foreman and Mr Edward Curling, farmer, Poor Law guardian, parish overseer, what the French call 'cock of the village', were both on Courtenay's hit list, as was William Kay, Scottish bailiff to the banker Snoulton. The *Kentish Observer* claimed that Kay's labourers were told that 'the farm was as much theirs as Mr Snoulten's, and should be divided among them', and that Courtenay had sent a message to the bailiff 'warning him to make peace with God, as he was shortly coming to settle his account'.[45] After the shooting of the constable's brother, a young farm servant rode his draught horse through Hernhill to spread the news. As he passed a leading Hernhill farmer, he shouted out that Courtenay had killed the constable, and he will shoot a 'hundred more of you buggers before night'.[46]

When Courtenay assembled his followers on 29 May, he told them that 'all the country would be up, for the great jubilee was to come, and we must be with 'em'. 'I am going for a jubilee; any of you men that have nothing to do I shall fill your bellies with victuals, and nothing shall happen to you.'[47]

Now the term 'jubilee' had a precise meaning in the eighteenth and nineteenth centuries, one far removed from current usage. By 1838 it was understood in radical circles in both a millenarian and political sense—the two were usually combined—as a time of change in the world order and a righting of wrongs. The idea of a jubilee was promoted by different groups. On source, Malcolm Chase has argued, was Primitive Methodism, which throughout the nineteenth century 'gave much prominence to the idea of jubilee' as the year that would inaugurate the millennium. Another source for the idea was the group of radicals usually called the Spenceans.[48] Thomas Spence and William Benbow both used the imagery of the Levitical Jubilee (Leviticus 25), a time on every fiftieth year when the land was restored to those who had lost it. For Spence and his nineteenth-century followers, the Society of Spencean Philanthropists, the jubilee meant land nationalization, or rather the day on which English land would be reclaimed from the landlords and placed in the control of the inhabitants, parish by parish. He wrote a hymn, the 'Jubilee Hymn', to be sung to the tune of the national anthem, which was 'to be sung at the End of Oppression, or the Commencement of the political Millennium, when there shall be neither Lords nor Landlords, but God and Man will be all in all'.[49] For Benbow, whose pamphlet *Grand National Holiday* was published in 1832, the jubilee was a holy day, a national holiday for one month, when workers downed tools to elect a congress to discuss the reform of society. Benbow used the imagery of festivity and rest. In the Hebrew jubilee, he wrote, 'no servile work was done, and servants and masters knew no distinction'; 'the land lay untilled; the spontaneous produce was the property of the poor'. Clearly too, his intention was to demonstrate power, to show the lords and masters—'the consuming party'—the strength of the 'martyrs of labour'; to provide the oppressed themselves with an awareness of their own might: 'The knowledge we want is knowledge of ourselves . . . of our own power, . . . of the right we have to employ in action that immense power'.[50]

Although contemporaries (and some historians) have assumed a Spencean connection, it is impossible to establish direct influences upon Courtenay.[51] As we will see in a later chapter, there may have been a Bible Christian (an offshoot of Methodism) link with some of Courtenay's followers—although the evidence is slim. We do know that Courtenay was in London in 1832, and he may have visited the city earlier, when he was living in Cornwall, so it is at least possible that he encountered the Spenceans. Certainly his talk of a jubilee, and evidence that he intended to divide property, would fit comfortably with the intellectual milieu of Spence and Benbow, what Iain McCalman has called the 'millenarian–radical culture' of London Spenceanism.[42] For clearly, Courtenay's jubilee had a millenarian as well as a political edge.

There is no doubting the millenarian mood of 1838. Courtenay was a messianic figure, whose coming was said to have been predicted in *Revelation*: 'And I saw and beheld a white horse; and he that sat on him had a bow, and a crown was given unto him: and he went forth conquering and to conquer.'[53] Religion provided the ideological fuel for hopes of amelioration; it fired out-and-out resistance. Courtenay drew on the whole repertoire of chiliasm. A labourer recalled that Courtenay had said that he was 'Christ come down from the cross'. Some of his followers referred to him as 'the saviour', and he styled his hair and beard in the manner attributed to Christ and depicted in the religious prints which we know adorned the walls of the cottages of many of the agricultural labourers. He was said to have shown people the nail marks on his hands as proof that he had been nailed to the cross. After his death it was believed that he would rise from the dead. Lydia Hadlow, mistress of one of the Hernhill day schools, wife of one of the rioters and sister of the leader, Wills, refused to believe that Courtenay was dead: 'no, no; you can't kill him; it is not the truth; it is not possible'. She expected his resurrection on the third day.[54]

Courtenay's more spectacular antics are in keeping with the idea of a millenarian-inspired rising. Witnesses attested to his claim that he was not like earthly men; 'I fell down from the clouds and nobody knew where I came from.' He said that all he had to do was to place his left hand on the muscle of his right arm and 10,000 would be slain. He pretended to shoot out the stars with tow steeped in oil and with iron filings, so that when he fired his pistol the shots emitted sparkles of light. He convinced some of his followers that they were invulnerable to bullets. When Courtenay lay dead, his lover, Sarah Culver, attempted to revive him with water—he had told her that if he appeared dead he would only be sleeping. Indeed, we find a curious, though not unexpected, mix of magic and millenarianism, folklore and Christianity. Courtenay was almost a combination of white witch and messiah. William Wills believed that Courtenay could hear everything that was said even though he was a mile away.[55]

Millenarian imagery and general millennial anticipation are present in the writings of both Benbow and Spence, the two radicals mentioned earlier as a possible influence on Courtenay. J. F. C. Harrison and W. H. Oliver have shown that millenarianism was a common currency of the age; in fact, the 1820s and 1830s witnessed an intensification of millennial excitement.[56] London was an important centre. Here, the Irvingites, led by Edward Irving, were extremely influential, attracting large crowds to their meetings, calculating the date of the second advent—14 July 1835, Christmas Day 1838. Not that there was anything remotely radical about the social and political doctrines of Irving, but, as Oliver has demonstrated, more radical figures were influenced by the urgency of the teachings about the shortly-to-be-expected reign of Christ.[57] And we can actually establish a link between Courtenay and Irving. The medical notes of the superintendent of the Kent County Asylum mention that Courtenay 'said he had heard Mr Irvine several times & considers him a Prophet'.[58]

The main argument against the theory of a projected millenarian insurrection is that only two of the rioters carried firearms. That the labouring population had access to guns was confirmed later by those who visited their cottages; and the prosecutions of poachers which dot the Petty Sessions records for the period show that there was no shortage of firearms in the neighbourhood. And yet, if the movements of Courtenay and company on 29 and 30 May are seen as a recruitment march or drilling for *future* insurrection, the fact that they carried only sticks is not so much at variance with my hypothesis. It would square too with the evidence of witnesses that real mobilization was scheduled for the following Sunday, Whitsun, and with the claims of magistrates that men did indeed arrive later from neighbouring parishes to join a rebellion that had been nipped in the bud by the massacre in the wood. In the light of the casualties of the Thursday afternoon, one could argue that the local authorities had every reason to emphasize the potential danger from the agricultural labourers. But their correspondence does seem to indicate a real fear of insurrection.[59]

Of course, as a recruitment march, the perambulations of Courtenay's band could hardly be said to have been a success. Groups of men working in a gravel pit and in a hop field refused to down tools to join him. It is instructive to compare the abortive Courtenay rising with other examples of nineteenth-century protest.[60] The roving band of labourers did not really use coercion to recruit, as was done in most of the major protest movements of early nineteenth-century England and Wales: the East Anglian riots of 1816, the Pentrich rising of 1817, Swing in 1830, the Merthyr riots of 1831, anti-Poor Law protest in 1835, the Newport rising of 1839. The Courtenay rioters did not seem to have any immediate target, no limited, attainable goal. The protesters of 1830 and 1835, for instance, had viable goals. They forced wages up, or they coerced the officials of the New Poor Law to pay money instead of tickets. They employed a degree of force that was largely absent from the 1838 insurrection. In 1835 bands of determined men, flying pickets in fact, moved from village to village in Kent, achieving what has been described as that 'critical mass' necessary for success. Indeed, given the context of early nineteenth-century Britain, violence was a common and 'necessary weapon'. As David Jones has argued, it provided a few (temporary) victories for those who had no permanent association to defend their rights.[61]

The aims of Courtenay and his followers, on the other hand, were, as we have seen, vague, non-specific, and various. Force was used once or twice to get people to join, and certainly to ensure that they stayed with the small group in those final hours, but it was never on the scale of Swing or the Newport rising. This absence of physical force is a bit of a puzzle, for the labourers proved themselves handy enough with cudgels in their engagement with the military, and we will see that several of them had convictions for violence. One of the problems with the Courtenay episode is that it was nipped in the bud after the shooting of the constable's brother. We will never know what would have happened if Courtenay had been allowed to continue mobilizing for a little longer. However, there is a real sense in which Courtenay had already let the moment slip before he embarked on murder. The death of Nicholas Mears, the constable's brother, may well have been a mark of frustration.

So what do we have? Vague aspirations for a jubilee of the poor, with land redistribution and retribution upon the rich? Millenarian visions of a servile war? It is impossible to be more precise than this. Courtenay never penned an 1838 manifesto; people joined him from various motives. One old man said that he had gone with the band 'without knowing what he was to do, save to work Sir William's bidding'. Others claimed that they had followed him because he had promised them plenty to eat and plenty to drink.[62] The rising is a superb example of what John Walter has termed the 'politics of Cockayne', referring to the folk myth of a fantasy land of idleness and superabundance, of hopes for a world turned upside down.[63] A time of eating and drinking, singing and marching, a brief respite from the troubles of merely existing. And who knew? Perhaps tomorrow would bring the jubilee! But, overall, there seems enough evidence to suggest that the affair in Bosenden Wood was the result of an abortive insurrection, and that, strictly speaking, it, and not the famous Swing rising of 1830, was the last revolt of the farm labourers.[64]

5
Courtenay

WHAT do we know about 'Sir William Courtenay', the leader of the abortive rising of 1838? We have encountered him in the immediate months before the Bosenden Wood battle, but what of his earlier background?

There are so many historical barriers. Courtenay was an impostor; the last decade of his life was lived out in fantasy. He craved fame. He had visions, it seems, of becoming a great popular leader, perhaps another Orator Hunt. And so he acquired a new identity, that of a gentleman, and courted popular approval. In the end he opted for the ultimate imposture: he claimed that he was Jesus Christ. John Tom's contemporaries (for John Nicholls Tom was his real name) colluded in his dreams. The rural, labouring inarticulate were in awe of his independence, his bearing, his familiarity with the scriptures and way with words. The craftsmen of Canterbury embraced his radical populist rejection of Whig and Tory. The men of property and the medical specialists were more worried by his demagogic and religious delusions than by his usurpation of a title and identity. His nineteenth-century biographer (although 'biography' is hardly the appropriate word) merely added to the elaborate patchwork of fact and fantasy, with assertions of numerous radical connections and an invented journey to the Middle East.[1] His twentieth-century biographer, for all his thoroughness and good intentions, presents Tom as a Victorian oddity.[2]

To arrive at the real personality behind the façade, the historian, almost like the restorer of old paintings, has to peel off the gloss and the dirt, bit by bit. The end result may be an object of exposed brilliance; the nagging danger is that, after all the effort, there may be nothing there at all.

Tom was born in St Columb in Cornwall in 1799, the son of innkeepers Charity and William Tom. He attended schools locally and in Launceston. At the age of 18 he began work as an articled clerk in St Columb. After about three years in this position, he kept an inn (briefly) in Wadebridge and then took a job in 1820 as a clerk to a firm of wine merchants in Truro. By the end of the 1820s, it seems, Tom, who was now married, had acquired his own business in wine-and-spirits and malting. His wife, Catherine, the daughter of a prosperous market gardener, had brought some money into the marriage, so it was probably this, with perhaps some assistance from his parents, that enabled Tom to set up trading in his own right.[3]

But it was a troubled time for Tom, now in his late twenties. His mother was committed to the Cornwall Lunatic Asylum. His business burned down in 1828 in a fire which resulted in an insurance claim of nearly £4,000. By the end of 1831, Tom himself was receiving treatment for 'derangement of intellect'. We have the depositions of the two doctors who treated him in Truro from December 1831 till January 1832. They tell us something of the state of provincial, nineteenth-century psychiatry, but little of Tom's actual complaint. He was suffering from 'a very violent fit of apoplexy', 'conjestion of the Brain'. One of the medical men, William Henry Bullmore, gentleman and surgeon, demonstrated a familiarity with the current terminology. Tom, he felt, suffered from 'monomania', making 'constant allusions to Scripture'.[4] 'Monomania', an influential psychiatric term in early nineteenth-century Europe, meant mental derangement on a few (usually one) subjects: the afflicted could appear quite rational in other respects.[5] It was a term popular with the mad-doctors, presumably because of its elasticity—the world must have seemed full of potential monomaniacs. But the remedy inflicted upon this patient was far more traditional: Tom, the doctors' depositions note, was bled.[6]

The future Sir William Courtenay was back in business by April 1832, for in the middle of that month he sailed from Truro to Liverpool to sell a cargo of malt. From Liverpool he travelled to Birmingham; we know this because it was from there that he wrote to his wife, telling her he was about to go to France. Then he disappeared. His family advertised for his whereabouts, in newspapers in France and England. They heard nothing more of him until July 1833, over a year later, when they learned that a man who fitted Tom's description, but who called himself 'Sir William Courtenay', was in prison in Maidstone. The handwriting of the 'two' men seemed to check, so Catherine Tom and another relative went to Maidstone to identify him. But although they recognized him, 'Sir William Courtenay' refused to acknowledge them.[7]

Although that year between 1832 and 1833 was a blank for Tom's family as far as his movements were concerned, we have some idea of what he was doing. We know that between May and August 1832 he was in London, using, according to the Kent newspapers, the name 'Squire Thompson'.[8] It was a year that saw the passage of the Reform Bill, and in these few months in London Tom may well have encountered the ideas of the radical Spenceans and William Benbow. It is almost certain that he saw the popular leader Henry Hunt (Orator Hunt) in action; and we know that he heard the millenarian preacher Edward Irving.[9]

By August 1832 he was in Kent, at the Rose Inn, Canterbury, an eccentric figure to say the least, claiming first to be Count Rothschild and then Percy Honywood Courtenay, Knight of Malta. The bogus Courtenay must have been an avid follower of the affairs of the landed families. The Courtenays were an old and at one time powerful baronial family from the West of England. The earldom of Devon, held by them, had lain dormant for almost three centuries until claimed by a member of one branch of the family, William Viscount Courtenay, in early 1831. The real Courtenay had left shortly afterwards for the Continent (there were whispers of 'unspeakable offences'), leaving the way open for Tom to assume his place. But the bogus Courtenay also laid claim to several recently deceased estates. Hales Place at Hackington (near Canterbury) was one, the owner, Sir Edward Hales, having died in 1829 without an heir. The other was Evington, in Elmstead (also near Canterbury), the home of the Honywood family. Sir John Courtenay Honywood had died shortly after Tom's arrival in Canterbury, and he was able to acquire Honywood's valet and various items of clothing which had belonged to the late baronet. Not that 'Courtenay' filed suit for any legal claim; he merely let it be known that he held 'papers' which proved his right to these various estates.[10] This imposture, one assumes, endowed him with some respectability and permitted him, because of his 'expectations', to survive on credit. He may also have been living off the proceeds from the sale of the malt in Liverpool. There were rumours of oyster barrels full of sovereigns arriving for 'Courtenay' every fortnight.[11]

Courtenay (as we will now call him) began to establish himself as the champion of the poor. His flamboyance went down well with the craftsmen and tradespeople of Canterbury. He was active too in the area surrounding Canterbury. We know that Boughton-under-Blean was part of his social arena because he penned a song about the village in 1833, because it was established in a perjury case that

32 Courtenay campaigning in Canterbury in 1832, from a contemporary print. *Source*: Dawes collection.

33 Contemporary oil portrait, believed to be of Courtenay. *Source*: Dawes collection.

he attended church there, and because the Boughton register of baptisms shows a few children named in his honour in 1833 and 1834.[12] An old woman recalled, many years later, that as a child she had witnessed Courtenay's visit to Whitstable in a coach; people had said that he was a man who was going to do good.[13]

In December 1832 Courtenay threw himself into politics,

standing as a candidate for the City of Canterbury. He polled well. His opponents, both Liberals (the Hon. Richard Watson and Viscount Fordwich), gained 834 and 802 votes respectively; Courtenay got a respectable 379. Courtenay clearly had a popular following in Canterbury. In true electioneering style his followers took the horses out of harness and drew him around the city in his coach. 'They marched up St. Dunstan's singing "Rule Britannia",' an eye witness remembered in the 1880s. After the votes were counted, Courtenay was treated as the victor rather than the vanquished; a drum-and-fife band marched him back to the Rose Inn.[14]

He also stood for East Kent, but here he was out of his depth. He had no power base, and his following in the Boughton area, for what it was worth, would have been mainly among the labouring class, the non-franchised. So Courtenay appeared on Barham Down, a lonely figure next to the five hundred farm labourers clad in white and orange, the paid entourage of the Tory Sir Edward Knatchbull, and the party of Sir William Cosway, the Liberal candidate, who carried blue banners and whose band played 'Rule Britannia'.[15] Courtenay ended up with a derisory four votes. As the vicar of Hernhill, the Revd. Charles Handley, noted with a mix of assurance and contempt, 'it was one thing to come before the mob at Canterbury and a very different thing to offer himself to the gentry and freeholders on Barham Downs'.[16]

Sir William Courtenay, KM, still saw himself as the champion of the poor. From March to May 1833 he printed a paper, the *Lion* or the *British Lion*, 'for the cause of liberty upon christian principle', aimed, Courtenay claimed in one issue, at the 'lower orders'. The *Lion* sold for 2d. a copy, and Courtenay planned to have agents take it to the villages on Saturdays so that working people could read it on Sundays. There is no evidence that it was distributed in any great numbers—the British Library has but one surviving issue.[17]

The year 1833 was not a good one for the 'companion of the cottager and the friend of the poor'. He was committed for swindling a waiter at the Rose Inn, obtaining money under false pretences. That he still enjoyed popular support is clear from the reaction to his arrest by the city magitrates. The *Kent Herald* reported that anonymous letters were sent to the city authorities, threatening a second 'Bristol affair' (i.e. a repetition of the Reform Bill disturbances in Bristol in 1831). A crowd assembled around the

Guildhall; stones were thrown; a company of the Rifle Brigade had to be brought in.[18]

In July Courtenay was in court yet again, this time facing a charge of perjury. Some Faversham fishermen had been accused of smuggling spirits. A government cruiser had intercepted a fishing boat suspected of smuggling, and there had been a chase, during which the revenue cruiser had fired into the sail of the fishing smack. The government crew had observed some tubs being thrown off the suspected smuggler, a common means of landing contraband. During the trial at Rochester of the suspected smugglers, Courtenay, in full regalia and complete with small scimitar, had appeared for the defence. He claimed that the tubs in question had not come from the fishing boat but had been floating off the Kent coast long before the encounter with the revenue cruiser. As a result of this patently false testimony, he was tried for perjury at the Summer Assize, and gaoled. The vicar of Boughton was able to show that at the time Courtenay claimed to have been near the Goodwin Sands he was in fact in church in Boughton-under-Blean, acting as sponsor for the christening of the child of a naval captain. The conviction carried the penalty of seven years' transportation.[19]

Courtenay was never transported. He served three months in prison, and was then transferred in October to the Kent County Lunatic Asylum. He remained there for exactly four years, until he was released under a Queen's pardon. He refused to rejoin his family, returning instead to the Boughton area in October 1837. We already know the story thereafter.

Let us now look in greater detail at Courtenay's earlier political ideology and activity. I am convinced that Courtenay has to be seen as but one of a whole range of nineteenth-century popular demagogues who surface again and again in the discontent of the period. The Pentrich 'rising' of 1817 had Jeremiah Brandreth. The Swing riots of 1830 had Hampshire's 'Captain Hunt', just one of the many colourful leaders to emerge at the popular level during the unrest of that year. In the Kent anti-Poor Law troubles of 1835, too, much of the agitation was led by a labourer called Major Murton, also known as 'The Judge'. And, of course, as it has been established recently, demagogic and charismatic leadership was vital for the Chartist movement. Few of these figures were to attain the popularity of Henry Hunt or Feargus O'Connor, but as a group they deserve, and await, a historian.[20]

34 Courtenay—Knight of Malta, from a contemporary print. *Source*: Dawes collection.

If Courtenay is re-examined in the light of recent work on the nineteenth-century demagogue, his behaviour seems more intelligible. We need to set him in the tradition of his better-known contemporaries Hunt and O'Connor.[21] Not that I presume to claim for him the status of these two radicals; it is just that Courtenay makes more sense as a political personality if set in the context of nineteenth-century demagogic and charismatic leadership.

During his politicking in Canterbury in 1832, Courtenay carried a sabre, grew his hair and beard long, and dressed flamboyantly in crimson velvet, trimmed with gold and with matching mantle, cap, silk stockings, and Turkish slippers. In one of his election addresses, he began the proceedings 'in the most extraordinary manner, bounding over the heads of those before him, and alighting on the table in a theatrical attitude'.[22] There is certainly no trace of deference in his attitude to the other candidates; he mocked them and punctured their rhetoric with behaviour which must have appeared socially eccentric.[23] The Revd. Charles Handley, who was convinced that from the beginning Courtenay was out to make a name for himself, described the 'baronet' in some detail:

In order to make himself conspicuous & excite notice he affected great singularity in his dress, never appearing dressed like other people but always in some singular fashion . . . his handsome & commanding figure, of which he was to the highest degree vain, was always set off by some singularity of dress, his long hair was parted on the forehead and thrown back behind his ears, his beard was allowed to grow to its full length. . . . His address was open & cordial, his manner graceful though highly theatrical, his elocution fluent & energetic, though rambling & inconclusive, & it may with truth be said that he was in everyway wch calculated to impose on the credulity of the multitude.[24]

A leading Chartist, George Julian Harney, said that a popular chief 'should be possessed of a magnificent bodily appearance, an iron frame, eloquence or at least a ready fluency of tongue . . . great animal courage, contempt of pain and death, and be not altogether ignorant of military arms and science'.[25] Courtenay had many of these attributes. He stood 6 foot tall at a time when an agricultural labourer over 5 ft. 6 in. was considered exceptional.[26] *The Times* reporter who saw Courtenay's corpse in 1838, and who had also known Hunt, remarked on the uncanny resemblance between the two men.[27] Like the popular leaders of the nineteenth century, Courtenay posed as the gentleman leader who had sacrificed all for the good of the labourer and the mechanic. In Courtenay's case, of course, it was a real imposture. In the campaign of 1832, he had presented himself as a man 'willing to throw up his Barony to become more extensively the Friend of the People'. 'Sir William Courtenay stood forward as the Poor Man's Friend.'[28] The rhetoric is identical to that of Hunt or O'Connor. In 1838 Courtenay symbolically discarded his finery for the simple smock of the farm labourer, the rural equivalent to O'Connor's adoption of the fustian jacket. Like the Chartist, he had a finely developed sense of what has been termed 'class without words'.[29] And, like O'Connor

35 Courtenay—gentleman, from a contemporary print. *Source*: Graham Hudson.

and Hunt, he had charisma—in the real sense of the word; for Courtenay became a religious as well as a political leader.

Courtenay's early political ideas similarly should be seen in terms of late eighteenth- and early nineteenth-century radicalism. He seemed to be in the right places at the right times: in Birmingham and London, the two key centres of radical pressure for parliamentary reform, at the height of reform agitation (April/May 1832).[30] We catch glimpses of Courtenay's rhetoric in reports of his campaign speeches in 1832 and in his newspaper, the *British Lion*. In many ways, he provided standard radical fare. Economic and social change would come as the result of the promotion of parliamentary reform. 'Universal Suffrage and Annual Parliaments is the only remedy . . . This one obtained, away go those monsters of Old England's oppression.' If elected, Courtenay promised reform of the House of Commons and more:

> he would abolish tithes, he would remove the burden of taxation from the shoulders of the poor, and place it on those of the rich—he would sweep away Corporations, and render the choice of Aldermen and Commoners more agreeable to the public taste—and, finally, he promised a return to the olden time, when roast beef and plum-pudding, and nut-brown ale were not so hard of attainment as at present.[31]

Courtenay's rhetoric is an interesting example of the way in which patriotism was used as an oppositional weapon in the nineteenth century, a phenomenon of nineteenth-century radicalism taken up only recently by historians.[32] His invocation of the roast beef of old England would have been appreciated by other radicals, as would the symbolism of the title of his newspaper, the *British Lion*, and his election-speech references to 'patriotism and true liberty', to 'true feelings of English blood', and to English freedom and English bondage.[33] He wrote a song called 'Liberty' which was to be sung to the tune of 'The Conquering Hero':

> Hark! Old England's pris'ners groan—
> 'Tis a deep and mournful tone,—
> From oppression to be free,
> And enjoy true liberty.[34]

Its chorus was: 'Britons must be—will be free: Truth bears off the victory.' The language is very reminiscent of radical ballads at the time of Peterloo.[35]

There are other genuflections towards radicalism. Courtenay opposed flogging in the army.[36] He called for the raising of wages to boost the economy through consumerism. He suspected that the government's Irish policy was a rehearsal for repression at home.[37] However, his outraged declaiming against oppression, his radical rhetoric, was combined with a curious mix of religious rambling (and it is rambling), with his claims that he was the King of the Gypsies, Prince of Arabia, and King of Jerusalem, and with equally vehement outbursts about republicanism and atheism—against Voltaire and the 'infidel' Paine.[38]

Even with a willingness to rethink parameters and definitions of radicalism, one cannot get away from the overall bizarreness of

Courtenay's ideology. But there is an underlying logic to the speeches and political manifestos—indeed, to his actions. Courtenay saw himself as the champion of the poor, a patriot, for neither Whig nor Tory but for the people, hostile to the rich and Old Corruption but loyal to King and God. In short, he was what we would call a populist, undeniably an opportunist, if, as would turn out, a spectacularly unsuccessful one; hero of the artisan and shopkeeper in Canterbury in 1832 in the first election after the passing of the Reform Act; champion of the seafarer in 1833 when he perjured himself on behalf of the suspected smugglers; saviour of the agricultural labourers in 1838 when he appeared before them, clad in a simple smock and gabardine.

Courtenay's great moment came in 1838, when he played a crucial role in the mobilization of the farmworkers. He presented them with a vision (however vague) of the future, a way out of their predicament (if only temporary). Not that the agricultural labourers were incapable of producing their own leaders. But in what was still a deferential society, Courtenay seems to have provided the kind of status-support helpful for those who wished to reject the hegemony of the landed élite and their brokers, the farmers. When the farmer Edward Curling attempted to get 'his' men back after they had deserted their work to join Courtenay, saying 'They are my men', 'I provide for them', Courtenay replied, 'I don't know that you do *provide for them*' (my emphasis).[39] Courtenay questioned; he provided an alternative to the prevailing assumptions of obedience. He was a Robin Hood-like figure who was seen as a friend to the poor.[40] And the man clearly had charisma. All the themes of Courtenay's leadership—the charisma, the independence, the feigned status, the charity, even the terror—come through in the wonderful description by one of his followers:

Oh, Sir, he could turn any one that once listened to him whatever way he liked, and make them believe what he pleased. He had a tongue which a poor man could not get over, and a learned one could not gainsay, standing before him. He puzzled all the lawyers in Canterbury, and they confessed that he knew more of law than all put together. You could not always understand what he said, but when you did it was beautiful, and wonderful, and powerful, just like his eyes, and then his voice was so sweet! And he was such a grand gentleman, and sometimes latterly such an awful man, and looked so terrible if any one ventured to oppose him, that he carried all before him. Then again he was so charitable! While he had a shilling in his pocket, a poor man never should want . . .[41]

122 The Rising

One of the most intriguing issues of the Courtenay affair is the question of John Tom's madness. Was he mad at all? The Boughton farmer, George Francis, told MPs that right up until the day of the battle he was sure that Courtenay was sane; 'and those who conversed with him said they never saw anything insane in any respect in his conduct'.[42] The vicar of Hernhill, Charles Handley, was convinced that Tom's insanity (like his religion) was an 'artful contrivance'. According to Handley, Tom had calculated that a plea of insanity would save him from the consequences of failure in his planned rising of 1838. It was 'a retreat to fall back upon, in case they should be unsuccessful'. He 'would plead his disorder in justification of crimes, not committed, but intended; he would say, they call me a madman; it is of no consequence therefore what I do, I cannot be punished.'[43] Certainly, Courtenay's bouts of mental instability came at convenient times. The first saved him from personal (and perhaps business) crisis in 1832—he sailed to Liverpool, disappeared, and began a new life under an assumed identity. Insanity saved him too from transportation in 1833, for an Act of 9 Geo. IV enabled those in prison who were certified as insane to be transferred to an asylum. Did Courtenay fake insanity as a means of escape?

This hypothesis would be difficult to maintain in the face of many of Courtenay's actions in 1838, dealt with in Chapter 4, his behaviour in the election of 1832, and his posturings in court in 1833 (the very thing that had landed him in prison). We also have the case-notes taken when Courtenay was in the Kent County Asylum. Do they provide any clues?

> William Courtenay states his belief that the Saviour never slept as the Holy Ghost would not let him Sleep. . . . He also believes that there are some Jews who never sleep. He condemns the Earth as deceitful because it is an object & mutable . . . . He acknowledges himself to be a dangerous character, & that if he had been returned for Canterbury he should have been sent to the Tower. He would have followed no party but have cut the speeches of all parties to pieces. He wd first have attacked the Throne, then Lord Chancellor Brougham. A Conspiracy wd have been formed against him which might have cost him his life & which he considers may have been saved by his being sent to the Asylum. He thinks no man can stand against his talents as a speaker, though he considers himself as nothing in himself. My dear child, he says, I am in myself a non-entity . . . . Every thing depends upon self, & selfish implies Lucifer. A Pig is the most selfish animal in existence & a sheep the least, hence pork is the most indigestible Meat, & Mutton the most digestible. He maintained that Pork required

strong faith to digest it, because a Pig was the most selfish animal in existence.... He spoke of himself as possessing more faith than any man in existence. His life was a very mysterious one which time must elucidate as it was incommunicable.... He represents himself as not being under the influence of his senses & says he has no smell, but that he lives entirely by faith.... Predicts that some great calamity is about to befall this Country for its sins. The causes of Materialism are the effects of the Creator.... He considers a Tory an Alkali & a Whig an Acid. He regards Locke & Sir I Newton as two of the greatest fools that ever lived.[44]

The only date on the notes is 26 January 1834, but these observations were presumably recorded over a period of time. They are difficult to decode. The religious enthusiasm and the anti-rationalism were not uncommon in the early nineteenth century. There is a faint echo of the visionary William Blake in the references to Newton and Locke. The document has a tortured air about it; it hardly seems to reflect a mind that is at ease. Courtenay was clearly troubled mentally, but can we say that he was mad? Roy Porter has shown that the famous Samuel Johnson walked a narrow path between mental instability and madness.[45] The same may have been true of John Tom.

What is important in the end is not whether Courtenay was mad or sane by any objective gauge—if such criteria ever exist. Madness is a social construct, a notoriously slippery concept. 'Beyond the initial hard core of easily recognizable behavioural and/or mental disturbance,' the historical sociologist Andrew Scull has argued of the nineteenth century, 'the boundary between the normal and the pathological was left extraordinarily vague and indeterminate.' Insanity 'was such an amorphous, all-embracing concept, that the range of behaviour it could be stretched to encompass was almost infinite'.[46] Furthermore, nineteenth-century England was an age of madness: the classification and care of the insane became professionalized and institutionalized. The result, not surprisingly, was a rise in the percentage of the population designated as mad.

Tom's 'madness', then, is interesting for what it represents. Like the case of Pierre Rivière, which occurred in France three years earlier and which has been documented and analysed by Michel Foucault and others, the Courtenay affair provided a focal point for the 'intersection of discourses'.[47] There are intriguing similarities between the two events. Rivière, a French peasant who had killed his mother, sister, and brother, claimed initially that God had ordered him to do it, and later that he had feigned religious mania as a defence for his actions. His priest (like Courtenay's minister!) did not think that Rivière was mad. Like Courtenay, Rivière was proclaimed by the medical specialists to be insane; his lunacy was 'simply the deplorable result of true mental alienation'. His family had a history of mental instability. 'Indeed, heredity', wrote Dr Vastel in his assessment of Rivière, 'is one of the most potent causes of the production of madness.' Monomania explained Rivière's irrationality on some subjects and rationality on others: 'it is a daily occurrence for the most irrational mental defectives to write letters of the most rational sort'. The law, however, denied Rivière's 'religious monomania'. His bill of indictment referred to his 'feigned' madness. There was a gap too between the medical verdict and opinions at the popular level. When fellow villagers were questioned about Rivière's state of mind, they defined his irrationality in terms of his fear of women, his cruelty to animals, his solitude, and his at times frenetic behaviour—not in terms of religious monomania.[48] For Foucault and Robert Castel, Rivière's case represents a confrontation, 'a strange contest', where the law and medicine battled over the custody of the offender. A struggle between two discourses, which, in the final analysis, was competition for power.[49]

Courtenay never stood trial for his homicide, so there was no battle over custody. Nor is my reading of Tom's case as clear-cut as Foucault's dossier on Pierre Rivière. But we will see that different concepts of madness did fasten upon the person of Courtenay. That is why it is so difficult to resolve the issue of his insanity. We do not even know precisely why he was committed in 1833. He had refused to acknowledge his family and was, as the Superintendent of the Kent Asylum certified, labouring 'under delusions respecting his person and property', claiming that he was Sir William Courtenay, Knight of Malta, when others had identified him as John Tom from Truro.[50] Was he committed because of this, or because of his 'religious delusions', the monomania noted earlier by his Cornish physicians? Or was it because of popular pretensions, 'his power of misleading ignorant people'? In 1834 the Asylum Superintendent informed Courtenay's friend, George Francis, that, while Courtenay himself was harmless enough, he could not answer for the 'conduct of others who might be excited by his unsound and extravagant opinion'.[51] 'I took him home from the asylum', Francis told a Parliamentary Select Committee, 'under the promise that he never would have anything to do with the lower class of people.' 'I told him that he had promised me not to go among the lower classes of people, and that he had likewise said he never would address a mob.'[52]

After the events of 1838, Courtenay's madness was simply assumed by newspaper reporter, lawyer, judge, and politician. At the post mortem Courtenay's brain was declared to be in a 'high state of inflamation', which was taken to explain his state of mind. The *Kentish Observer* and other papers carried a report from the *Atlas* which invoked authorities such as Pinel and Esquirol to point out the foolishness of releasing Tom into the very environment that had created his malady—the aim of incarceration, of course, was to remove the patient from whatever had nurtured the ailment.[53] For the medical specialists of the time, monomania must have seemed an attractive explanation for Courtenay's complaint: sound enough, even cunning, on some issues, but obsessed with religion and personal fame.

Several of the newspaper accounts drew comparisons between Courtenay and the seventeenth-century Quaker James Nayler, who had been punished by Parliament for blasphemy, and with the more recent enthusiasm of Joanna Southcott. The impression given was that such religious zeal, 'religious ravings', as the defence lawyer of the 'rioters' put it, was out of keeping with the temper of the times.[54] Although admittedly writing thirty years after the event, Charles Dickens provides a perfect example of this kind of sentiment. Courtenay, Dickens wrote, was a 'dangerous maniac', a man in a 'state of raving religious insanity'. Such fanaticism was explicable in the 'dark ages' or the Reformation but aberrant in the context of nineteenth-century England.[55]

If religious delusion loomed large in élite explanations of Courtenay's behaviour, however, it did not feature in perceptions at the popular level. Courtenay's religious claims were more acceptable in the rural communities. When prompted by the defence lawyer to recall Courtenay's 'madness', the signs that witnesses came up with were to do with the impostor's behaviour rather than his claims of divinity. He shouted, expressed anger, rolled his eyes about; he 'appeared to me a crazy man, completely frantic and mad', 'quite frightful and frantic'.[56] As J. F. C. Harrison has observed, when it came to definitions of madness, there was a gap between polite and popular culture.[57]

Courtenay, the impostor, was never quite what he seemed. Life was an act. He played a role, his assumed identity; but even then

36 Courtenay—Byronesque figure, from a contemporary print. *Source*: Dawes collection.

could not resist the urge to go over the top. His antics at the Canterbury election were described as '*à la* Kean' (with reference to the famous nineteenth-century actor Edmund Kean).[58] He hovered on the edge of madness: sane to some, insane to others, not always for the same reasons. While a quest for fame governed many of his actions, however, we need not doubt the sincerity of his attachment to the radical cause. He was a popular demagogue, even if at times it seemed as though he had imbibed the scent rather than the substance of radicalism.

There is something almost fictional about Courtenay. His story has many of the ingredients of early nineteenth-century melodrama and romantic literature. Biographical romance about a popular hero, the lure of the 'oriental and exotic', a 'knight' determined to reclaim his rightful inheritance: all are commonplace in the popular fiction of the 1830s and early 1840s. And these themes were to be found in both the drawing-room reading of the bourgeoisie and the cheap working-class fiction of the towns in what was a considerable overlap of literary tastes.[59] It is a cultural overlap which perhaps helps to explain some of Courtenay's appeal to the wives of Kentish farmers as well as the craftsmen of Canterbury, and which provides new resonance to the story of the 'ladies of Canterbury', who in 1833 kissed his hands and his clothes and threw a glass of gin cordial into their hero's mouth as he was led off to prison.[60]

Here was a swashbuckling hero, a traveller to the Middle East, so he claimed, a man of exotic dress and manners. (It was said that his travels overseas were responsible for his strange demeanour.) For at least some of the knight's followers, it must have seemed like fantasy becoming reality. Courtenay might almost have stepped out of a page of early nineteenth-century literature. It is appropriate that the widely read novelist William Ainsworth—now largely forgotten, though in his time arguably more popular than Charles Dickens—found a place for Courtenay, as the Knight of Malta, in his book *Rookwood*, published first in 1834.[61]

The events of 1838 have a touch of the Gothic and the melodramatic about them, too. Like many a Victorian villain, Courtenay shoots and stabs the hapless 'constable' Nicholas Mears. He acts without mercy; his eyes blaze and his pistol smokes. The victim sobs before he is finally dispatched with a dagger. The prints illustrating the affair could have come straight from a work of contemporary popular fiction.

I began this chapter with the metaphor of the restoration of paintings. With Courtenay, we never really get beyond his persona, the lacquer and the gloss. To all intents and purposes, John Tom *was* Sir William Courtenay. In an age before fingerprints and passport photographs, it was relatively easy to assume a new identity: Natalie Davis's *The Return of Martin Guerre* has recently provided us with a spectacular case of an impostor in sixteenth-century France.[62] England in the 1830s stood on the threshold of a new era of surveillance; on matters of identity, it was not too far removed from the world of Martin Guerre. Who was to say who he really was if 'Sir William Courtenay' stuck resolutely to his story,

37 Courtenay in *Rookwood* (1850 edition). He is the figure carrying the sword.

denying family and former friends? Even those who were sceptical colluded, unintentionally, in the lie. In Courtenay's trial for perjury in 1833, the prosecution said, 'Whether he called himself Perken Warbeck, or Napoleon Buonaparte, with that they had nothing to do: they would try him by the name by which he called himself.'[63]

Others were certainly taken in by Courtenay. Francis, who from his testimony before the Select Committee does not appear to have been a fool (he has had a bad press), 'really thought that Thom was telling me the truth'. He 'considered him to be the Lord Courtenay that he described himself to be'. It is interesting and, given the argument of this chapter, appropriate that the warrant for the removal of Tom to the Lunatic Asylum refers to him as 'William Courtenay alias Sir William Courtenay'. Francis told the Parliamentary Committee that when Courtenay was in the Asylum he did not have his head shaved like other patients and did not wear institutional clothing. In other words, he was treated like a privileged inmate.[64] The burial entry in the register at Hernhill reads 'William Courtenay *alias John Tom*' (not vice versa). Perhaps Tom has had the last laugh![65]

And yet what matters really is not Courtenay, or Tom, but his social endorsement. As the Chartist Feargus O'Connor observed at the time, 'if Courtenay was mad, how woeful must be the condition of those men who will even follow a mad man in the hope of change'.[66]

6
The Rioters

WHO were the rioters of 1838? We learn precious little about them from the pages of Rogers's *Battle in Bossenden Wood*; he was concerned with Courtenay and his story rather than with his followers. Contemporaries dismissed them as a band of ignorant and deluded labourers. Neither approach is satisfactory if we are going to take the insurrection of 1838 seriously. From a list provided at the time by the Reverend Handley, a similar document in the Home Office papers in the Public Record Office, and from Liardet's survey, we know of over forty men who either were with Courtenay in Bosenden Wood or left the band just before the confrontation with the military.[1] This information, together with my extensive research on the parishes of Hernhill and Dunkirk, including family reconstitution, enables a detailed study of the rank-and-file of an insurrectionary movement of a kind, as far as I am aware, never attempted in any study of popular protest in Britain (in any historical period).

The statements of trial witnesses provide a further half-dozen names of men, mostly from Dunkirk or Boughton, who entertained Courtenay and his followers in the few days before the massacre, or who attended his meetings. This list includes the old man Wooley (we do not know his first name), who said that he would have sold his bed from under him 'to serve Sir W. Courtenay'.[2] Another was William Kennett, who allowed meetings in his home and who must have known Courtenay earlier, for one of his children, baptized in October 1833, was named 'William Courtenay Kennett'.[3] William Branchett, an agricultural labourer, was standing by his door in Boughton Street on 29 May (the Tuesday: Oak Apple Day) when Courtenay and his party passed; they asked him to join them and he did. The Thomas Brown who led Courtenay's horse, according to Branchett, was probably the son of the Dunkirk small farmer/fruiterer John Brown, whose other son, Daniel, was on the Home Office list. George Hawkins, and William Stevens, a labouring man living at Boughton, both of whom appeared as witnesses at the trial, were with Courtenay when Mears, the constable's brother, was killed. Stevens claimed that he had remained with the men all night, 'because I was afraid to go away'.[4] None of these men were with the rioters when they clashed with the soldiers.

There is little disputing the role of Hernhill in the rising of 1838. Of those who perished in Bosenden Wood, four were from Hernhill and four from Dunkirk. Of those taken up in the wake of the rising, ten were from Hernhill, two from Boughton, and two others from nearby Selling and Whitstable.[5] It is not always easy to allocate individuals to a particular parish; people, we have seen, moved locally from parish to neighbouring parish. But of our file of forty-four would-be insurrectionists, twenty-eight (over 60 per cent) came from Hernhill, six from Dunkirk, four from Boughton, and six from undetermined places.[6] The preponderance of Hernhill recruits is assured, even if the six unknowns are assumed to be from either of the two other parishes.

What is immediately striking about the rioters is their ordinariness, for in many ways they represent a cross-section of the local population. Twenty-nine out of the forty-four (66 per cent) were either labourers or agricultural labourers; six (14 per cent) were farmers; six (14 per cent) were employed in trades and crafts; the remaining three (7 per cent) were farm servants. These figures are not widely different from the breakdown of male occupations for Hernhill and Dunkirk for the census of 1841[7] (see Table 11).

The labourers varied in circumstance and age. Stephen Baker, aged 22 when he was killed, was described as 'an inoffensive young man' who was earning 2s. 3d. a day as a labourer at the time of the rising.[8] He was married, with no children, and was probably supporting his parents Thomas (also an agricultural labourer) and Mary Baker, who were both admitted to the Faversham Union

TABLE 11 Occupations of the rioters

Occupation	No. of rioters	% of rioters	% of Hernhill male population with same occupation (1841)
Farmers	6	13.6	14.6
Trades	3	6.8	4.0
Crafts	3	6.8	7.3
Agr. labourers/ labourers	29	65.9	55.0
Farm servants	3	6.8	13.9

workhouse shortly after their son's death.[9] William Rye, also from Hernhill, was another agricultural labourer killed in the rising. He was a married man in his forties with four surviving children. His wife, Sarah, who was older than him, had had a total of eight children, three of whom had died as infants. She was a sickly woman. Liardet claimed that Rye was in constant employment, receiving 2s. 6d. a day; however, we know from the overseer's accounts for Hernhill that he was on constant poor relief during the 1820s and 1830s and that he could not pay his rent in 1834.[10] Edward Rigden Curling, who was imprisoned for his role in the rising, was a 33-year-old looker (or shepherd) who had lived in Hernhill all his life. He and his 28-year-old wife, Charity, had been married for seven years and had three young children. Curling was in constant employment, working on the marshland property of John Cobb at Waterham.[11] One final example of someone from the labourer/agricultural labourer category is provided by William Burford, out of work at the time of the rising. Although Burford was born in Boughton and married there in 1831, he seems to have lived and worked at Westwell (near Charing) at some stage. He was resident in Dunkirk in 1838. Burford was described by Liardet as a 'decidedly bad character ... suspected to be concerned in several depredations that had been committed', and his wife, Emma, had brought a charge of assault against him in 1836. (She was arrested in 1838 after she had followed the rioters into the wood attempting to persuade her husband to leave Courtenay.[12])

The majority of the farmers involved were small farmers. Edward Wraight and Noah Miles had the largest properties. Wraight owned about 20 acres and rented more than 30. Miles, who was also the occupier of two public houses, owned a 14-acre farm and rented an equivalent amount of land.[13] He was a lone Whig voter in a Tory stronghold. (Wraight voted Conservative in 1832 and 1837.)[14] Both men had large families; both were in their fifties or sixties. Miles's wife Mary—Edward Wraight's sister—was dead by 1838. They had had eleven children: one was dead, and the survivors ranged in age from 12 to 35. The Wraights had six surviving children out of a total of eleven. (Three had perished as infants and two as children.) He was described as 'a man of a sullen, uncommunicative character, extremely tenacious of his rights'.[15] Two of his sons are on the list of insurrectionists; two of his daughters were married to followers of Courtenay.

Alexander Foad, imprisoned for a year for his role in the affair, was an archetypal small farmer. An owner-occupier of 8 acres at Dargate Common, he had been in the parish for about six years. Born in Reculver, Foad met his Chislet-born wife, Mary Barnett, in Ospringe, presumably when he was in service there. He left his service in 1822, married in 1823, and took his own farm in Ospringe until he moved to Hernhill.[16] The Foads were in their forties, with at least three children, two under the age of 12. Thomas Mears Tyler, whom I have also included in the small farmer category, although he was described by contemporaries as a labourer, owned 3 or 4 acres and a cottage.[17] He was single, and in his late twenties in 1838. Transported for life for his part in the rising, he was considered to be one of the leaders in mobilizing the farm labourers. William Wills, a 46-year-old, who was transported too as a ringleader, was a downwardly-mobile small farmer. He came from a Hernhill farming family who at one stage had occupied Lavender Farm. If his parents had owned any land, it would soon have been dissipated among the huge Wills family, such was the inheritance custom in Kent. Wills was renting 13 acres in the 1830s, but by 1838 he was living at Fairbrook, working for the farmer George Francis, and was being described as an 'ex'-small farmer, distressed and drunken and dissolute in his habits.[18] His wife, Lucy, the daughter of another rioter, Charles Hadlow, and more than twenty years Wills's junior, was pregnant when they married in 1835. They had two young children. Finally, there was Wills's brother-in-law, John Hadlow (married to Wills's sister Lydia), bailiff at Lavender Farm for the absentee landowner Julius Shepherd, and tenant of 4 acres of land at Dargate.[19] Lydia Hadlow had ten children, two of whom were dead by 1838. The rest ranged in age from 3 to 21: two of them, Henry and John junior, were involved in the riot. The existence of this peasant phalanx, two of whom were transported as recognized leaders of the rising, is an important confirmation of Mick Reed's recent highlighting of the role of the small farmer, the family producer, in nineteenth-century rural protest.[20]

The three craftsmen were a shoemaker from Boughton, William Nutting, and two Hernhill carpenter-cum-hurdlemakers, Peter and Thomas Adams. All were single and in their twenties. All worked with their fathers. The Adams brothers were half-brothers of Thomas Mears Tyler. Of the three rioters employed in the trades sector, two, James Miles (son of Noah) and James Goodwin (son-in-law of Edward Wraight), kept beershops; the other, Edward

Wraight junior (son of Wraight senior and Goodwin's brother-in-law), was an agricultural labourer and a higgler or petty dealer. The Goodwins had six children aged from 2 to 20 years (one had died when young). Mary Miles was pregnant at the time of the rising, and she had five surviving children under the age of 10 (two others were dead). Sarah Wraight had six children ranging from 1 to 10 years (she too had lost a child). James Goodwin was the poorest of these tradesmen, constantly drawing on poor relief during the 1820s and receiving blankets and bread in the 1830s. But the others had recourse to aid in 1830 and received parish bread.[21]

Finally, there were the farm servants. We have details about only one of the three, George Griggs, a 23-year-old unmarried man from Dunkirk. He was one of ten children of the blacksmith William Griggs and his wife Ann. William, a son of a blacksmith himself, was born in Selling but had settled in the Ville in the early part of the century, renting a cottage and an acre of land.[22] He was dead by 1838. In 1836 George Griggs had become involved in one of the many disputes between employer and employee which can be found in the Petty Sessions records for the period, in his case with the Boughton farmer John Pell, who had accused George and a fellow servant in husbandry of being 'impertinent and negligent in their service'.[23] By 1838 he was a farm servant to Edward Curling, receiving yearly wages and board. He perished in Bosenden Wood; his elder brother Thomas, an agricultural labourer, was wounded and imprisoned for a year.

The rioters represented a fair cross-section of the population of Hernhill and Dunkirk in other ways, too. Ninety per cent of the Hernhill insurrectionists had been born within five miles of Hernhill. (The figures for the whole population of Hernhill in the census of 1851 are 80 per cent.) These figures disguise an element of geographical mobility. Courtenay's follower, the agricultural labourer William Knight, who was born in Hernhill, married a pregnant Ann Millington in All Saints, Canterbury, in 1826.[24] Several of the six children that they had had by 1838 were baptised in Canterbury, yet William was receiving relief in Hernhill at that time, so there must have been movement between the two places.[25] Richard Foreman, another agricultural labourer, imprisoned for his part in the rising, was born in Selling, baptized in Hernhill, and married in Seasalter (to Sarah Longbottom, a Seasalter woman). George Bishop, arrested and discharged in 1838, was born in Hernhill but married his Sandwich-born wife in Chartham in 1828.

James Miles, the beershop-keeper, was a servant in Faversham in the late 1820s when he met his Chilham-born wife—the result was an illegitimate child.[26] But the point about all this mobility—and there are other examples—is that, as we have seen in a previous chapter, it was all within a specific social arena, that crucial five-mile radius.

The crude literacy level of the rioters was also not totally at odds with that of the local area. Of those for whom we have details of literacy from the marriage registers, mostly Hernhill people, 40 per cent were able to sign their names and 60 per cent made their mark. The figures for male literacy in the parish of Hernhill, as we saw in Chapter 2, were 48 per cent literate and 52 per cent illiterate. (Illiteracy in Dunkirk was much higher, but there are too few rioters from the Ville to make any meaningful comparison.)

Even their moral profile, if we should call it that, was remarkably similar to that of their fellow parishioners: 54 per cent of the wives of rioters were pregnant when they stood before the altar, a figure only slightly higher than the 50 per cent of prenuptial pregnancies in Hernhill and Dunkirk during the first half of the nineteenth century.

Yet the Hernhill rioters were not really a representative sample of the parish populations. What is most noticeable—indeed, readers may have already seen it in the case studies a few pages earlier—is the age structure of Courtenay's followers. We have the ages of forty of them, varying from the 17-year-old John Fuller to the 65-year-old William Harvey. If the spread of ages is matched against the Hernhill male population of equivalent age groups, then the overrepresentation of middle-aged insurrectionists becomes immediately clear (see Table 12). Nearly 60 per cent of the rebels were in their thirties or forties compared with just under 35 per cent of the equivalent Hernhill population. Their average age was 34.9 (median age 33), in contrast to the Swing rioters, the anti-Poor law agitators of 1835, and the incendiaries of the 1840s, whose average ages were all in the mid to late twenties.[27] As might be predicted from the age profile, most (68 per cent) were married. The figures for the Hernhill rioters alone are even higher, both for the proportion married and the number of middle-aged men. A third of Hernhill males in their thirties turned out to support Courtenay, or about half of the parish's agricultural labourers in that age group.[28]

These men, most of whom we have already encountered, made

TABLE 12 Age structure of the rioters

Age	No.	%	% of Hernhill male population in same age group (1851 census)
15–19	4	10.0	17.5
20–29	10	25.0	25.0
30–39	12	30.0	16.0
40–49	11	27.5	18.5
50–59	1	2.5	12.5
60–69	2	5.0	10.5

up the central core of the insurrectionaries in Bosenden Wood: George Bishop, George Branchett, William Burford, William Coachworth (or Coatsworth), Edward Rigden Curling, Alexander Foad, Richard Foreman, William Foster, James Goodwin, Charles Hadlow, John Hadlow, Charles Hills, William Knight, James Miles, William Packman, William Price, William Rye, Henry, John, and William Spratt, Edward Wraight junior, James Wraight, and William Wills. The majority of those imprisoned, transported, or killed in 1838 came from this group of men in their thirties and forties. Some of those mentioned as being with Courtenay and his followers, but who were not actually on the Home Office's black list, were in their thirties also: William Kennett, Thomas Dalton, and William Branchett.

The key to the role of this group is a type of mid-life crisis very different from our current understanding of the term. They were victims, most of them, of the poverty cycle, married men with several dependent children not yet old enough to bring in any kind of supplementary income or to assume child-care responsibilities so that the female householder could find outside work.[29] The only group for whom it is possible to make any meaningful comparison with the local population is the twenty-eight Hernhill rioters. They belonged to twenty-five family households and, as Table 13 shows, had more young children per family than the general population. The average family size with children under the age of 12 was 3.5 in the Hernhill census of 1851: for the rioters' families the figure was 4.3. (Both figures include single and childless households.) The rioters were clearly those under the most pressure from the poverty cycle, those with the most young mouths to feed. Moreover, four of

TABLE 13 Dependency structure of the rioters

| | No. of children under the age of 12 ||
	Hernhill rioters	Hernhill parish, 1851
No. per family of		
Heads	25/25 = 1.0	129/129 = 1.0
Wives	23/25 = 0.9	115/129 = 0.9
Children under		
12 yrs. old	60/25 = 2.4	203/129 = 1.6
TOTAL	4.3	3.5

the Hernhill men's wives were pregnant at the time of the insurrection.

Even those with older children may have been in difficulty. The historical demographer David Thomson has argued that, given the economy of nineteenth-century England, low wage, and surplus labour, 'employable' children were a dubious asset. His calculations of the weekly resources of agricultural labourers in 1838—a fortunate coincidence of date—indicate that the poorest families in his sample were those with the *most* children in their earning years. Put simply, if jobs were short and wages low, grown-up children were not exactly a boon to the family economy.[30] Here too, the Hernhill rioters may have been in trouble: nineteen had ninety-five surviving children, an average of five children (young *or* old) per rioter.

Of course, this analysis flies in the face of nineteenth-century efforts to disassociate poverty from the troubles of 1838. Liardet, for one, was eager to demonstrate that poverty and the New Poor Law had nothing to do with the rising. The annotated list of the Revd. Handley and the enquiries of Liardet established that most of the Hernhill rioters were employed at the time of the trouble. Seventeen of the twenty-eight were in work; seven more were small farmers or self-employed. Only four were out of work. Quite apart from the fact that this was in May, not the worst month for unemployment, Liardet ignored the longer-term perspective. The parish records would have shown the lawyer that fifteen of the rioters (54 per cent) had been in receipt of some kind of parish relief in the 1820s and 1830s, either in the form of cash, bread, or directed labour, or as gifts of guernsies or blankets at Christmas

TABLE 14 Social structure of the rioters: rental values

Value (£)	Rental value of property occupied by Hernhill rioters		Rental value for parish, 1838 (known indwellers)	
	No.	%	No.	%
1–5	14	70	21	37.5
5–10	3	15	10	17.9
10–25	1	5	8	14.3
25–50	2	10	5	8.9
50–100	—	—	8	14.3
100–300	—	—	4	7.2
TOTAL	20		56	

time. Ten rioters had indeed been provided with a jacket or blanket during the winter of 1837. And fourteen of the fifteen assisted men fell under Handley and Liardet's employed category.[31] The rental lists for Hernhill also put the lie to attempts to minimize the collective poverty of the protesters. Seventy per cent of that parish's rioters were in the rental brackets £1–£5 a year (the bottom bracket), whereas for the parish as a whole less than 40 per cent fell into this range.[32] (See Table 14). This suggests that the rioters were drawn disproportionately from the lower rungs of parish society.

It is interesting that the insurrectionists were not all the respectable men that George Rudé has led us to believe made up his rehabilitated crowds. No fewer than fourteen had been in trouble with the law: five for assault, two for wood-stealing, three for suspected theft, one for poaching and theft, one for possessing smuggled drink, one for misbehaving in the poorhouse, and one for riot.[33] Most were poverty-related crimes, in keeping with the sort of experience that has been outlined above.

Liardet was misleading about poverty and unemployment among the rioters because he ignored wider factors. It is this long-term perspective, rather than relative levels of poverty, that explains the social basis for Courtenay's insurrection. For the insurrectionaries had one further thing in common: a shared historical experience. They and their families had experienced the transition (rupture is probably a more appropriate word) from the Old Poor Law to the New. The New Poor Law had been in force for a mere three years, so even the youngest rioter had had first-hand experience of it. What I have in mind, rather, is the long-term experience of an old system, which was replaced by the new as dependency ended and the rules were changed almost overnight. Those rioters who were in their thirties and forties had this longer-term experience of poverty and insecurity.

William Knight had received poor relief in the winters of 1822–3, 1823–4, and 1826–7, when he had also been employed on the roads. From the winter of 1827 until March 1830, he was almost constantly in receipt of some kind of parish help, ranging from a few shillings to several pounds a month. He clearly relied on parish aid to supplement, and sometimes to replace, paid labour. In fact, his life was inconceivable outside the framework of parochial assistance: the parish paid for the laying out of his dead father, for the coffin made by John Foreman (£1. 2s.), and for the body bearers at the funeral.[34] Charles Hadlow, the 47-year-old agricultural labourer and parish vermin-catcher, had a similar history of indigence. The parish provided occasional relief in the early 1820s, including burial and coffin expenses for two of the Hadlow's ten children (three died in infancy). From late 1822 to July 1830 (when the overseers' accounts stop), he received almost continuous parochial assistance. The parish paid his rent occasionally, provided help for his wife when she was in confinement, bought him mole traps and a pair of shoes, and covered the cost of his move to parish accommodation at Bessborough. In January 1830, when his wife was ill, he received £3. 4s. 6d. in assistance. At times he got 14s. a week; 2s. 3d. a day in 1829. He worked occasionally on the highways, too.[35] William Rye, whom we have already encountered as an agricultural labourer, provides a third detailed case study. As with Hadlow and Knight, poor relief was part of his everyday survival; regular payments throughout the 1820s, sometimes small amounts, a matter of a few shillings a month, at other times £1 or more. Help varied from 4s. 6d. for a spade to £5 for overdue rent. Once again, the overseers' accounts record payments, quite literally, for help from the cradle to the grave—they provided for the birth of the infant Jane Rye and for her funeral a few weeks later.[36]

Although it would be tedious to provide similar details, the beershop-keeper James Goodwin (six children) and the agricultural labourer John Spratt (five children) had relief profiles almost identical to those above. The agricultural labourers William

Packman (three children under 12), James Wraight (four children under 12), William Coachworth and William Foster (both with five children under 12) had also relied on the parish for assistance in the late 1820s.

It was at the dependency of the Knights and Ryes of the village world that the New Poor Law was aimed. As we saw in Chapter 3, gaps in the historical records preclude any systematic charting of the transition, but all the indications are of a greater astringency in administration even if the banned outdoor relief continued. In 1829 the future rioter Knight, with a wife and three children, was receiving 11s. a week in poor relief: in 1837, ill, with a wife and *six* children, he was awarded 7s. a week (3s. in money and 4s. in kind) by the Faversham Poor Law Union.[37] It is little wonder that he followed Courtenay, he claimed, 'because he said he would give us plenty to eat and plenty to drink'.[38] The 1838 rising was a protest against the removal of the crutch of the Old Poor Law.

In the 1820s the parish supported men like Rye and Knight. After 1835 they had a 'choice': marginal survival, or into the workhouse. Rye and Knight did not go into the hated workhouse, but another insurrectionist, George Branchett of Dunkirk, did. Indeed, the accounts of the New Poor Law contain the annals of his family's suffering. In May 1837 he and his wife Sarah (Gower), who were both ill, received 6s. a week outdoor relief to support their six children (less than half the sum they would have received before 1835). Sarah died in November, and George applied for funeral expenses. A few days later he was admitted to the Union House at Faversham with his children; the Master's report book records that he arrived on a Saturday night, applied to be discharged on the Monday, and then asked to be readmitted on the Tuesday. He was still there in February 1838, for he applied 'to be allowed a few hours liberty to seek work'. (Perhaps, as during the preceding winter, he hoped to get some work tying hop-poles in bundles.)[39] He was out of the House by the end of April, but his four youngest children were all dead (two in the workhouse, two shortly after they left). The Boughton parish register records that one of the children died in the workhouse at Ospringe, so the family seems to have been split up. Again, Branchett had to ask the Union for coffins.[40] With his family thus depleted, the Dunkirk labourer had nothing to lose when he confronted the military in Bosenden Wood. It is not surprising that he was among those killed. Even Liardet had to admit that Branchett's 'misfortunes and distresses had left him peculiarly open to the alluring promises of Thoms'.[41]

These individual chronicles explain one of the main impulses behind the abortive rising. So far we have looked only at the middle-aged cadre, but some younger men may have had similar motivations. Thomas Baker and John Harvey, the fathers, respectively, of Stephen Baker and Phineas (or Finnis) Harvey, had relief profiles during the 1820s very similar to that of the most indigent rioter.[42] Both lost their sons in the rising of 1838. Thomas Mears Tyler, another of the younger insurrectionists, had already served time for his part in the anti-Poor Law disturbances of 1835.[43] There seems enough evidence to describe the Courtenay affair as an anti-Poor Law rising.

It was more than shared experience which bound together the rioters of 1838. Kinship was clearly a crucial factor in mobilization. Many of the rioters were related. The Wraights were linked by marriage to Noah and James Miles, and to William Packman and James Goodwin who had married daughters of Wraight senior. George Bishop was a cousin. William Wills was at the centre of another kinship group. Wills's sister Lydia was married to John Hadlow senior. (He was therefore the uncle of two other rioters, John junior and Henry Hadlow.) Wills in turn was married to one of Charles Hadlow's daughters. Hadlow was also Thomas Griggs's brother-in-law. The other groups were smaller. Thomas and Peter Adams were Thomas Mears Tyler's half-brothers. The Boughton labourer Samuel Eve was married to William Nutting's sister, Mary. The three Spratts, William, Henry, and John, were brothers. Just over half of the rioters, then, had relations among those who supported Courtenay—five kin groups consisting of 8, 7, 3, 3, and 2, respectively.[44]

Nor can one overstress the role of the community. There is ample evidence in this study for the sociologist Craig Calhoun's claim that 'traditional communities were the crucial social foundation for radical collective action'.[45] Those who supported Courtenay lived in clusters, in hamlets. The Hernhill rioters came mainly from Dargate and Bessborough (see Maps 3 and 4). One can trace their patterns of residence in the tithe return of 1840, in the overseers' accounts, and in the rate book for 1837. Eight lived at Bessborough at some stage: the Mileses, Wraight junior, Bishop, Packman, Knight, and (for a while) Wills and Charles Hadlow. John Spratt, Foad, Goodwin, James Wraight, Wraight senior, the Hadlows,

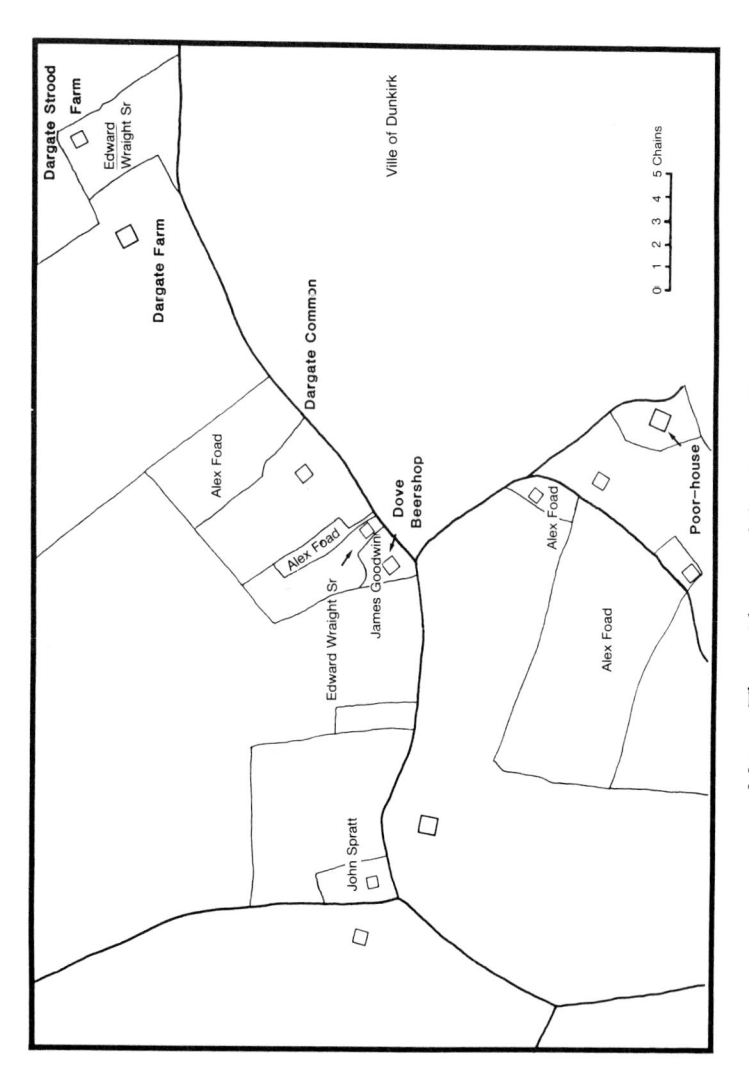

MAP 3 The residences of the rioters: Dargate

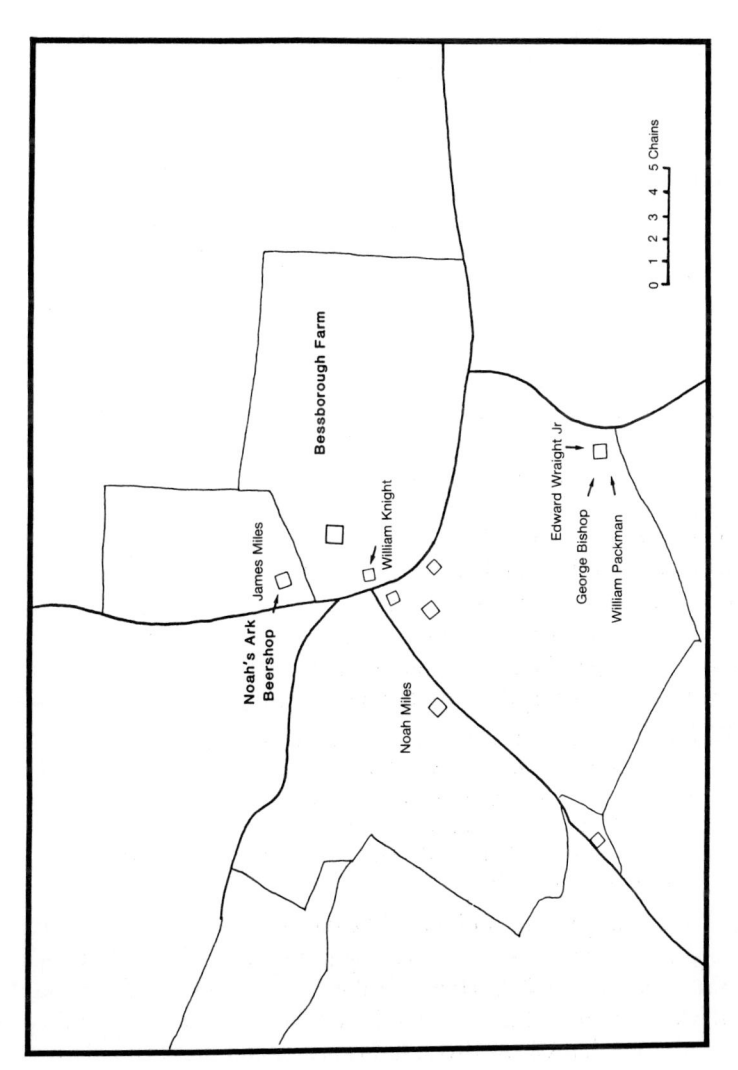

MAP 4 The residences of the rioters: Bessborough

Rye, and Finnis Harvey's father either owned or occupied land or rented cottages at Dargate Common. Goodwin's beershop, the Dove, was situated at Dargate, and James Miles ran his father's beerhouse, Noah's Ark, at Bessborough in the 1830s; they would have been the social centres for their respective hamlets. We know that future rioters met in the beerhouses to discuss social and religious issues.

Several of Courtenay's followers worked together. Eight were employed at various stages by William Kay, the banker Snoulton's bailiff. Four of Edward Curling's farmworkers actually downed tools to join Courtenay. At the trial Curling testified that he knew most of the prisoners and had hired them at one time or another.[46] Many had worked together in poor relief gangs—further evidence of the role of poverty in the forging of a common identity. Some laboured on roads; the overseers directed others to dig the land of local farmers. Foster, Packman, Knight, James Wraight, Charles Hadlow, Goodwin, Finnis Harvey's father, and Stephen Baker's brother worked in such gangs in 1829, labouring for the landowner Shepherd and on the farms of William Wraight, Curling, and John Foreman.[47]

The abortive rising in 1838 was fuelled by socioeconomic discontent, but it was religion that gave it much of its drive. For if 1838 saw the last of the revolts against the New Poor Law, it also marked the last of England's millenarian risings. Sarah Hills, Edward Wraight junior's wife, recalled that William Wills had visited her cottage in the days before the rising:

we had some ale; and, says he, 'Have you heard the great news, and what's going to happen?'—'No', says we, 'William Wills; what be it?' And he said, the great Day of Judgment was close at hand, and that our Saviour had come back again; and that we must all follow him. And he showed us in the Bible, in the Revelations, that he should come upon a white horse, and go forth to conquer.[48]

And sure enough, she continued, 'the day after, as we were coming in our cart from market, we met the groom leading Sir William's white horse'. Lydia Wills (John Hadlow's wife) said that Courtenay had claimed that Christ had selected his body for his second appearance; 'that Christ dwelt in his heart; and that his body was the temple of the Holy Ghost'. 'He had assured her . . . that the millennium was at hand, and that the reign of the saints was approaching.'[49]

The women of Hernhill have so far remained partially hidden in our story, but of course they suffered the same hardships as their fathers, brothers, and husbands. Their absence from the drilling and the fighting should not blind us to their role in the events of 1838. They sang hymns at the meetings held in the days before the battle, and composed a song 'against some person that had injured them'.[50] The kinship links that I mentioned earlier were almost exclusively female links. Magistrates complained that wives and daughters had urged their men to turn out for Courtenay.[51] The women were certainly responsible for much of the religious mobilization. Handley and Liardet were convinced of the part played by Lydia Hadlow (sister of one rioter and wife of another). The latter described her as the 'oracle of the community'. Regarded by her 'ignorant neighbours' as a prodigy of learning, she 'misused' her knowledge of the Bible and her influence as mistress of one of the day schools.[52]

The evidence that much of the ideological drive may have come from the women is tantalizing. They were there when Courtenay gave his followers the sacrament and anointed them with oil to ward off the soldiers' bullets. A charcoal burner remembered that Courtenay had then sat on the ground 'with his back against a tree like, and there was all the women a crying and praying to him'.[53] Women invited Courtenay to their homes to meet their friends. His friendship with Sarah Culver was his entry into William Culver's farm at Bosenden. When a visitor had called at Bosenden to see 'old Culver', he had found Sir William asleep in front of the fire; 'Sarah rose up and with her finger to her mouth said gently, "Hush, hush, the Saviour is sleeping. You must not wake him." '[54] Sarah Wraight and Lydia Hadlow retained their faith in Tom after his death. Wraight told Liardet that she was certain that the slain Courtenay would rise from the dead; 'after poor Edward was taken prisoner, me and a neighbour sat up the whole of that blessed night reading the Bible, and believing the world was to be destroyed on the morrow'. Hadlow claimed that 'even if Sir William . . . had been deceived in some respects, he was nevertheless a holy man inspired by God, and that if he had even gone astray himself, he had led her (to use her own expression) into heavenly paths'.[55] There seem to be traces, then, of what Deborah Valenze has termed 'cottage religion' or 'the religion of the hearth', where women played a large role in a religiosity centred in humble households—although paradoxically, as we will see, the links in our case were with the established church rather than with the sects.[56]

We saw in an earlier chapter that the ability to sign one's name, a functional definition of literacy, may have underestimated those able to read. There is some evidence that in the case of women it was a substantial underestimate. T. C. Smout, in a particularly illuminating study, found that, of a group of women involved in a religious revival in an eighteenth-century Scottish village, only one in ten could write but all of them could read.[57] Writing was not considered necessary for women: at all social levels it was usual for higher percentages of women to sign their names with a cross or mark. And yet, more females than males attended the schools which taught reading. In Hernhill in 1851, only 13 per cent of agricultural labourers' sons were at school compared with 40 per cent of their daughters: 58 per cent of the sons of farmers compared with 65 per cent of their daughters.[58] So there may well have been some foundation to the claim that the reading facility of the women had helped to mobilize the 1838 insurrectionaries. It was said that in Hernhill more women than men were able to read, 'and it is thus that they have been enabled to do so much mischief . . . they availed themselves of their power of reading the Scriptures, which to them or their husbands was a book they could not open, to distort tenets, not very clear in themselves, into proofs that Thom was the promised Messiah'.[59]

A gentleman told a journalist that many of the rioters were Methodists.[60] In an earlier chapter we placed Wesleyan Methodists and Bible Christians in the hamlet of Dargate during the 1820s, which, we saw, was a core area for Hernhill protesters. In a wider arena, still within travelling distance of Hernhill and Dunkirk, Canterbury and Faversham provided a range of dissenting voices.[61] It is *possible* that a lingering Bible Christian enthusiasm was tapped by Courtenay and his followers in 1838, but there is no firm evidence that this was the case. All we know for certain is that, if there were any noncomformist influences, they were not expressed in terms of congregational commitment. William Branchett, the Boughton labourer who was with Courtenay's group at one stage but who left before the confrontation with the military, had been to a Methodist chapel, and his children were at the chapel school.[62] But only one rioter, the shoemaker William Nutting, can be identified firmly as a Methodist, and this was ten years after the battle in Bosenden Wood. None of the known Dunkirk and Hernhill Methodists turned out for Courtenay. When the would-be messiah attempted to mobilize a gang of men working in a gravel pit near Sittingbourne and the men refused to join him, he dismissed them as 'a set of Methodists'; 'It is of no use talking to you.'[63] It is an ironic footnote to the debate over Methodism and the threat of revolution in eighteenth- and nineteenth-century Britain that the religious milieu of the Courtenay rising seems to have been that of the Anglican church!

Foster, Rye, Baker, and Harvey, all of whom were killed in the rising, were described as regular church attenders; the slain George Griggs had been a star pupil at Handley's Sunday school. Alex Foad and Charles Hadlow went to church and received communion.[64] Even more interesting is the fact that several of the Hernhill followers of Courtenay were members of the church band, including the leader of the church singers, William Wills. As we shall see, a journalist from *The Times* who attended the funeral of those killed in the battle noted that the bulk of the church choir was either dead or in Maidstone gaol.[65] (A study of working-class association and politicization in nineteenth-century France has suggested that the secular choral societies were agents of socialization: the Hernhill church choir provides an unexpected rural, religious, English comparison.[66])

The fact that the remainder of the insurrectionaries were not described as regular attenders at church suggests that their links with the church were not strong. But this does not mean that religious influences should be discounted. When Liardet visited the homes of the dead rioters, he noticed that several of them had possessed religious books. The reputed sheep-stealer Burford and the farmer Edward Wraight, who had refused to go to church 'to hear a man who robbed him every day of his life by taking tithe', had in their homes a Testament and 'one or two other books of a religious nature'.[67] As we saw in Chapter 2, few people who owned books in Hernhill and Dunkirk possessed other than religious material. People who went to school to learn to read were taught to read the Bible; 'Indeed, the usual answer in the district to the question "Can you read?" is, "Yes, a little in the Testament." '[68] Twelve of the rioters could read and write and eighteen could read only: only thirteen (30 per cent) were totally illiterate. In other words, 70 per cent were able to read. And even illiteracy did not totally preclude biblical influences. After the riot, *The Times* reporter encountered a labouring man who 'took from his breast a few pages of the Testament containing the whole of the Revelations; a mark was made at the 6th chapter; and the man told me that he could neither read nor write himself, but that his wife read the book to him every night, and said that some such person as Sir William Courtenay was spoken of in it'.[69] The prints on the walls of the cottages, too, were primarily scriptural in subject matter.[70] It was this kind of cultural myopia, Liardet claimed, that largely explained Courtenay's following.[71]

PART III
The Aftermath

7
Repercussions

IT would be foolish to compare the Courtenay affair with Peterloo, Pentrich, or Newport—in terms of scale and impact, it matched none of those. Yet the battle does not deserve the silence it has been accorded in the history books, for what the Chartists called the 'horrible butchery' of Bosenden Wood sent ripples across the nation. The affair quickly became entangled in party politics. The Conservatives would have liked to have made political capital out of the Whig government's predicament. The party machine was feeding information to the centre from 31 May on; letters from the magistrate Norton Knatchbull to his father, Sir Edward Knatchbull (a future Paymaster-General), were in turn passed on to Sir Robert Peel. But the problem was that, while the government—the Home Secretary, Lord John Russell, to be precise—was responsible for Courtenay's release from the Kent County Asylum a matter of months before the trouble, a local *Tory*, the aforesaid Knatchbull, had been deeply involved in the actual suppression of the band of agricultural labourers. And the Tories were reported to have supported Courtenay in his bid for political power in Canterbury in the early 1830s. So, in the end, the Conservatives had to be content with claims that Courtenay had been freed through Whig electoral patronage, allegedly in return for the vote of Tom's (i.e. Courtenay's) father—what they referred to as 'a Cornish job'. For their part, the Whigs were able to point out that the Tories had whipped up anti-Poor Law feeling for their own advantage in the recent election and that the nation had now reaped the consequences. It was a somewhat contradictory position to take, given that Whigs were simultaneously denying that the labourers' protests had anything to do with opposition to the New Poor Law.[1]

Journalists and others descended upon the area, notebooks in hand, quizzing 'the peasantry'. It was as if they had entered some strange land; the cultural gap was immense. The agricultural labourer was encountered as a different species: William Wills, one of the rioters, was described as having 'the glance of a wild Indian or a wild beast'.[2] The Central Society of Education carried out a survey of the affected parishes, which has since become a vital historical source. The investigator, a barrister named Frederick Liardet (whom we have already encountered), questioned people in beershops, in their cottages, and in the fields. How many rooms per family were there? How clean were their dwelling places? How many wives could sew and bake? What did people do of an evening? (Not surprisingly, few admitted to resorting to the beershop.) How many gardens had flowers—a sign of civilization? Did cottagers keep livestock? How many households possessed books? Were there any prints on the walls (like flowers, a gauge of 'cultivation in the cottager')? How many children attended school, and of those how many could write or read?[3] The people of Hernhill, Boughton, and the Ville of Dunkirk must have felt like the old Breton in P.-J. Hélias's *The Horse of Pride* who said, after some anthropologists had left his village, 'We've been eaten by the mice.'[4]

The English press, in both London and the provinces, devoted space to the trouble in Kent, ranging from the prints in *Wilson's Wonderful Characters* and the *Penny Satirist* to the *Morning Post*'s phrenological anlaysis of Tom's head ('a compact wreck of masculine beauty and moral deformity'[5]). There were predictable comments on the 'worse than barbarous credulity', 'brutal ignorance', 'moral degradation', and 'grovelling' superstition of the poor; one could expect such goings on in Scotland or Ireland, but in Kent![6] Some held the Church responsible. The irony of the situation was not lost on commentators, that the scene of this 'dreadful superstition' was a few miles from the seat of the Church of England. Have you 'been to Canterbury and counted the number of churches?', asked the *Kent Herald*.[7]

The Chartists provided an interesting alternative to the prevailing discourse. At a dinner in Manchester given by the MP for Oldham, John Fielden, Feargus O'Connor suggested that a monument should be erected in memory of the followers of Courtenay, that is for those who fell in opposition to the New Poor Law.[8] The London Democratic Association petitioned Parliament for an inquiry into the affair. Bronterre O'Brien, we saw earlier, wrote of the 'assassination' of the labourers in Bosenden Wood: 'I repeat that Courtenay and his followers were murdered for no other purpose than to enforce the infernal New Poor Law Act.' For a brief moment, the dead farm labourers found a place in the rhetoric of radicalism. In Newcastle in June, a speaker at a demonstration for universal suffrage ended his oration with the words, 'Let them remember Peterloo and Canterbury (Cheers and "We will").'[9]

Other than the wounded, few of the 'rioters' had been taken prisoner on the spot. But the constables and military managed to pick them up later, aided by the verbal and written lists provided by the vicar of Hernhill, a relieving officer, and other local office holders and employers who had recognized parishioners or workmen among Courtenay's band.[10] (It is easy to see why rioters sometimes blackened their faces and dressed in women's clothing to avoid detection in a close-knit community.) Oral evidence collected fifty or sixty years later revealed that several men had hidden with neighbours or relatives—in one case in a faggot stack—to avoid detection, returning when they heard it was safe. One man fled first to a brother at Badlesmere (south of Faversham) and then to Ramsgate where he found work as an ostler.[11]

Those captured and rounded up later were taken to the White Horse Inn in Boughton. Before long, there were twenty-seven prisoners incarcerated there and the yard was 'filled with their weeping and fainting wives and children'.[12] A company of soldiers remained in the area for several days; more special constables were sworn in. The Revd. Poore, JP, hoped that 'the terrible Example' that had taken place would 'prevent any future Disturbance'. The Assistant Poor Law Commissioner for the province, E. Carleton Tufnell, believed that 'The worst gang in the county has been broken up & thoroughly annihilated, & people regret that they were not all shot, instead of only 10'; 'I thus get rid at a blow of 40 of the worst characters in [Kent].'[13] And yet those on the spot, Poore included, seemed to fear either that there would be a bid to free the prisoners or that a rising would be attempted. It was said that before he had murdered Mears, Courtenay had engaged men to meet him on the Sunday. Poore reported on the 1 June that 'Several came to day from distant parishes to join him but on hearing the result of Yesterday they hastily left the Neighbourhood.'[14]

The bodies of Bennett and those of most of the dead rioters were taken to the Red Lion Inn at Dunkirk, close to the scene of the action and on the main London to Canterbury road. They were separated, in death as in life, as if proximity would lead to contamination or dishonour. Lt. Bennett's corpse was placed upstairs in the Inn itself, while those of the rioters lay in the stable. Here they remained on exhibition. The *Kent Herald*'s correspondent was there.

154 The Aftermath

The bodies . . . were lying cold and stark on the straw. They were evidently all common labourers in agriculture, with one exception—that of a man who was shot through the heart, and in whose breast the perforation of the bullet was distinctly visible. The eyes of all were wide open, and the glare of them from being stripped from all intelligence was horribly frightful.

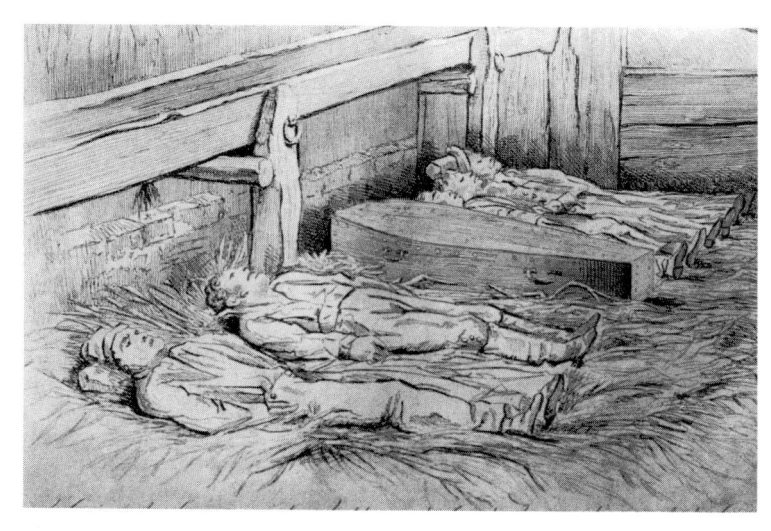

38 The dead rioters. *Source*: *Life and Extraordinary Adventures of Sir William Courtenay* (Canterbury, 1838).

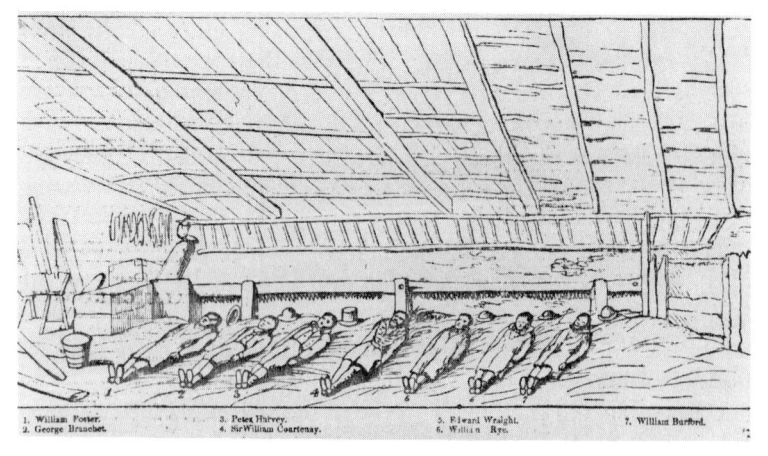

39 The dead rioters. *Source*: from a drawing in the *Weekly Chronicle*, 10 June 1838.

As for Lt. Henry Boswell Bennett,

His fate is universally lamented. He was a very fine looking young man, the only son of an Irish gentleman of good fortune and family. He has died with the reputation of having been an excellent officer and a perfect gentleman.[15]

The memento-hunters and the curious descended upon the area in droves. The landlord of the Red Lion claimed that 20,000 people had visited the neighbourhood in the space of a few days. On the Sunday, Gravesend thronged with 'respectably-dressed' people who had come from London by steam-boat.[16] The trees at the scene of the affray were stripped of bark, blood-stained earth was scraped up by souvenir hunters. Locals realized the commercial possibilities of the relic trade: 'strands of Courtenay's beard' and 'pieces of his smock' were snapped up by Canterbury jewellers to be made into brooches; bludgeons were hurriedly cut and coloured with animal blood to feed the insatiable market. An elderly woodcutter recalled that any old button said to have belonged to Courtenay would sell readily.[17]

Not all were souvenir hunters; some must have sought relics in the real sense of the term. There were those among the labouring population of the area who believed that Courtenay and his dead followers would 'rise again' on the Sunday (the third day). A board appeared on the tree under which Courtenay had fallen, and hooks were driven into the trunk to prevent its removal: it read, 'Our real true Messiah, King of the Jews'.[18]

The authorities took such chiliasm seriously. There was debate about the best way of disposing of Tom's body. If he was buried secretly by night, out of the area, it would avoid publicity and any further disturbance. However, it might cause resentment or, even more important, fuel the rumours that the 'saviour' would rise again from the dead. The Revd. Handley and Mr Julius Shepherd, not a resident of Hernhill 'but a considerable landed proprietor in the parish', agreed that it was best to bury Courtenay 'in open day in the churchyard of the parish [Hernhill] which he had so frightfully agitated, lest it should be supposed by some of his ignorant admirers that Thoms had suddenly disappeared in the night, and might be expected again from heaven to revisit earth'.[19]

As the *Morning Chronicle* put it, in words that would have gladdened the heart of Charles Dickens's Mr Gradgrind, only 'facts' could dissipate such 'foolish notions' and 'fancies'. 'It was ... for the purpose of meeting assertions with facts, and of

40 Courtenay's corpse on display. *Source: Wilson's Wonderful Characters* (no date), Bodleian Library, Oxford.

beating down their delusions by the evidence of their own senses, that the body of Courtenay was exposed to the view of all who chose to look upon him.' He was then to be buried publicly, so that the labouring population would be 'sure that his body was in their presence committed to the earth'.[20] The representatives of the press were to be there so that 'the peasantry hereabout'—as *The Times* put it, exaggerating the power of the printed word in a culture that was still strongly oral—'might be really convinced, by seeing it in the papers, that he was dead and buried'.[21]

And so, at the Red Lion Inn, Courtenay, clad in linen, was placed in an unmarked coffin and covered with sawdust. The lid was screwed down, witnessed by a dozen of the 'most respectable persons in the neighbourhood', while the 'peasantry' stood outside. Then at 10 a.m. on 5 June, with an obvious attempt to avoid anything approaching a funeral procession, the dead messiah was conveyed to Hernhill churchyard in a van, at a smart trot, surrounded by constables, with the gigs and horses of the gentry and farmers at the front instead of at the rear, and with the labourers running along behind. As the van turned down the road to Staple Street, *The Times* reporter noticed ten women on the ridge of Boughton Hill, quietly observing the proceedings. There were about sixty people at the church, some by the graveside, others in a nearby field. One man had a bandaged head; others were recognized by reporters as having been in custody in Faversham in connection with the 'riot'. The *Morning Chronicle*'s man noted their 'sullen indifference or stolid ignorance'. Punishment pursued Courtenay to the grave: death proclaimed the social order. Tom was to be denied any hint of social, let alone divine, legitimation. The coffin, without a pall or covering, was conveyed direct to its unmarked grave instead of into the church, as was the custom. The minister, Handley, read only the parts of the service necessary for interment in consecrated ground, omitting the section concerning the 'resurrection of the body to a life of immortality'. Not so much as a bell marked this rite of passage; not so much as a mound of earth acknowledged Courtenay's consignment to the ground. A watch was placed on the grave to prevent the removal of its contents.[22] One of those watching the grave was told several months later that despite his vigilance Courtenay's body had been carried secretly to the house of the Culvers. 'He never dared to speak about it until years afterwards.'[23]

Courtenay's followers were buried in the afternoon. They were not buried alongside him, as had been planned, but in other parts of the churchyard with their families. They were given a proper burial. The bell was tolled as the bodies approached the church. First came Stephen Baker, aged 22, attended by eight mourners, including his wife and father, 'sobbing as if their hearts were breaking'. Then, one by one, came the corpses of William Foster, 33, William Rye, 46, Edward Wraight, 62, Phineas Harvey, 27 (accompanied by his father 'in an agony of grief'), and William Burford, 33. All were attended by mourners; there were five young women in Rye's train, two of them his children, one of them his sister, whose 'affliction was excessive'. The minister met each coffin at the church gate and led the small processions into the body of the church. When all were inside, the bell stopped tolling. *The Times*'s correspondent noted that all the caskets were of oak, with ornamental black studs and black coffin plates. All except for Harvey's, that is, which had a silvered plate and ornaments. It was duly noted that all were buried at their own expense: 'a proof that poverty had no share in producing those disturbances'. It was, of course, no such thing; and we know, furthermore, that the coffins of Burford, Foster, Rye, and Baker were paid for by the Faversham Poor Law Union. Handley was in tears as he read the funeral service, laying 'peculiar emphasis' on the lesson taken from the 15th chapter of St Paul's Epistle to the Corinthians (the text omitted from Courtenay's burial): 'Be not deceived—evil communications corrupt good manners—awake to righteousness and sin not—for some have not the knowledge of God. I speak this to your shame.' Then, one by one in reverse order, the bodies were conveyed to their graves. The total ceremony had lasted some two hours.[24] There were two remaining dead rioters. George Griggs, aged 23, was buried in Boughton. There appears to have been a dispute over the fate of the body of the 49-year-old pauper George Branchett. A grave was dug for him in Hernhill after his comrades had been laid to rest, but he seems finally to have been interred in Boughton. As with most of the others, poor relief provided for his coffin.[25]

Reporters had an opportunity to observe, first-hand, the aftermath of the Courtenay affair, its impact upon the communities involved. As we saw, neighbourhood and kinship links were important in the mobilization of the 'rioters', so the repercussions for relatives were all the more devastating. It was difficult to fall back on neighbours and kin for emotional and material support because they too had been affected. At one stage in Hernhill, over thirty inhabitants (all male) were either dead, wounded, or missing as a result of the affray. Journalists wrote, movingly, of a community in grief. A woman sat outside a cottage, the last in a row of 'neat' labourers' dwellings. 'Her back was to the road, and her eye fixed on the house, while every moment her body could be observed shaking and trembling as if she were struggling against some frightful emotion.' 'In walking through the village I heard the voice of wailing in almost every house.' There is little sign here of the inurement to the emotional consequences of death which, according to some academics, poverty is supposed to bring. 'One poor young woman, whose brother has been committed to Maidstone gaol for wilful murder, was sitting at a door, pale and seemingly exhausted, and stupified by grief. Another woman I heard singing most dolefully to a young child she held in her arms, and ever and anon breaking off to bewail her dear, dear husband.' A week later, a reporter attended Hernhill church to assess the mood of the congregation. It was as if 'some great national calamity' had occurred; St Michael's church was a 'house of mourning'. Labouring men, with black crepe on their hats, gathered in the churchyard. 'I should conjecture that of the male labouring population two-thirds were in mourning of some description or other.' He counted over thirty women in the centre aisle of the church 'dressed in deep mourning'. 'There was no psalmody attempted. Not even a hymn was given out. The great body of the rustic choir was either among the dead or among the captives in Maidstone gaol.' In Boughton, too, 'there was a gloom on the faces of a larger portion of the labouring classes'.[26]

The Faversham Poor Law Union awarded temporary outdoor relief to the needy wives, widows, and children of those either killed in the riot or in prison for their role in the affair; but at the end of June, six of the ten applicants were ordered into the workhouse 'on the ground of bad character'. If the Courtenay affair was a movement of protest against the New Poor Law, it was the Poor Law that emerged the victor.[27]

Over thirty men and two women were arrested in connection with the affray, appearing either before the Coroner's Inquest at Boughton or at the Petty Sessions at Faversham in early June. Of these, sixteen men faced the Assize Grand Jury in August, charged with murder; and of these, ten proceeded to trial, two for the murder of the constable's brother and nine for the murder of Bennett. (One man, Mears, was charged with both.) On the eve of the trial the radical, Bronterre O'Brien, predicted its outcome.

'Most probably the accused will be found guilty of murder, with a recommendation of mercy from the jury; and the Whigs, to show their merciful bearings, will commute the sentence to transportation for life.'[28] We will see that his assessment was not wildly inaccurate.

The Chartist press also alleged the class nature of the law. The odds were stacked against the followers of Courtenay: 'The Coroner's jury and the Magistrates who committed them are all persons *of that class which thrives by the New Poor Law Act.*'[29] Again, the Chartists had a point. From the perspective of the charged agricultural labourers, British justice could hardly seem disinterested. When they appeared before the Petty Sessions at Faversham, the rioters found that those on the bench included the very magistrates who had led the troops against them four days before: the Revd. Handley and Sir Norton Knatchbull on the bench, the 'squarson' Poore in the chair. The proceedings here— and later at the Assizes, where the Grand Jury reads like a roll-call of the Kentish élite (an earl, a viscount, sirs, esquires, and hons.)— are almost a textbook illustration of Douglas Hay's claims for the law as an instrument of class power. It is all there. The defence attorney is brow-beaten. The prisoners have no financial assistance to conduct their defence. Justice is selective: a few are chosen for punishment, the others are spared to produce what Hay has called 'gratifying deference'.[30] 'When you return to your homes', Poore warned the lucky ones,

> recollect not only that the law has extended its mercy to you, but also that you are bound to show gratitude for it. I hope that your masters, not withstanding what has happened, will again receive you into their employment, and that you will display your gratitude to them by protecting not only their lives, also their property.

And there was an iron fist in the velvet glove of mercy:

> Some of those who were discharged from this place on Saturday have been so unwise as to make improper observations against individuals residing on the spot. That might operate to your injury if we were inclined to make use of our advantage. But, in the discharge of our duties, we cannot suffer our minds to be biased by any such considerations. Recollect, however, that there are many lives now suspended on a thread. Be sure you abstain from anything which may by possibility accelerate their fate.[31]

The judge at the Summer Assizes in August, Thomas Lord Denman, Lord Chief Justice, was a former Whig Attorney General, described in the nineteenth century as 'a steady Liberal and a sound free-trader'. Denman's career straddled the first half of the century, and indeed, from the perspective of the bar, the bench, or the House, forms part of the history of radical causes. In 1817, as a lawyer, he had defended (unsuccessfully) those allegedly involved in the Pentrich rising. In 1819, in the immediate wake of the Peterloo massacre, Denman, now in Parliament, spoke out for the legality of the suppressed meeting, saying that it was 'improperly dispersed'. He represented and defended Queen Caroline in 1820 in the Queen Caroline affair, a radical *cause célèbre*. Denman's nineteenth-century biographer described him as 'a bold denouncer of all oppression and wrong, a firm and enlightened advocate of all useful reforms'. Yet by the 1830s he was far from popular with radicals. He was made Attorney General in 1830, in the administration of Earl Grey. In 1831 he conducted the prosecution of the Swing rioters and then proceeded to initiate prosecutions against the prominent radicals Richard Carlile and William Cobbett for allegedly encouraging them. He prosecuted the Bristol rioters in 1832, and in the same year declined to save three men condemned to death for rioting in Nottinghamshire. (Many had expected him to show clemency as Whig Attorney General.)[32]

The trial of the 'rioters' deserves more attention than it has been given. Denman set the agenda in his address to the Grand Jury. First, he argued that what had occurred was in fact a riot: a large body of armed men were parading the country 'to the peril of the lives of individuals and the disturbance of the public peace'. Second, the magistrates had acted to curtail the disturbance by issuing warrants for the apprehension of the 'principals in the riot', and as a result, 'one of the officers' entrusted with the execution of the warrant was shot during the course of his duty. Third, if any magistrate or constable, or indeed any individual acting lawfully to preserve the peace, is killed, it is murder. Fourth, that if a party is in 'tumult' and someone is killed, then all involved are guilty of murder. Denman ended by nailing his political colours to the mast. Hostility to the New Poor Law, he felt sure, had nothing to do with the disturbance—not a law 'which tends so greatly to the alleviation of the distresses, and extends relief so largely to the poorer and more unfortunate classes of society'.[33]

Thomas Mears and William Price were tried first for the murder of the brother of the constable, who was now being described, conveniently, as 'the constable'. They were convicted, largely on the

41 Thomas Mears. Source: *Life and Extraordinary Adventures of Sir William Courtenay* (Canterbury, 1838).

42 William Price. Source: *Life and Extraordinary Adventures of Sir William Courtenay* (Canterbury, 1838).

principle established at the start of the trial, that, if a group of people are engaged in unlawful activity and a person is killed attempting to control that activity, then those involved are all accountable. In other words, the two men were convicted as principals rather than as accessories to Courtenay.

The lawyer for the defence was able to cite a case, known as the Sittinghurst case. A number of people had assembled for a riot, constables had appeared, and some of the group came out of the house and killed one of the officers. Those in the house at the time were acquitted because they had assembled for a different purpose. The defence also disputed that Courtenay and his men had assembled for an unlawful purpose. It questioned, in other words, the Crown's claims that a riot had been in progress; no money had been extorted, no unlawful act had been committed up until the death of the constable (at the hands of Courtenay). The defence also pushed the line that Courtenay was mad and that his followers therefore could not be held accountable for his actions. Presumably the madness argument would prevent the conviction of the accused as *accessories* to Courtenay, but it did not, Denman argued, prevent their conviction on the second count, as *principals* in the death of the constable: if 'the prisoners were aware of the malignant and unlawful purposes of Courtenay, and were aiding, assisting, abetting, maintaining, and comforting him in acts fatal to life, there could be no doubt but that they were by law guilty as principals upon this charge'.[34]

It is interesting that the defence did not make more of a ploy used by the presiding judge himself in 1817, when he was a mere lawyer defending the Pentrich 'rebels'. For Denman had then argued that the rebel rank-and-file were simple men, dupes of their charismatic and forceful leader, Jeremiah Brandreth. Ironically, Denman's description of Brandreth was very similar to the descriptions of Courtenay: 'an eye like no eye that I ever beheld before, of a countenance and figure formed for activity, enterprise and command. Even the dark, strange beard he wore, and his singular costume, seemed to accord with his wild and daring character.'[35]

There are niggling aspects about the case, particularly for the historian who has the private correspondence of magistrates in front of him as well as the statements of witnesses. Was it a riot? I have argued that it was more than a riot: an abortive rising, in fact. But within the context of the evidence presented at court, it was never convincingly demonstrated that what had happened was a riot in the *legal sense* of the term. Definitions in the courtroom had a touch of the *ex post facto* about them: men were engaged in activity that JPs felt was a riot; one of the men sent to detain the leaders was killed; *ergo*, the activity they were engaged in was a riot. But Denman was at a loss to account for the motivations of the 'rioters', who had assembled 'without any apparent cause, without any apparent suffering or deprivation'. He muttered about crimes near to 'high treason', but there was no state trial, presumably because the government would have found it difficult to establish the precise nature of the sedition.[36] If the group was dangerous, why had only one constable (*he* had enrolled the help of his brother and an assistant) been sent to serve the warrants? Nor is it possible to establish what, precisely, the warrants were for. Some accounts say they were for the apprehension of the principals in the riot; others suggest that they were to be served on individuals for behaviour that had nothing to do with rioting, on farm servants who had breached contract by leaving their employ to join Courtenay.[37]

When the prisoners charged with the murder of Lieutenant Bennett saw that the crown had secured conviction for the murder of the constable's brother, they pleaded guilty. Given the principle of culpability established in the first trial, there seemed even less point in disputing their responsibility for the second death. They threw themselves on the mercy of the court.[38] Again there are worrying aspects, although, given the plea, these were never aired in court. The riot act had not been read; in other words, the 'rioters' had never been given the opportunity to disperse. And there is some doubt about whether the magistrate in charge (there had to be one, by law, when the military suppressed a contentious gathering) ever ordered the troops to fire. In the inquest on the death of Bennett, Poore actually said that he had *not* given any orders to fire.[39]

As predicted, the Whigs showed their 'merciful bearings'. Denman donned the black cap twice to pronounce the death sentence, and then to announce that the lives of the convicted would be spared. Thomas Mears and William Wills (considered to be Courtenay's ring-leaders) were to be transported for life, William Price for ten years. Edward Curling, Alexander Foad, Richard Foreman, Thomas Griggs, Charles Hills, and Edward Wraight were each to be imprisoned for one year, at hard labour; with a month in solitary confinement.[40] The prisoners, 'who were all bathed in tears, severally bowed their thanks'.[41]

8

Epilogue

WHEN P. G. Rogers added his postscript to the *Battle in Bossenden Wood*, he claimed that, apart from some minor details on the fate of Wills, there was 'hardly any trace' of what happened to the others involved in the Courtenay affair.[1] Is this really the case, or do we know a little more of the fate of the would-be insurrectionaries and their families? One might anticipate that a community rent by the divisions of 1838 would be broken, irreparably; that those involved would have moved quietly out of the area after they had finished their prison sentences to a kind of voluntary exile to match the forced transportation of their leaders. But this did not happen. Perhaps the guilt of the community became focused on the memory of Courtenay as the villain who had led them astray.[2] Possibly a collective amnesia settled on the hamlets of Hernhill and the cottages of Dunkirk. Whatever the reason, most of the families remained in the area, in Dunkirk, Hernhill, or Boughton.

The only ones to move were the kin of some of those killed in the rising. The suffering of the Branchetts continued. Twelve-year-old Benjamin and 17-year-old Mary were in the workhouse in 1839, where the boy died of consumption at the end of the winter. Elizabeth, aged 15, seems to have fared better. After a few months in the workhouse, the Poor Law Union paid for her travel and clothing so that she could go into service in London. We do not know what became of her after that.[3] The family of the dead William Rye was scattered. His wife, Sarah, died on poor relief in 1840 after she had been discharged from hospital as an incurable case. One son, William, was in Seasalter in 1851, a labourer, married with a child. Charlotte and Harriett, the daughters, were both in the Faversham workhouse at various stages in the 1840s and early 1850s, destitute, and (both of them) unmarried mothers of illegitimate children. Two of the Rye illegitimates were called William, presumably in memory of the women's dead father.[4]

It is an eery experience, thumbing through the census returns for 1841 and thereafter, encountering demographic profiles of those who had confronted the military in Bosenden Wood.[5] The parents of the dead rioters Finnis Harvey and Stephen Baker were in Dargate in 1841 and 1851. The Bakers, who died in the 1850s, lived in the parish's new homes for the poor. Next door to them in 1851 were the Coachworths, William and his new wife Hannah (widow of the rioter William Foster, another of those killed in 1838). They lived at Dargate with a total of seven children, including the products of both previous marriages. The Fosters and Coachworths (William was of course another follower of Courtenay) had been living next door to each other when the Census of 1841 was taken. Two of the stepchildren would marry, and into this century Coachworths and Fosters lived in adjoining homes.

The Coachworths and Bakers were numbers 37 and 39 on the census enumeration. James Wraight was number 36. A widower since 1846, he remained in Dargate until his death in the 1870s in the household of his son Elias. James's brother Edward Wraight junior and his wife Sarah (Hills), who at the time of the rising had lived in a cottage at Bessborough, were still in that hamlet in 1881. Edward was 77 years old by then. Sarah died in 1884; Edward was then admitted to the Ospringe Union house where he died two years later. They had a total of twelve children, ten of whom survived into adulthood. Wraight had two neighbours at Bessborough at the time of the rising, both of whom were involved. One, George Bishop, was still in Bessborough in 1841. He moved shortly afterwards and ended his days in Dargate in 1882. The other neighbours, William and Harriett Packman, were in Dargate by 1841 and were still there in 1881 when William, aged 79, died. After the rising the Packmans had gone on to produce a total of ten children, three of whom, aged 7, 4, and 2, were buried on the same day in 1846, presumably as the result of some accident or infectious disease.

Others lived out long lives in the area. Alex and Mary Foad remained at Dargate; both died in the 1880s when they were in their eighties. Richard and Sarah Foreman lived sometimes at Bessborough, sometimes at Dargate, with a total of eleven children, three of whom died as infants or children and two as young adults. When Richard died in 1894 he was 96 years old; Sarah lived into our century, dying in Whitstable in 1900.

The Goodwins remained in Dargate, running the Dove beerhouse. James Goodwin was a widower by the 1860s, and when he died in 1875 he handed the premises on to his son Edward, the child that

Mary Ann Goodwin was carrying at the time of the rising. The other beershop owner, James Miles, moved with his shop, Noah's Ark, from Bessborough to High Street. James and Mary were there for the 1851 Census but died in Canterbury (James in 1871), so they must have moved out of the area some time in the 1850s. It seems that he fell out with his father, Noah, for he is the only one of the farmer/publican's ten surviving children not mentioned in his will of 1853.[6] Noah, another follower of Courtenay, lived out the rest of his life at Bessborough.

Charles and Tamsen Hadlow appear in the 1841 Census with their five children and two grandchildren, the offspring of the transported William Wills. Charles, recently widowed, moved to Faversham in the 1860s and died there in 1866, probably in the workhouse. As we have just noted, Wills's children, aged 3 and 5, were with their grandparents in 1841. The daughter, Helen *Courtenay* Wills, died in 1842. The son, Willam junior, was a farm servant in 1851 on the farm of John Butcher. In 1854, the boy, now working for another local farmer, was charged with absconding from service—he had attempted to run away to sea but had been rejected because of his height.[7] Lucy Wills, the transported insurrectionist's wife, moved to Chartham. The Chartham Census of 1851 lists one Lucy Wills, housekeeper, widow (sic), aged 35, born in Hernhill, living in what was obviously a common-law marriage with Daniel Cozens, a 42-year-old widowed agricultural labourer, and their children Jane and Harriet Cozens, Daniel Wills (who was 2 and born in Chartham), and an infant Mary Cozens Wills.

We have but sketchy details on a few remaining families. Edward Rigden Curling and Charity (Brown) Curling were in nearby Graveney in 1851, where he was employed as a shepherd. By 1861 he was back in Hernhill, residing at Lavender Farm. He ended his days in an almshouse in Whitstable, where he was interviewed by a local paper in 1888 on the fiftieth anniversary of the rising.[8] Thomas Griggs, badly wounded in Bosenden Wood, was in Staple Street in 1841 and at Waterham in 1851. He fades from the scene afterwards, presumably to Canterbury, where he died in 1854. William and Ann Knight were in Staple Street in 1841 and in Boughton thereafter. John Hadlow and his wife Lydia (Wills), one of the women blamed for being a driving force behind the rising, were in Boughton in 1841—Hadlow was described as a butcher. They then returned to Hernhill, to the hamlet of Staple Street, where Hadlow was listed as a small farmer and grocer. Lydia and her husband were still there when they died in the 1870s. Their sons, the rioters Henry Hadlow, a gardener in 1841, and John, a baker, had set up home in Boughton; both married.

Of the twenty-eight would-be insurrectionists from Hernhill, four were killed and two transported; all of the twenty-two survivors, apart from one temporary move to Graveney, stayed in the immediate locality.[9] It may have been that Dargate became a haven of sorts for the followers of Courtenay: about half of the families were living there. As far as I am aware, there is no evidence that they found solace at the hamlet's new Wesleyan chapel, although they may have sought comfort in the Goodwin's beershop next door, which underwent refurbishment later in the century (see Plate 43).

It is hard to determine whether the emotional wounds healed along with the physical injuries. At a day-to-day level life continued as usual. The Foads' 16-year-old daughter Mary was a servant in the household of the rioters' old enemy Edward Curling.[10] The bailiff William Kay acted as executor for the will of Sarah Spratt (John Spratt's widow).[11] Curling's account book shows numerous transactions from 1839 to 1841 with those who had considered him a foe in 1838. James Goodwin continued to buy his sacks of potatoes from Crockham farm, and the Curlings sold pigs to Wraight junior, Packman, and Foreman. James Miles purchased a cow and a calf. Goodwin hired a garden at Sand Hole. Thomas Griggs was a tenant in one of Curling's cottages. Edward Curling junior ploughed and carted for Alex Foad.[12] Economic necessity, on both sides, would have ensured that such dealings continued, but it is impossible to know how cordial these relations were. One assumes that the agricultural labourers and small farmers tried to put the trauma behind them. When the vicar of Hernhill met Foad after his release from prison, he asked the smallholder how it was that someone such as himself, a man with 'a little freehold property', 'of fair education and knowledge of the world' ('having lived several years in gentlemen's service'), could have become embroiled in such an affair? Foad's only reply was that he 'could not tell how it was that he was deluded'.[13] J. W. Horsley junior, the son of the first minister at Dunkirk, recalled that in his early boyhood it 'was not desirable to mention "The Fray" as it was called at Dunkirk or Herne Hill, as so many had friends implicated'.[14]

43 The Dove, Dargate, in the process of refurbishment, c.1890. *Source*: Len Rooks photography.

Given that the rising was overwhelmingly a Hernhill affair, it is ironic that outside attention focused upon Dunkirk. Just as the dead Courtenay provided a target for internal reprehension, external attention was concentrated upon the Ville. In direct response to the rising, the extra-parish became a parish, with a new church and school. Unruly Dunkirk was civilized with a vengeance.

Considering the nature of the district, there could hardly have been a more bizarre choice of the parish's first minister than that of John William Horsley, a High-Church Anglican and disciple of Newman and Manning.[15] Surviving fragments of a journal give the initial impressions and encounters of a stranger in a strange land. The new church, he noted, was on top of Boughton Hill, exposed to the elements; 'all round are almost interminable woods, known generally by the name of the Blean Woods and covering all the hills round about.' In his search for lodgings (his house was yet to be built), the young curate encountered a Methodist grocer who suggested the home of a co-religionist William Berry, a tradesman and farmer who lived across the road from the church on Boughton Hill. Horsley replied that he 'should not like to lodge there, if they are Methodists'. 'Methodists, Sir,' retorted the grocer, 'why you must not be so nice as all that. I should like to know why you don't like with [sic] Methodists. Let me tell you, they are very good people—We're all Methodists here, Sir [at Boughton Street]—Not live with Methodists indeed . . . . The sooner you get rid of your prejudices the better, Sir.'[16]

Undeterred, Horsley set about creating a High-Church haven in the wilds of Blean. Before long—for he lived only until 1846—he had introduced monthly communion, the beating of parish bounds on Rogation Day, and the observation of saints' days and Ember and Litany days. (Instead of the day and the month in the parish baptismal register, the unprepared demographer encounters Advent Sunday, Feast of the Epiphany, Feast of St Mathias.) The new church acquired the beauties of holiness, with carved oak altar rails, a colourful altar cloth, and a specially commissioned chandelier to light the church during festivals. It also had a barrel organ of the type that was to replace the old church bands throughout England. Boys in surplices (among the first in village churches) did the singing alongside some agricultural labourers clad in smocks. And Horsley instituted cottage garden shows to encourage the habit of cultivation among his parishioners.

Only day labourers were permitted to enter; prizes were awarded for the best fruit, vegetables, flowers, and honey.[17]

We do not know how the people of the Ville survived this cultural buffeting. Horsley's correspondence about the propriety of administering communion to an adulterer and the rite of baptism to Wesleyans suggests a precision that may not have been welcomed either by his parishioners or by his ecclesiastical superiors. His refusal to allow parents to be sponsors of baptisms was said to have been unpopular with the neighbourhood, although presumably it approved of his abolition of fees for the same ceremony.[18] There is no evidence, however, that his policies kept people away from the church. Attendance in the Religious Census of 1851 was even higher than in Hernhill.[19]

It certainly seems that over the years the inhabitants of the parish made use of the new schooling. Of those farmers and labourers and their wives in Dunkirk in 1851 for whom we have details of literacy, 74 per cent of the men and 78 per cent of the women were unable to sign their names; by the next generation—their children marrying in the 1860s and 1870s—the illiteracy figures had dropped to 31 and 33 per cent respectively, better than those for the same groups in Hernhill.[20] By 1888, fifty years after the rising, the vicar of Dunkirk, the Reverend W. J. Springett, could pronounce the parish 'no longer distinguishable from any other Christian and civilized neighbourhood'.[21]

Finally, what of the three men transported to Tasmania? George Rudé has traced their fate in the New World.[22] They arrived together on the Pyramus at the end of March 1839, almost a year after the events that had led to their transportation. After the ship's arrival they were sent to different parts of the island. Thomas Mears Tyler, described by the ship's surgeon as intelligent, trustworthy, and well-behaved, worked in Hobart as a gardener on the governor's domain. He was in trouble repeatedly: for staying out all night, for being drunken and insolent, for frequenting the pub on a Sunday. His unruliness cost him a flogging, solitary confinement, and a spell of six months' hard labour on the roads. He received a conditional pardon in 1851 and went, it was said, to the diggings on the Australian mainland, where he made 'a hundred pounds'. William Price, a married man who had been sentenced to a lesser term of ten years, was assigned to the south, to Brighton. Despite two brushes with authority for misconduct, he earned a ticket of leave in 1844 and a conditional pardon several years later.

William Wills, the third offender, served his time at Longford in the north of the island, emerging with an unblemished record. After his conditional pardon he attempted to return to England, sending out feelers, through a mediator, to the vicar of Hernhill in the hope of being reunited with his family. Handley relayed the news of the death of Wills's daughter and discouraged him from returning partly because he was aware of Lucy Wills's new domestic situation. However, he did suggest that Wills's son could join him in Australia.[23] Nothing came of it. Handley wrote his letter in 1853, the year before Wills junior, who may well have been attempting to join his father, tried to run away to sea. As far as we know, none of the three rioters ever returned from Australia.

In some respects they were the lucky ones. Back in the Old World, the social divisions remained. The condition of the agricultural labourer fluctuated in the nation at large. The late 1840s saw a collapse in prices and wages and a predictable rise in unemployment. Incendiarism increased dramatically: the Kent Fire Insurance Company's payments for farm fire losses skyrocketed in the period 1849–51.[24] As Alan Armstrong has demonstrated, real wages remained stagnant throughout the 1850s and 1860s but rose thereafter.[25] There is some evidence that local resentments remained. After 1838, the occasional farmer was dragged off his horse late at night in a Dunkirk lane and beaten up, or stoned as he rode by a group of labourers.[26] Poaching continued; one of those arrested, for setting wires for pheasants in Blean Wood in 1861, was William Coachworth, probably the son of the rioter. Wood theft was rife.[27] But whatever the material condition of the agricultural and other labourers of Hernhill and Dunkirk, it would have been unlikely— no doubt inconceivable, given the massacre of 1838—that protest would have taken anything other than a covert or muted form. Even arson, the last resort of resistance, seems to have stopped in the immediate area.[28] Organized protest must have seemed an impossibility. In 1878 the Kent and Sussex Labourers' Union had members in Faversham, Teynham, Canterbury, Harbledown, Selling, in Chilham and Chartham where labourers in the KSLU were being locked out of their cottages, and as near as Boughton-under-Blean; but none in Hernhill and Dunkirk.[29]

PART IV
Implications

9

Rural Life and Protest in Nineteenth-Century England

WHEN Richard Cobb reviewed Eric Hobsbawm and George Rudé's now classic study of the agricultural labourers' rising of 1830, *Captain Swing*, he suggested that one of the weaknesses of the book was the absence of a close contextual analysis of any of the small rural communities involved in the unrest. He finished with the call: 'And now to the study of Lower Hardres.'[1] (Lower Hardres is the Kent village, south of Canterbury, where the Swing rising began.) When, over ten years later, in the pages of the *Journal of Peasant Studies*, Roger Wells, Andrew Charlesworth, Mick Reed (and others) debated the nature of agrarian discontent in nineteenth-century England, one of the few things they could agree on was the need for more locally based studies of everyday life.[2] My book can be seen as a response, perhaps somewhat belated, to these calls.

The Battle in Bosenden Wood, or the Hernhill Rising of 1838 as it should now be called, was the last battle fought on English soil; it was the last revolt against the New Poor Law; England's last millenarian rising; and the last rising of the agricultural labourers. It was a product of tensions in nineteenth-century rural society, none of which was sufficient in itself to produce a conflagration but which together help to explain the abortive insurrection. Class tensions between farmers and labourers, declining wages, the pressures of a demographic revolution, were compounded by a harsh winter and a localized crisis in the agrarian economy. The situation was exacerbated too by state intervention in the form of the New Poor Law of 1834. We have seen that the Whigs were simply wrong in their denial of the role of hostility to the New Poor Law in the rising of 1838.

In 1838 agricultural labourers and their wives, most of them from Hernhill, but some from Dunkirk and Boughton-under-Blean, mobilized in the cottages and lanes of the villages and hamlets of the Blean. They were humble men and women, several of whom could not read and write. Some had been in trouble for assault and theft. They did not include all the 'hard men' of the area: I know of Dunkirk 'roughs', habitual offenders, who were not there with Courtenay in the woods. But the criminal profiles of several of his followers show that those who confronted the military included men for whom violence was no stranger. The use of family reconstitution and close contextual work alongside more traditional historical analysis has yielded some unexpected insights into the social basis of the rising of 1838. The roles of kinship and neighbourhood, the part played by the sharp experience of poverty (revealed by painstaking reconstruction of individual profiles), the pressures of marital fertility, could never have emerged from more orthodox use of the sources. The demographer is often accused of writing history without politics: 1838 has demonstrated that it is possible to link family reconstitution with the actual historical drama of events. Both types of history could benefit from a liaison.

The place of women in the rising further demonstrates the potential of the micro study. If the rising had happened before 1810, it would have appeared as a 'men-only' riot in John Bohstedt's recent *Past and Present* article on the role of women in riot in late eighteenth- and early nineteenth-century England, because the Hernhill women were not out there on the streets, or rather in the lanes, to be counted—they did not have any part in the protest if a 'role' is defined in terms of actual physical participation in conflict.[3] Too many (male) historians of protest, Joan Scott has observed in a recent critique of this aspect of the work of E. P. Thompson's *Making of the English Working Class*, write women out of the agenda, seeing them at best as providers of support or backup for the men.[4] Hernhill in 1838 provides a different perspective: here, women played a vital role in mobilization.

The affair is still shrouded in mystery; historians should not be ashamed to admit their failures as well as their successes. I have argued that the weight of the available evidence suggests that Courtenay and some of the agricultural labourers had visions of an insurrection of the labouring classes, with the seizure and redistribution of the land into smallholdings and with retribution upon the rich. There seems little support here for Eric Hobsbawm and George Rudé's claim that the demand of land was not a concern of the rural proletariat.[5] Whether this social amelioration was to be achieved primarily by human agency, by divine intervention, or through a combination of the two is still unclear. We do know that the motives of the participants varied. For some, the marching at the end of May was almost a carnivalistic release from the burden of everyday existence, a time of eating and drinking and singing: hymns, and bread, tobacco, and beer by the 'pailful'.

It has to be said that, while the labouring families of Hernhill and Dunkirk led a marginal existence, their general predicament was little different from that of other communities. In some respects they were better off than their rural class contemporaries. Why, then, did the insurrection take place in Hernhill and not elsewhere? Perhaps the situation in Hernhill merely demonstrates the dire straits of other nineteenth-century rural communities, the truth of the old maxim that the really desperate never revolt. Alternatively, benign conditions (relatively speaking) may have brought their own penalty: the added, and very real, burden of larger surviving families. We will not be able to answer such questions until historians have done the empirical groundwork.

Some would argue that what distinguishes 1838 from other examples of nineteenth-century protest is its millenarian edge. After all, it was a millenarian rising led by a messianic figure. This has been sufficient to prevent the episode from being taken very seriously by historians of the nineteenth century, who seem to be blinded by the spectres of Swing and Chartism or who gaze expectantly towards agricultural trade unionism later in the century. The Hernhill rising was in the wrong place at the wrong time. Hobsbawm and Rudé stress the uniqueness of the abortive millennial revolt; it was part of a retreat into religion after the defeat of Swing—the chiliasm of despair—'an escape from, rather than a mobilization for, social agitation'.[6]

Certainly I would not want to dispute the importance of religion in the events of 1838; it is one of the themes of this book. What I do contest is the uniqueness of the Hernhill context. If the rising had drawn the bulk of its support from Dunkirk (where indeed Alan Everitt and David Vincent have centred it), or even from Boughton (where Rudé places it), then, with some justification, the episode could be dismissed as an aberration.[7] If one were to pick a likely scene for unrest, then the Ville, with its unruly population, absentee landowners, and lack of church control, would be a prime candidate. Boughton too was a likely prospect, for it had a long-established nonconformist population, and a large number of craftsmen, those with the literacy and independence denied to agricultural labourers, the sort of people who often made up the nucleus of protest activity. And yet the bulk of support for

Courtenay came from Hernhill, a parish with a resident vicar, a parish that would score high in the gauge of Anglicanism in the 1851 Census of Religious Worship.

Herein lies the significance of the Hernhill rising. It cannot be dismissed as a freak event in an unusual part of the country. Of course, there is no such thing as a *typical* English rural community—this and other micro studies demonstrate a remarkable diversity down to the hamlet level. But what was so unique about Hernhill? The point about the rising there is that it could have occurred in *other* parts of the nation; the lawyer Liardet stressed that conditions in that parish—material and mental—were not vastly different from those in communities elsewhere. My impression—and at this stage it can be no more than an impression—is that there was a hidden potential at the popular level throughout nineteenth-century England, which could have been tapped by radical activists. It surfaces from time to time in the historical accounts. Anti-Poor Law protesters spoke of the 'Law of God' being 'torn asunder by the Laws of Man' and quoted 'texts of scripture illustrative of the tyranny and injustice' of some of the provisions of the new Act.[8] In the Ampthill riots of 1835 in Bedfordshire, one of the crowd used the Bible to demonstrate to the magistrate that the new law was 'contrary to the Word of God'.[9] Eileen Yeo has certainly demonstrated the importance of religion in Chartism.[10] Nigel Scotland has highlighted the vitality of biblical allusion, quotation, and imagery in agricultural trade unionism during the 1870s.[11] At the moment, we do not know whether the relative silence of the history books is because the agitators failed to realize this hidden potential or because many historians have yet to recognize the strength of the religious factor in early nineteenth-century protest. Of course the other possibility is that the religious milieu of Hernhill was unique and that religion was unimportant in 1830 and 1835. I will be happy to be proved wrong, provided the right questions are asked.

If the 'cottage religion' of Hernhill and Dunkirk before and after 1838 was not unique in the village world, all we are left with is the role of Courtenay. However much the sources conspire to throw Courtenay into the limelight (the community, the government, the local vicar, and the defence lawyer all needed a scapegoat, and the literary world loved a colourful character), however much it goes against the grain to be construed as advancing, even remotely, the 'great man view of history', however much we remain alert to the role of women in 1838, and to the acts and aspirations of the men who did the marching and fighting, it still remains that Courtenay played a vital part in the events of 1838. I have shifted him away from the centre, but he is still there, on stage. Again, this suggests unrecognized possibilities for popular mobilization. If the charismatic Chartist leadership—popular demagogues not unlike Courtenay—had turned their attention to the rural areas, the history of mid-nineteenth-century England might have been very different.

Yet we know that there was no widespread rural insurrection in the last century. Why not? What does this study tell us more generally about rural life and protest in that period? The questions of hegemonic control and labouring passivity dog the historian of nineteenth-century rural England—indeed, dog peasant studies *tout court*. Sometimes the issues are taken seriously, as in the debate on deference initiated by the work of Howard Newby and the discussion engendered by Roger Wells's article on the structural reasons for covert protest in nineteenth-century England.[12] Sometimes the barriers to resistance at the labouring level are merely assumed rather than analysed. Thus, in his recent history of the English farmworker, Alan Armstrong gives the issue little more attention than a nod in the direction of Newby, and digs about the high church attendance figures for agricultural labourers in the 1851 Census and the fact that there were more farmworkers' wives in the Women's Institute in the 1930s than there were husbands in the trade unions.[13]

One of the greatest constraints against labouring protest was what James Scott, following Marx, has termed 'the dull compulsion of economic relations', the actual day-to-day grind of mere existence.[14] The struggle for survival seemed unremitting. We saw that wage rates in Hernhill and Dunkirk were higher than in many parts of England and that, between them, these parishes provided opportunities for female and child labour. But the general impression of the standard of living of farmworkers in Hernhill and Dunkirk is that, even in more 'fortunate' Hernhill, it was a thin line between survival and destitution. Poverty, inadequate diet, sickness, the pressure of large families, and competition for work: this was the reality of labouring life. The late Raymond Williams once wrote of the 'mutuality of the oppressed',[15] and we have seen that there were attacks on farmers. Yet as Chapter 3 has shown, some of the despair and anger could be turned, self-destructively, into the labouring community, with labourer against labourer, man against woman and child. There is at least some support for the argument that most of the energies of the rural proletariat would be channelled towards making ends meet, and that the little life that remained was dissipated in self-destructive activity.

The seeming interminability of their predicament must have been another barrier to any kind of widespread labouring resistance. Not that the period lacked major social change: it witnessed a population boom, the decline of farm service, the division of society into landlord, farmer, and labourer, the creation of an agricultural proletariat for whom there was insufficient constant work. But the point about this substantial change is that it occurred over time, gradually. As Wells has reminded us, the 'evolutionary nature of the multi-dimensional British agrarian revolution served to secure mass acquiescence: change was too slow for the genesis of a past "golden age" notion in workers' minds.'[16] It was difficult to hit back against, indeed even to identify, something that ground on so slowly and relentlessly. Sudden change is more likely to provoke resistance than piecemeal transformation. So it was that the implementation of the New Poor Law prompted riots in 1835—and targets were obvious. Nor is it pure coincidence that particularly savage winters preceded the Swing rising and the trouble in Hernhill in 1838. A glacial social structure left the rural proletariat with slim hope for improvement. They were, we saw in Chapter 1, a socially static group, denied any formal political voice in the nation. A few would marry into local farming families—not many, but perhaps enough to blunt class consciousness (an area of research which it is worth pursuing). Most would continue to live in the manner of their parents before them.

Of course, force, or fear of repression, was the ultimate inhibitor. Control was exercised at different levels. We saw that in our part of Kent the great landlords maintained what we could call a hidden presence, government by remote control. Effective day-to-day power was in the hands of the local farming élite and a few others: the employers, cottage landlords, parish 'big men'. The power of the British state was not obvious in the everyday activity of the local parish constable (the professional police force came later to Kent) or in the Petty Sessions deliberations of the nearby Justice of the Peace. Yet the local population found in 1838 that the troops would be called readily enough if they were needed. We see the various layers of intervention at work in that episode, with the farmer Curling's attempt to dissuade 'his men' from following Courtenay, with the gentleman Knatchbull's shadowing of the labouring band, with the military solution in Bosenden Wood, and with the former Attorney General's trial of the survivors. It is inconceivable that bare-faced repression failed to have an impact on the governed. The lessons of 1830—the nationwide mass transportations and the executions—were etched deep in the rural mind. The public hanging of the Packman brothers on Penenden Heath in 1830 must have sent shock waves through the cottages of the Blean. When Courtenay spoke against the workhouses and asked a group of labourers to join him, one replied that 'he must have sufficient grounds shown him for putting his own neck into jeopardy and the country into disturbance, before he joined in such an expedition'.[17] The 'magisterial murders' of 1838 provided further demonstration—if it was needed—of the power of the state and the perils of any kind of resistance.

Finally, there was the great hurdle of ideology. This grew out of the situation of the rural proletariat; it was rooted in their experience. As Newby has written,

Any consideration of the agricultural worker's perceptions of his own subordination must begin with a very simple point. Above all, the system which has brought about his economic and social subordination is an awesome and apparently irrevocable fact. It is *there* and possesses a reality in comparison with which all alternatives appear abstract and putative.... It is a fact of life as permanent, as tangible and as easily observable as the physical features of the countryside around them. It is, in other words, *natural*, and all suggested alternatives are consequently impractical, unrealistic and doomed to inevitable failure.[18]

The fatalism, the limited horizons, of the agricultural labourers are legendary. George Sturt called them 'the humiliated'. 'Being born to poverty and the labouring life, they accept the position as if it were entirely natural.'[19] It is easy for us to mock labouring passivity and fatalism, though perhaps, given Britain's current predicament, we should have more empathy and understanding than at any other moment of our own lived historical experiences. Under the conditions described, there was surely a simple logical realism to much of the inaction. When the proto-sociologists descended upon Dunkirk, Hernhill, and Boughton in the wake of the unrest of 1838, they were told by a labourer that half a loaf of bread was better than no bread at all, and that it was 'not for such as us to resist the law and the whole British power'.[20] Who are we to dismiss this as false consciousness!

If part of the answer lies with the actual experience of labouring life, much also can be explained by ruling-class ideology. The agricultural labourers were encouraged to look to those who controlled wealth, as Sturt put it, as if they were the source of it[21] — a myth that the privileged still like to purvey. Inequality was portrayed as both natural and inevitable. The stress was on order and privilege, and on a reciprocity based on unequal power; respect and support for superiors by inferiors, periodic charity, and the occasional protection of inferiors by superiors ('crumbs from the table, relatively speaking', in Keith Wrightson's graphic phrase[22]). Such values were pure seventeenth- or eighteenth-century patrician, but the nineteenth-century farmer had co-opted something of this code, even if his workers no longer lived under his roof and the ethos sat uneasily with the spirit of the New Poor Law. For whatever reason, some of this deference was internalized. In 1838 there were touching scenes of a dying farm servant handing his watch over to his master, of farmers and gentry testifying on behalf of the good character of their rebellious some-time employees.[23]

Let us return to the lawyer Liardet, who carried out that useful survey of the area in 1838. Among those he talked to were a shoemaker in the Faversham workhouse and a man from Dunkirk. It is worth quoting the encounters in full. The shoemaker was in his late twenties, with a wife and five children. Determined to demonstrate that the family's predicament was the result of its own 'culpable neglect', Liardet asked the man if 'he did not calculate, before marrying so early, his means to support a wife and family'. The man replied 'No, sir,—never gave it a thought—never thought of anything—you see, sir, we an't used to look forward.' When asked if he would have listened to advice, his answer was, 'Why, perhaps not, sir, if it came from the like of one of us, sir; but if it had been a gentleman like you, I think I should.'[24] The next interview was in Dunkirk.

Talking one day with some men in the ville of Dunkirk, I observed, it was a pity there were no gentry in the neighbourhood. 'Well,' said one fellow, 'for my part, I see no good they are to us; all they do is make hard laws to grind us down. There was my poor brother clapt into prison, and his wife and family left to starve, all because he had killed a few hares.'—'Well,' said I, 'what right had he to kill other persons' hares?'—'Other persons', indeed! why weren't they as much his as another's?'—'Because he had no property in the land which fed them.'—'Ay, that's just it, but he ought to have had though.'—'How! do you mean to say everybody ought to have land?'—'Yes, to be sure I do; look here now, didn't God give the land to *all*?'—'Well, what of that?'—'Why, then a few can't have no right to the whole of it.'—'But I say they may.'—'Then how do you make out that?'—'Suppose every man had had his share, I suppose you'll allow he had a right to do what he liked with it?'—'Why, yes; I can't say no to that.'—'Well, then, suppose one man wishes to sell his share, and another wishes to buy it, they would have a right to do so.'—'Why, yes; no doubt of that.'—'Well, suppose, after that, the buyer saves up more money, and sets up a shop, and clears a good deal, and other men see what he is doing and want to do the same, but they have no money, and they offer their land to him and he buys it; has he not a right to do so?'—'Yes, to be sure, if he gives them the money for it.'—'Well, then, you see here is a man who has got a good deal of land, and others have lost theirs, and you own it's all right?'—'Ay, ay, that's all well enough; but our squires didn't all get their land in that way.' 'Perhaps not, but then those they got it from did.'—'But if a man makes money and buys land, hasn't he a right to leave it to his children, or to anybody else he chooses?'—'Why, I can't but say but what he has.'—'So, my friend, you see one man may have half a county, and another not half an acre, and yet the last has no fair right to complain.'—'Why, sir, to be sure you do make it out somehow, there's no denying that; but then it's a hard case that one man's good should be another man's harm.'—'But it is not: suppose a rich man were to come and build a cotton-mill in your neighbourhood, and your children could earn 10s. a week each in it, you wouldn't think there was much harm in that?'—'Harm! no, indeed; it would be the best thing ever happened to us; for you see, sir, we are often puzzled to get work here.'—'Well, but how much would it take to build such a mill, and fit it up with machinery?'—'Why, I can't tell; but I suppose a great deal.'—'Then I can tell you a very moderate-sized one would cost £20,000.'—'Indeed? that's a main sum!'—'Do you think the poor people in any place could ever club such a sum together?'—'Never, sir,—not if they lived to the age of Adam, and tasted nothing stronger than water.'—'So, then, if the rich man didn't come and build the mill, the poor people never could do it.'—'No, that's certain.'—'Then you see the wealth of the rich man in this case is a real advantage to the poor?'—'To be sure it is, sir; and I was quite a fool like not to see it before.'—'But did you never read of such things?'—'No, never, sir.'—'Did you ever see the Penny Magazine?'—'No, can't say as I ever did.'—'But you read the newspaper?'—'No, I can't say as I can undertake for that; but I read a little in the Testament.'—'But you talk of these things with your neighbours?'—'No, sir, not much of that; you see, sir, though some of us are 'cute enough in some things, we aren't quite up to what you have been talking of, and there an't no one here as can talk of these things to us.'[25]

The encounters are far from simple. For a start, as readers will have gathered, they were not on equal terms. The cultural and class barriers are obvious. Here was an outsider, an educated bourgeois, confronting a poor shoemaker and a man who was presumably a cottager or woodsman. Liardet came in the immediate wake of direct state repression, a military massacre, so would have been a figure of authority in the context of his appearing as well as in his demeanour—his accent, mode of discourse, and bearing. There was also a hidden agenda, although those questioned would scarcely have been aware of it. Liardet was a member of the pressure group, the Central Society of Education, which, as David Vincent has discussed, set out to show that 'a moral regeneration of [the] labouring poor would be an effective first step towards the creation of a stable, hierarchical society', and whose president, Lord Chief Justice Denman, would actually preside, in his capacity as Assize judge, at the trial of the surviving rioters.[26] Liardet's report, useful though it is, is a manifesto as well as a survey, calling for a 'sound system of national education', for 'exertion on the part of the legislature and the wealthier classes of society to introduce the benefits of education among the mass of the people—teaching them not merely to read and write, but to cultivate the prudential virtues, and learn to provide better for themselves, than any charitable assistance can do for them'.[27]

It is plausible to read Liardet's encounter with the labourers as a particularly clear example of the hegemonic process. Here we have an unequal relationship, of interaction based on inequality of power. The educated, class superior versus the ill-educated, social inferior. Moreover, Liardet was the interrogator, the questioner: his social subordinate has to respond to the lawyer's verbal agenda, as in day-to-day life, where the socioeconomic choices of the powerless are predetermined by class inequality, the given agenda of power. On the face of it, Liardet, in true hegemonic form, convinces. It is in the interests of the exploited that they are exploited: ' "Then you see the wealth of the rich man in this case is a real advantage to the poor?"—"To be sure it is, sir; and I was quite a fool like not to see it before." ' We do not have the intonations of speech; the body language is lost. We are forced to see things, in this instance, through the eyes of Liardet, even when the document provides the illusion of direct reportage.

But there is a nagging doubt about all this labouring reasonableness. It seems to escape the Central Society of Education's man, but it is there in black and white for the historian: 'you see, sir, though some of us are 'cute enough in some things, we aren't quite up to what you have been talking of, and there an't no one as can talk of these things to us'; 'Why, perhaps not, sir, if it came from the like of one of us, sir; but if it had been a gentleman like you, I think I should.' Was it really a triumph for the lawyer; a case of gratified deference? Or were the humble having a laugh at the high? Even if they were not mocking him openly, how do we know that this did not happen as soon as he left the beershop or the workhouse? And, given the weighted conditions of the interaction between lawyer and labourer, what is remarkable in the Dunkirk interview is the overtness of many of the criticisms of the social order.

The attraction of the concept of hegemony as a key for unlocking the complexities of social relations in any historical period is that, defined correctly, it explains and allows for resistance as well as control.[28] The hegemonic group (or groups) maintains its position not merely by naked force, but also by dominating what Marx and Engels called the means of intellectual production, by shaping ideas. Hegemony determines the parameters of the possible; it inhibits the development of social, political, or cultural alternatives to the status quo and the prevailing ideology. But we need to think in terms of an impulse towards domination, a striving for control (conscious or otherwise) which can never be all-encompassing. It inhibits but cannot preclude alternative views of the social situation. Hegemony certainly narrows the options, constrains; it does not prevent resistance. This is why James Scott has warned against inferring ideological support, 'even from the most faithful compliance' on the part of the subordinate group, and why Howard Newby stresses the ambivalence of a rural working-class culture which combined elements of both conservative deference and radical resistance.[29] Resignation does not mean lack of resentment. The middle-class observers who visited Dunkirk, Boughton, and Hernhill also detected 'a general dislike and envy of the wealthy classes'; 'very erroneous notions prevailing respecting the rights of property'; 'a total ignorance of the advantages resulting to society at large from the institution of the law of property'. Indeed, they encountered feelings towards the rich that were 'not merely envious but vindictive'. Hence the 'charities of the [rich] are regarded but as the return of a miserable fraction of the wealth they have extorted from their own labours, and are received by them with ingratitude and sulleness'.[30] These are attitudes that would normally be hidden from the historian and which might be concealed from contemporaries by the outward show of deference—although it is interesting that they were not concealed in this instance.

Given all the constraints listed in the preceding pages, it is truly remarkable that there was any rural labouring resistance at all. But protest there was. The agricultural labourer did resist—before and after 1830. What is so fascinating about the protest of the nineteenth century is the way in which, even with all the constraints, the labourer jostled for a place in the sun. It was extremely difficult for agricultural labourers to congregate, actually to get together, in other than small numbers; there were few agencies for potential political socialization. Yet in 1838 they made use of the meagre resources at their disposal: Oak Apple Day, the beerhouse, the church band (though not the Friendly Society)—all played a role in mobilization. The nature of labouring work in the rural areas did not encourage wide-ranging solidarity. Apart from the divisions between the 'constant man' and the casual labourer, and competition for scarce work, the actual work units were usually small. Gangs of men on poor relief who were directed to work on the roads or on the properties of local farmers rarely numbered more than a dozen men (in this part of the country, at least). Then there were the constraints of localism, that five-mile social arena, the 'inescapable cage'[31] of the agricultural labourer. It was difficult to break outside the local mould. The potential bonds of solidarity in rural labouring protest, then, were based on a combination of class and ties to the hamlet and family. They were potentially strong, but implied small cells of protest, fragmented in a national or indeed a regional sense. Yet again, the humble practised the art of the possible. Strong localized responses could occur, and in 1830 provided the illusion of a nation-wide rising. Hence the importance of violence in rural protest. 'The typical agent of propagation' in 1830 'was the itinerant band, which marched from farm to farm, swelling its numbers by "pressing" the labourers working in the fields or in their cottages at night.'[32] In 1838 the ties of kin, class, and neighbourhood combined to mobilize some of the labouring men and women of Hernhill and Dunkirk.

Many historians of popular protest assume that literacy is a prerequisite for effective political action and consciousness. This assumption lies behind Hobsbawm and Rudé's comments about the superior literacy and noticeable radicalism of the village craftsmen, and is explicit in John Stevenson's comment that the rural labourers, 'hindered by illiteracy and less frequent exposure to the world of pamphlets and newspapers, lagged almost a generation or more behind their urban counterparts in the forms of their protest'.[33] At one level, it is difficult to argue. Radical literature can generate tremendous ideological questioning, presenting alternatives to the mental cage of the status quo. Printed ideas can feed on one another. It is impossible to conceive of Chartism, for example, without the power and role of the press.[34] But we should not therefore believe, as Keith Thomas has warned, that those without literacy 'lived in some sort of mental darkness, debarred from effective participation in the great events of their time'.[35] The Dunkirk man who talked to Liardet about the gentry also told the lawyer that, because God gave the land to all, 'a few can't have no right to the whole of it'. He did not read the newspaper, but he did read 'a little in the Testament'. Ideas and values could be transmitted verbally. People could read aloud, as the Hernhill women did in 1838. Courtenay and his followers were to recognize the cultural mix of orality and literacy in the mobilization techniques that they employed: the use of symbols and songs as well as graffiti.

The drama of Swing, 1835, and Bosenden Wood should not divert attention from other, arguably more important, forms of protest, 'the quiet, unremitting guerrilla warfare that took place day-in and day-out'. For our area also provides examples of what Scott has described as the 'weapons of the weak', everyday forms of resistance and 'individual self-help', ranging from pilfering to sabotage and arson.[36] Presumably this is what Mick Reed had in mind too when he urged the importance of examining worker–employer conflict, neglected in favour of more spectacular but less common 'protest'.[37] There are several local examples of individual labouring resentment, of the powerless hitting back at the local power brokers with the only means at their disposal, ranging from sullen intransigence to violent intervention, from muttering in the beerhouse about firing a wood-dealer's stack to stoning a passing farmer in a Dunkirk lane.[38] We have the cases of the servants in husbandry brought before the Petty Sessions for being 'impertinent and negligent in their service',[39] of the labourers who refused to labour in the fields of local farmers when directed by the parish overseer,[40] and of youths who absconded from the workhouse.[41]

There seems little to be gained by awarding marks for modernity, for charting some kind of linear progression towards trade unionism and modern political organization. Arguably, the American historians eager to hunt traces of the modern political (as opposed to the pre-political!),[42] and the British historians keen to pin-point a precise conversion from overt to covert protest,[43] have both got it wrong. It is the background noise of nineteenth-century protest that is important—the continual negotiation and contention, the grumbling, the acts of 'self-help' and revenge—rather than the brief crescendos of Swing and the anti-Poor Law movement. The two forms, whether we call them 'overt' and 'covert' or 'protest' and 'conflict', continue together.

This book does not support bland assumptions, *à la* Armstrong, about the general passivity and inertia of the labouring population. It is true that one of the important lessons of the abortive affair of 1838 is that it throws into sharp relief the barriers against effective mobilization. Courtenay and his core of followers were able to build upon social discontent and, for a brief moment, to breach the bars of accommodation. Personal charisma, claims of divinity, millenarian hopes, promises of the Land of Cockayne, and the bonds of kinship and neighbourhood stirred some labourers and small farmers in Hernhill and Dunkirk, and then failed to carry the movement beyond the local community.

Yet 1838 should not be remembered for its failures. It should be recalled rather for its vision of an alternative world. A 'great day of judgement' is close at hand, one of the rioters etched in lime on a barn door; 'Our rites and liberties We Will have.'[44] The religious dimension of 1838 is a sharp lesson to historians who continue to equate attachment to the Church of England with ideological conformity. It is quite clear that the inhabitants of the cottages of Hernhill and Dunkirk moulded and adapted their 'Anglicanism' to suit and reflect their predicament.

Finally, the events of 1838 should be remembered for the dignity of the humble participants. The insurrectionists, Courtenay included, do not deserve to be condemned for eternity as lunatics or dupes, or, worse still, to be forgotten entirely. Even today, the physical presence of Hernhill's St Michael's church proclaims the divisions, the hierarchies, in the surrounding hamlets of the past. Inside the body of the church there are the marble and brass tablets to the landed Dawes family and stained glass windows for the Boughton gentleman, Percy Groves. Outside sit the limestone headstones of the lowlier but prosperous farming and trading families. As for the labourers, most have no memorial at all except for an entry in the parish register which is now kept in Canterbury. If this book acts as their final memorial, and, in the process, breathes some imaginative life into those memories, I will be content.

NOTES

Introduction

1 E. P. Thompson, *The Making of the English Working Class* (Harmondsworth, 1974), 881.
2 P. G. Rogers, *Battle in Bossenden Wood* (Oxford, 1961). Graham Hudson has persuaded me to use the nineteenth-century spelling of 'Bosenden' (with a single 's') rather than Rogers's 'Bossenden'.
3 J. F. C. Harrison, *The Second Coming: Popular Millenarianism, 1780–1850* (London, 1979), 213–15; Thompson, *Making of the English Working Class*, 880–1; G. Rudé, *Protest and Punishment* (Oxford, 1978), 120–2.
4 J. Stevenson, *Popular Disturbances in England 1700–1870* (London, 1979), 350, n. 40.
5 J. O. Baylen and N. J. Gossman (eds.), *Biographical Dictionary of Modern British Radicals (1770–1870)* (2 vols.) (Brighton, 1979, 1984).
6 E. J. Hobsbawm and G. Rudé, *Captain Swing* (Harmondsworth, 1973), 242.
7 J. E. Archer, 'Rural Protest in Norfolk and Suffolk 1830–1870' (University of East Anglia Ph.D. thesis, 1981); D. Jones, 'Thomas Campbell Foster and the Rural Labourer: Incendiarism in East Anglia in the 1840s', *Social History*, 1 (1976); J. Knott, *Popular Opposition to the 1834 Poor Law* (London, 1986); J. Lowerson, 'The Aftermath of Swing: Anti-Poor Law Movements and Rural Trades Unions in the South East of England', in A. Charlesworth (ed.), *Rural Social Change and Conflicts since 1500* (Humberside College of Higher Education, 1982); R. Wells, 'Rural Rebels in Southern England in the 1830s', in C. Emsley and J. Walvin (eds.), *Artisans, Peasants and Proletarians 1760–1860* (London, 1985), ch. 6; R. Wells, 'Resistance to the New Poor Law in the Rural South', in M. Chase (ed.), *The New Poor Law* (Middlesborough Centre Occasional Papers no. 1, 1985).
8 C. Tilly, *The Contentious French* (Cambridge, Mass., 1986).
9 M. Harrison, 'The Ordering of the Urban Environment: Time, Work and the Occurrence of Crowds 1790–1835', *Past and Present*, 110 (1986). See also his *Crowds and History: Mass Phenomena in English Towns, 1790–1835* (Cambridge, 1988).
10 J. Walter, 'A "Rising of the People"? The Oxfordshire Rising of 1596', *Past and Present*, 107 (1985); D. J. V. Jones, *The Last Rising: The Newport Insurrection of 1839* (Oxford, 1985).

Chapter 1

1. W. Cobbett, *Rural Rides* (Harmondsworth, 1967), p. 209.
2. F. Liardet, 'State of the Peasantry in the County of Kent', in *Central Society of Education, Third Publication*, 1839 (reprint, London, 1968), 88–9.
3. A. Everitt, *Landscape and Community in England* (London, 1985), 67.
4. PRO, MAF 68/35/11: Agricultural Returns 1866: Livestock; MAF 68/36/11, 12, 14: Agricultural Returns 1866: Acreages; *PP* lxxxv (1852–3), 330–1.
5. Everitt, *Landscape*, 73, 75.
6. E. Hasted, *The History and Topographical Survey of the County of Kent* (1797–1801) (reprint, London, 1972), vii, 19. For the malaria areas, see M. Dobson, ' "Marsh Fever"—the Geography of Malaria in England', *Journal of Historical Geography*, 6 (1980), esp. 359 (map).
7. KAO, U521 E2/195, 299, 311–12: Lambert Estate Papers.
8. Liardet, 'State of the Peasantry', 88.
9. See Alan Everitt's extremely useful 'The Making of the Agrarian Landscape of Kent', in his *Landscape*, ch. 4.
10. Ibid.
11. KAO, U2394 Z1: Family scrap-book of Revd J. W. Horsley; KAO U521 E2/153; Hasted, *History*, ix, 3–4.
12. A. Armstrong, *Farmworkers: A Social and Economic History 1770–1980* (London, 1988), 46.
13. R. Kain, 'The Land of Kent in the Middle of the Nineteenth Century' (University of London Ph.D., 1973), 345.
14. KAO, U521 E2/123–4, 146, 155.
15. PRO, MPZ 26: Reference Book or Terrier to the Plan of the Ville of Dunkirk 1827–8. The calculations are my own.
16. The phrase comes from K. D. M. Snell, *Annals of the Labouring Poor: Social Change and Agrarian England 1660–1900* (Cambridge, 1985).
17. KAO, PS/US7/41–2; Settlement Examinations for the Upper Division of the Lathe of Scray 1812–16; PS/US 8/20–1: Settlement Examinations for the Upper Division of the Lathe of Scray 1816–18.
18. For Hernhill today, see *Hernhill Now: Report and Analysis of the Village Appraisal Questionnaire* (Hernhill Parish Council, 1988). Harold Kay was kind enough to provide me with a copy.
19. These figures are based on an analysis of the Hernhill and Dunkirk census returns for 1851: PRO, HO 107/1626. For similar comparisons at the micro and macro levels, see J. Robin, *Elmdon. Continuity and Change in a North-west Essex Village 1861–1964* (Cambridge,

1980), 221, 252; M. Anderson, 'The Emergence of the Modern Life Cycle in Britain', *Social History*, 10 (1985).
20 This and the following come from my family reconstitution files for Hernhill and Dunkirk 1780–1850. The mean age at first marriage for 157 Hernhill women was 21.6 (median 20); for 139 men it was 24.6 (median 24). In Dunkirk the mean age at first marriage for 123 women was 22.3 (median 21); for 126 men it was 25.5 (median 24). Compare the national and county female mean marriage ages of 24.2–24.6 at mid-century: N. F. R. Crafts, 'Average Age at First Marriage for Women in Mid-Nineteenth-Century England and Wales', *Population Studies*, 32 (1978), 22–3. My figures are closer to those given by Dennis Mills in his study of the nineteenth-century Cambridgeshire village of Melbourn (also based on family reconstitution): D. R. Mills, *Aspects of Marriage: An Example of Applied Historical Studies* (Milton Keynes, 1980), 21.
21 Cf. M. Anderson, *Approaches to the History of the Western Family 1500–1914* (London, 1980), 19–20; Armstrong, *Farmworkers*, 102.
22 The mean completed family size (no. of births per women) of 182 Dunkirk and Hernhill women married between 1780 and 1850 was 7.3 (median 8.0).
23 The infant mortality rates were calculated from the parish registers by aggregative analysis. For the national average, see N. L. Tranter, *Population and Society 1750–1940* (London, 1985), 47. Again, some studies of nineteenth-century rural parishes provide figures closer to mine: see those summarized in Armstrong, *Farmworkers*, 38.
24 Family reconstitution data.
25 Again based on my family reconstitution. I plan to elaborate on this subject in a forthcoming study.
26 J. Robin, 'Illegitimacy in Colyton, 1851–1881', *Continuity and Change*, 2 (1987), 338. For comparisons with rates of prenuptial pregnancies in other parishes, see J. Robin, 'Prenuptial Pregnancy in a Rural Area of Devonshire in the Mid-nineteenth Century: Colyton, 1851–1881', *Continuity and Change*, 1 (1986), 115 (52% in Colyton); Mills, *Aspects of Marriage*, 14–15 (40% in Melbourn).
27 See e.g. his 'Characteristics of the Western Family Considered over Time', in P. Laslett, *Family Life and Illicit Love in Earlier Generations* (Cambridge, 1977), ch. 1.
28 My figures come from a breakdown of the census returns for 1851.
29 See the discussion in Anderson, *Approaches*, 22–33. A paper by Luc Danhieux gave me the idea of tracing the fate of households over time: L. Danhieux, 'The Evolving Household: The Case of Lampernisse, West Flanders', in R. Wall, J. Robin, and P. Laslett (eds.), *Family Forms in Historic Europe* (Cambridge, 1983), ch. 13. See also L. Berkner, 'The Use and Misuse of Census Data for the Historical

Analysis of Family Structure', *Journal of Interdisciplinary History*, 5 (1975).
30 The best guides are the 1840 tithe maps for Boughton, Blean, Harbledown, and Hernhill: PRO IR 30/17/41, 93, 166, 178; and a map of Dunkirk, drawn up in the late 1820s: PRO, MR 890.
31 This means that it was necessary for me to use the parish registers of these places in my family reconstitution work for Dunkirk for the period before the 1840s.
32 KAO, PS/US 14/14: Lathe of Scray Petty Sessions, 1820–33.
33 For example, KAO, U951 C37/34: Knatchbull papers; Liardet, 'State of the Peasantry', 115.
34 For an interesting discussion of the role of hamlets in a European community, see J. de Pina-Cabral, *Sons of Adam, Daughters of Eve* (Oxford, 1986), 126–7.
35 PRO, HO 71/39, pt. 1, 23: Clergymen's Schedules of Returns to Census 1831.
36 R. J. Olney (ed.), *Labouring Life on the Lincolnshire Wolds* (Sleaford, 1975), 9; J. Obelkevich, *Religion and Rural Society: South Lindsey 1825–1875* (Oxford, 1976), 11–14. For a recent critique, see S. J. Banks, 'Nineteenth-Century Scandal or Twentieth-Century Model? A New Look at "Open" and "Close" Parishes', *Economic History Review*, 41 (1988).
37 PRO, MPZ 26; Liardet, 'State of the Peasantry', 113–15; KAO, U951 C37/34.
38 J. M. Wilson, *The Imperial Gazetteer of England and Wales* (Edinburgh, 1870–2), iii: Hernhill; PRO IR 29/17/178: Hernhill Tithe Apportionment Award, 1840.
39 PRO, IR 29/17/41: Boughton Tithe Apportionment Award 1840; PRO, HO 107/471/11: Boughton Census 1841; *Post Office Directory of the Six Home Counties* (London, 1845), 273.
40 Somerset House, Will of Reverend Charles Richard Handley, 1873.
41 PRO, HO 107/473/12: Hernhill Census 1841; PRO, HO 107/1626.
42 Liardet, 'State of the Peasantry', 133.
43 PRO, HO 107/466/5: Dunkirk Census 1841; KAO, TR 2804/2: Sale Catalogue for Berkeley Lodge; KAO, U2394 Z1.
44 Calculated from PRO, IR 29/17/178; PRO, MPZ 26.
45 The information comes from Roger Kain's 'Data Files for Tithe Surveys: Kent Landowners *c.* 1840', held at the University of Exeter. I am extremely grateful to Dr Kain for allowing access to these invaluable files.
46 Obelkevich, *Religion and Rural Society*, 46.
47 What follows is based on the Hernhill tithe survey (PRO, IR 29/17/178). Additional information comes from my family reconstitution files, Kain's 'Data Files', and title deeds in the possession of Harold Kay of Hernhill. For landownership in Kent, and the methodology

Notes 195

involved in the use of the tithe surveys, see R. J. P. Kain, 'Tithe Surveys and Landownership', *Journal of Historical Geography*, 1 (1975).

48 CCDRO, Hernhill Highway Accounts 1813–27; Hernhill Churchwardens' Accounts 1782–1853; Hernhill Vestry Book 1835–61.
49 Obelkevich, *Religion and Rural Society*, 46.
50 KAO, PRC 32/70/141: Will of Stephen Butcher, 1834.
51 See M. Reed, 'Nineteenth-Century Rural England: A Case for Peasant Studies', *Journal of Peasant Studies*, 14 (1986); and his 'The Peasantry of Nineteenth-Century England: a Neglected Class?', *History Workshop*, 18 (1984).
52 For this and the following section, see Hernhill tithe survey and the 1841 and 1851 census returns.
53 Liardet, 'State of the Peasantry', 107.
54 Collection of Sandys Dawes, Mt. Ephraim (Hernhill): Farming Account Book of Crockham Farm 1837–46.
55 See PRO, MPZ 26, and the census returns for 1841 and 1851.
56 Liardet, 'State of the Peasantry', 117.
57 An individual's plots were sometimes scattered throughout the parish rather than consolidated into adjoining lots: this can be detected by co-ordinating the terrier book for Dunkirk (PRO, MPZ 26) with its map (PRO, MR 890).
58 Somerset House, Will of Olive Hadlow, 1876.
59 Family reconstitution files.
60 PRO, HO 107/1626: Boughton Census 1851.
61 CCDRO, Hernhill Churchwardens' Accounts 1782–1853.
62 Family reconstitution files.
63 Snell, *Annals of the Labouring Poor*, ch. 2; Obelkevich, *Religion and Rural Society*, ch. 2; E. J. Hobsbawm and G. Rudé, *Captain Swing* (Harmondsworth, 1973), chs. 1–2.
64 Anderson, 'Emergence of the Modern Life Cycle', 70.
65 I arrived at these figures by matching the Hernhill tithe survey against the census return for 1841.
66 Liardet, 'State of the Peasantry', 106.
67 PRO, MPZ 26. See also, KAO U1172 O24: Dunkirk Land Survey c.1860s.
68 PRO, MPZ 26.
69 Liardet, 'State of the Peasantry', 117.
70 Family reconstitution files.
71 KAO, PRC 32/71/293: Will of Sarah Spratt, 1849.
72 Hobsbawm and Rudé, *Captain Swing*, 40.
73 G. P. Selby, *The Faversham Farmers' Club* (Faversham, 1927), 63–4.
74 Liardet, 'State of the Peasantry', 73.
75 L. Davidoff and C. Hall, *Family Fortunes. Men and Women of the English Middle Class, 1780–1850* (London, 1987); L. Davidoff,

'The Role of Gender in the "First Industrial Nation": Agriculture in England 1780–1850', in R. Crompton and M. Mann (eds.), *Gender and Stratification* (Cambridge, 1986).
76 Calculated from KAO, Q/R Pr 2/11/24v–25v, 164v–165v: Register of Electors for East Kent 1837–8.
77 For literacy, see pp. 62–4 below.
78 Census returns for 1851.
79 See KAO, PRC, 32/69/390: Will of Edward Rigden, 1831.
80 The above comes from my family reconstitution files.
81 Ibid.
82 W. Howitt, *The Rural Life of England* (Shannon, 1971 edn.), 88 (first published in 1838).

Chapter 2

1 This estimate was arrived at by calculating the number of those on relief in Hernhill in 1830 (CCDRO, Hernhill Overseers' Day Book 1821–30) as a percentage of the number of those listed in the 1831 Census as being employed in agriculture (*PP* xxxvi (1833), 266–7). I also matched the list of those receiving parish bread in 1839 (CCDRO, Hernhill Sacramental Money 1810–61: relief lists) against those listed as agricultural labourers in the Census of 1841 (PRO, HO 107/473/12).
2 D. Gittins, 'Marital Status, Work and Kinship, 1850–1930', in J. Lewis (ed.), *Labour and Love* (Oxford, 1986), 251; E. Higgs, 'Women, Occupations and Work in the Nineteenth Century Censuses', *History Workshop*, 23 (1987), 60.
3 PRO HO/107/1626: Hernhill and Dunkirk census returns 1851.
4 KAO, PS/US 14/14, 86–7: Lathe of Scray Petty Sessions 1820–33; KAO, Q/SBe 146: East Kent Quarter Sessions, Michaelmas 1836; Q/SBe 173: Midsummer 1843.
5 KAO, Q/SBe 195: Epiphany 1849; CCDRO, Hernhill Churchwardens' Accounts 1782–1853: 1852/3.
6 KAO, Q/SBe 191: January 1848.
7 See Higgs, 'Women, Occupations'.
8 K. D. M. Snell, *Annals of the Labouring Poor* (Cambridge, 1985), ch. 1.
9 *PP* xxx (1834), 249, 255, 266; *PP* xxi (1843), 143–208; *Morning Chronicle*, 30 January 1850, 13 February 1850; *PP* xiii (1868–9), 80–4, 88–105, 270–94.
10 *PP* xii (1843), 150.
11 *PP* xii (1843), 203–4.
12 See sources in n. 9 above. For a good general account of female labour, which also draws on some of the Kent material, see J. Kitteringham, 'County Work Girls in Nineteenth-Century England',

in R. Samuel (ed.), *Village Life and Labour* (London, 1975), pt. 3.
13 *PP* xii (1843), 148.
14 See sources in n. 9 above.
15 For a systematic charting of the important role of child labour in an estate in another part of Kent, see Reading University Library, KEN 4/7/2: Labour Payments Goss Hall, Ash, Kent, 1838–48. Unfortunately, there do not seem to be any such account books for our area.
16 For rural housing, see J. Burnett, *A Social History of Housing 1815–1970* (Newton Abbott, 1978), 34, 43.
17 F. Liardet, 'State of the Peasantry in the County of Kent', in *Central Society of Education, Third Publication*, 1839 (reprint, London, 1968), pp. 100–1.
18 Family reconstitution data.
19 A. Kussmaul, *Servants in Husbandry in Early Modern England* (Cambridge, 1981), 26; J. Rule, *The Labouring Classes in Early Industrial England 1750–1850* (London, 1986), 80.
20 Calculated from the census return for 1851.
21 Liardet, 'State of the Peasantry', 117.
22 *Morning Chronicle*, 30 March 1850; Liardet, 'State of the Peasantry', 103, 117.
23 Collection of Sandys Dawes, Mt. Ephraim (Hernhill): Farming Account Book of Crockham Farm 1837–46.
24 A. Armstrong, *Farmworkers: A Social and Economic History 1770–1980* (London, 1988), 42.
25 For malaria, see M. Dobson, ' "Marsh Fever": The Geography of Malaria in England', *Journal of Historical Geography*, 6 (1980). Using aggregative analysis, I have charted the seasonal mortality pattern for Hernhill, Dunkirk, and Boughton (based on the burial registers): it is not that of a malarial area.
26 *PP* xvi (1839), 116: 'First Annual Report of the Registrar General'; *PP* xvii (1840), 108: 'Second Annual Report of the Registrar General'; KAO, G/FRA1/18v–19, 51v–52: Faversham Union Outdoor Relief; CCDRO, Harbledown burials 1837–40.
27 F. Markus Hall, R. Stevens, and J. Whyman, *The Kent and County Hospital* (Canterbury, 1987), 64–5.
28 CCDRO, Hernhill Overseers' Day Book 1821–30.
29 Markus Hall *et al*, *Kent and County Hospital*, 65.
30 KAO U251 E8.
31 KAO, PS/US7: Settlement Examinations for the Upper Division of the Lathe of Scray 1812–16; PS/US8: Settlement Examinations for the Upper Division of the Lathe of Scray 1816–18; PS/US9: Lathe of Scray Petty Sessions 1818–32: Nov. 1829, May 1830, June 1831, July 1831; KAO, Fa/JP 7/1: Lathe of Scray Petty Sessions 1832–9: 22 Nov. 1833, 17 Dec. 1833, 15 Aug. 1836; PS/US 10: Lathe of Scray Petty Sessions 1839–45: 1 Sept. 1842.

32 B. Short, 'The Decline of Living-in Servants in the Transition to Capitalist Farming', *Sussex Archaeological Collections*, 122 (1984), 147; M. Reed, 'Indoor Farm Service in 19th-Century Sussex', *Sussex Archaeological Collections*, 123 (1985), 232–3.
33 See the Petty Sessions references in n. 31 above, and KAO, Q/SBe 165: East Kent Quarter Sessions, Midsummer 1841; Q/SBe 201: Midsummer 1850.
34 *PP* xiii (1868–9), 281.
35 Collection of Sandys Dawes, Farming Account Book of Crockham Farm 1837–46.
36 Liardet, 'State of the Peasantry', 107.
37 *PP* xvii, pt. 1 (1837), 132–9.
38 Liardet, 'State of the Peasantry', 106–8; *The Times*, 9 June 1838.
39 *Kentish Gazette*, 9 June 1835. In 1830 in Boughton Street (in Boughton parish) labourers combined to force wages up to 2s. 6d. a day: E. J. Hobsbawm and G. Rudé, *Captain Swing* (Harmondsworth, 1973), 77.
40 *Morning Chronicle*, 6 March 1850.
41 F. Carlton, ' "A Substantial and Sterling Friend to the Labouring Man": The Kent and Sussex Labourers' Union 1872–1895' (University of Sussex M.Phil. thesis, 1977), 31.
42 See p. 43 above.
43 *Morning Chronicle*, 6 March 1850.
44 D. H. Morgan, 'The Place of Harvesters in Nineteenth-Century Village Life', in Samuel, *Village Life*, 55.
45 CCDRO, Hernhill Overseers' Day Book 1821–30; CCDRO, Hernhill Sacramental Money 1810–61; KAO, Q/C1/86: Insolvent Debtors' Records.
46 A phrase first used by the historian Olwen Hufton in her description of labouring life in eighteenth-century France.
47 *Morning Chronicle*, 30 March 1850.
48 *PP* xxviii (1834), 204; R. Arnold, *The Farthest Promised Land* (Wellington, 1981), 193, 195, 198–9, 209–10.
49 R. Jefferies, *The Toilers of the Field* (London, 1893), 100–1. (Most of the material was first published in 1874.)
50 PRO, TS 11/943/3412: Treasury Solicitor's Papers: Rex *v.* Henry and William Packman, 1830; *The Times*, 9 June 1838.
51 J. Obelkevich, *Religion and Rural Society: South Lindsey 1825–1875* (Oxford, 1976), 86.
52 KAO, Q/SBe 176: Easter 1844.
53 PRO, TS/11/943/3412; KAO, PS/US 9: March 1824; KAO, PS/US14/85: Lathe of Scray Petty Sessions 1820–33; Liardet, 'State of the Peasantry', 124.
54 KAO, PS/US 11: Lathe of Scray Petty Sessions 1864–8: 29 Sept. 1865.
55 KAO, PS/US 10: 6 May 1841.

56 KAO, Q/SBe 146: August 1836; Q/SBe 173: Midsummer 1843.
57 KAO, Q/SBe 176: Easter 1844; Q/SBe 178: Michaelmas 1844.
58 KAO, PS/US 11: 5 Sept. 1867.
59 KAO, Fa/JP 7/1: 20 Feb. 1838.
60 KAO PS/US 11: 29 Sept. 1865.
61 KAO Q/SBe 176: Easter 1844.
62 Calculated from the census returns of 1841 and 1851.
63 CCDRO, Hernhill Churchwardens' Accounts 1782–1853.
64 KAO, PS/US 9: 23 Feb. 1832.
65 This is in keeping with the findings of other local studies: J. Robin, *Elmdon: Continuity and Change in a North-west Essex Village 1861–1964* (Cambridge, 1980), 24–7, 182–4; D. Jenkins, *The Agricultural Community in South-West Wales* (Cardiff, 1971), 158; B. J. Davey, *Ashwell 1830–1914* (Leicester, 1980), 25. See also the valuable discussion (for the early modern period) in K. Wrightson and D. Levine, *Poverty and Piety in an English Village: Terling 1525–1700* (London, 1979), ch. 4.
66 KAO, U951 C37/34: Knatchbull papers; Liardet, 'State of the Peasantry', 109–12, 118–19; *The Times*, 9 June 1838. The number of students is calculated from the 1851 Census.
67 Liardet, 'State of the Peasantry', 109.
68 *PP* xii (1843), 167, 169; *PP* xiii (1868–9), 92–3, 270–1.
69 *PP* xii (1843), 171.
70 *PP* xii (1843), 169; *PP* xviii (1837–8), pt. 3, 135.
71 Liardet, 'State of the Peasantry', 109.
72 Taken from my family reconstitution files and based on the marriage registers 1800–50.
73 *PP* xix (1842), 456, 458, 459. For an exhaustive national study, see W. B. Stephens, *Education, Literacy and Society 1830–70* (Manchester, 1987).
74 D. Levine, 'Education and Family Life in Early Industrial England', *Journal of Family History*, 4 (1979), 368–80.
75 *The Times*, 9 June 1838.
76 R. S. Schofield, 'Dimensions of Illiteracy, 1750–1850', *Explorations in Economic History*, 10 (1973), 440; R. K. Webb, *The British Working Class Reader 1790–1848* (New York, 1971), 22.
77 My calculations from Liardet, 'State of the Peasantry', 109, 118, 122–3.
78 Ibid., 112.
79 Ibid., 108–9, 118–19, 122, 128.
80 Ibid., 124, 128–32.
81 For this mix in Britain in an earlier period, see R. A. Houston, *Scottish Literacy and the Scottish Identity: Illiteracy and Society in Scotland and Northern England, 1600–1800* (Cambridge, 1985), ch. 6; K. Thomas, 'The Meaning of Literacy in Early Modern

200 Notes

England', in G. Baumann (ed.), *The Written Word: Literacy in Transition* (Oxford, 1985).
82 Cf. Levine, 'Education and Family Life'.
83 PRO, HO 129/67/18–19: Religious Census 1851; KAO, U951 C37/34; Liardet, 'State of the Peasantry', 112–13.
84 Lambeth Palace Library, VG/3/3a/343–4: Visitation Returns 1864.
85 Obelkevich, *Religion and Rural Society*, 143.
86 CCDRO, Hernhill Churchwardens' Accounts 1782–1853.
87 Ibid.
88 For the rise and fall of the English church bands, see V. Gammon, ' "Babylonian Performances": the Rise and Suppression of Popular Church Music, 1660–1870', in E. Yeo and S. Yeo (eds.), *Popular Culture and Class Conflict 1590–1914* (Brighton, 1981), ch. 3. The quotation comes from Obelkevich, *Religion and Rural Society*, 147.
89 See p. 171 below.
90 KAO, U951 C37/34.
91 Liardet, 'State of the Peasantry', p. 123; KAO, M8/1B/5/1: Canterbury and Faversham Methodist Circuit Records: Baptismal Register, Wesleyan Chapel, Boughton 1838; KAO, M8/2E/5/1: Wesleyan Methodist Sunday School, Boughton Class Book 1833–8.
92 KAO, M8/1A/4: Wesleyan Methodist Preachers' Circuit Plans, Canterbury Circuit 1818–77; CCDRO, H/A/394, 399, 455: Applications for Registration of Dissenting Churches 1818–52; PRO, RG31: Places of Religious Worship: Returns for Diocese of Canterbury 1816–38; PRO, HO 129/67/31.
93 Family reconstitution files.
94 KAO, Q/C3R/E15: Letter concerning Dissenters in Boughton Blean, 18 July 1829; CCDRO, H/A/424, 457, 503, 905, PRO, RG31.
95 Family reconstitution files.
96 KAO, M8/1B/1/6: Faversham Methodist Circuit Quarterly Meeting Accounts 1839–50; PRO, RG4/926: Non-parochial Registers: Wesleyan Chapel, Faversham, Baptisms 1814–37.
97 PRO, HO 129/67/36; PRO, HO 129/65, no pagination (Canterbury).
98 KAO, Fa/JP 7/1: Faversham Borough Petty Sessions 1832–9: 4 Aug. 1836; *Primitive Methodist Magazine* . . . *1839*, 316–17.
99 *Primitive Methodist Magazine* . . . *1837*, 315.
100 *James Thorne of Shebbear: A Memoir* (London, 1873), 173.
101 KAO, N/MC 4/1: Sheerness Bible Christian Circuit Quarterly Meeting Minute Book 1822–52; PRO, RG4/880: Arminian Bible Christians, Sheerness Circuit, Baptisms 1823–37.
102 KAO, N/MC 4/1.
103 Ibid.; *Minutes of the . . . Annual Conference . . . [of the Bible Christians]* (1828–39) (which gives the numbers attending meetings); PRO, HO 129/67/50 ff.

104 KAO, N/MC 4/1.
105 Liardet, 'State of the Peasantry', 108–9, 111–12, 118.

Chapter 3

1 KAO, Q/SBe 166: East Kent Quarter Sessions, Michaelmas 1841.
2 KAO, PS/US 11: Lathe of Scray Petty Sessions 1864–8: 6 April 1866.
3 KAO, PS/US 11: 30 March 1868; Faversham Society, Manuscript Notebook/Account book of John Mears, Constable of Boughton 1825–36: 2 July 1836; KAO, Fa/JP 7/1: Lathe of Scray Petty Sessions 1832–9: 2 July 1836. For other cases, see KAO, PS/US 14/31, 122: Lathe of Scray Petty Sessions 1820–33.
4 *Kentish Express and Ashford News*, 12 February 1910: oral account of Elizabeth Arnold.
5 KAO, Q/SBe 191: January 1848.
6 KAO, PS/US 10: Lathe of Scray Petty Sessions 1839–45: 13 July 1844; Fa/JP 7/1: 6 Aug. 1835.
7 KAO, PS/US 14/142; Fa/JP 7/1: 2 Nov. 1837; Q/SBe 178: Michaelmas 1844.
8 KAO, PS/US 10: 15 Oct. 1839.
9 G. Rudé, *Criminal and Victim. Crime and Society in Early Nineteenth-Century England* (Oxford, 1985), 79.
10 KAO, Q/SBe 190: Michaelmas 1847; Q/SBe 173: Midsummer 1843; PS/US 9: Lathe of Scray Petty Sessions 1818–32: 1825.
11 KAO, Q/SBe 171: January 1843; Q/SBe 190: Michaelmas 1847. For pawning in Canterbury, see Q/SBe 146: Michaelmas 1836.
12 KAO, Q/SBe 176: Easter 1844; Q/SBe 178: Michaelmas 1844.
13 KAO, Q/SBe 132: June 1833.
14 F. Liardet, 'State of the Peasantry in the County of Kent', in *Central Society of Education, Third Publication*, 1839 (reprint, London, 1968), 96.
15 PRO, TS 11/943/3412: Treasury Solicitor's Papers, 1830: Rex. v. Henry and William Packman.
16 Faversham Society, Notebook/Account book of John Mears.
17 KAO, Q/SBe 145: Easter 1836.
18 KAO, PS/US 10: 4 April 1840.
19 KAO, PS/US 10: 24 Feb. 1843.
20 KAO, U521 E2/180–1: Lambert Estate Papers.
21 KAO, PS/US10: 20 Jan. 1842.
22 KAO, Fa/JP 7/1: 29 Sept. 1836; PS/US11: 4 Oct. 1866.
23 KAO, PS/US 14/118, 134, 154–5.
24 Liardet, 'State of the Peasantry', 101.
25 M. Waugh, *Smuggling in Kent and Sussex 1700–1840* (Newbury, 1985), 48, 49, 53, 57.
26 Liardet, 'State of the Peasantry', 114.

Notes

27 KAO, PS/US 14/6, 9, 11, 12, 14, 86–7.
28 KAO, PS/US 14/12.
29 PRO, TS 11/943/3412.
30 Liardet, 'State of the Peasantry', 134.
31 See J. G. Rule, 'Social Crime in the Rural South in the Eighteenth and Early Nineteenth Centuries', *Southern History*, 1 (1979).
32 E. J. Hobsbawm and G. Rudé, *Captain Swing* (Harmondsworth, 1973). See also Monju Dutt's superb Ph.D. thesis: 'The Agricultural Labourers' Revolt of 1830 in Kent, Surrey and Sussex' (University of London Ph.D. thesis, 1966).
33 Hobsbawm and Rudé, *Captain Swing*, app. iii: 'Table of Incidents'.
34 PRO, HO 52/8/9: Home Office Correspondence; *Kent Herald*, 18 November 1830; *Kentish Gazette*, 19 November 1830.
35 *Kentish Gazette*, 29 October 1830; *The Times*, 30 October 1830; KAO U2593 B45: Kent Fire Insurance Company Farm Fire Losses 1830–53.
36 *Kentish Gazette*, 23 November 1830; *Kent Herald*, 2 December 1830, 16 December 1830.
37 *The Times*, 4 November 1830; *Kentish Gazette*, 29 October 1830.
38 *Kentish Chronicle*, 28 September 1830.
39 KAO, U2593 B6/16: Kent Fire Insurance Institution Directors' Minutes 1830–2.
40 *Kentish Gazette*, 5 November 1830.
41 PRO, HO 52/8/39, 379.
42 PRO, TS/11/943/3412.
43 Ibid.
44 *PP* xxxiv (1834), 266; *Kentish Gazette*, 5 November 1830; Hobsbawm and Rudé, *Captain Swing*, 258.
45 *PP* xxxvii (1834), 508.
46 *Kent Herald*, 30 December 1830.
47 CCDRO, Blean burials 1830.
48 PRO, TS/11/943/3412. Another of Courtenay's followers, also a distant relation of Wraight, was a man called George Bishop, but he was not the same person as the Blean incendiarist.
49 *Kent Herald*, 7 May 1835, 4 June 1835, 11 June 1835; *Kentish Gazette*, 9 June 1835. See also David Hopker's useful pamphlet, *Money or Blood: The 1835 Anti Poor Law Disturbances in the Swale Villages* (Broadstairs, 1988).
50 KAO, Q/SBe 140: Special Sessions 1835.
51 See pp. 87–8 below.
52 *Kentish Gazette*, 9 June 1835; KAO, Q/SBe 140.
53 KAO, Q/SBe 144: January 1836: Calendar of Prisoners.
54 CCDRO, Hernhill Highway Accounts 1813–27.
55 Calculated from CCDRO, Hernhill Overseers' Day Book 1821–30.
56 Ibid.

57 D. Thomson, 'Provision for the Elderly in England, 1830 to 1908' (University of Cambridge Ph.D. thesis, 1980), 16.
58 KAO, G/F AM 2–3: Minutes of the Board of Faversham Union 1836–42; G/F RA1: Faversham Union Outdoor Relief.
59 KAO, G/F AM1/196: Minutes of the Board of Faversham Union 1835–6.
60 KAO, G/F RA1/19v–20; G/F AR 11: Faversham Union Outdoor Relief Book: Dec. 1836.
61 KAO, G/F AM1/23, 64–5.
62 PRO, MH 12/5054: Ministry of Health Poor Law Union Papers 1836–9: 23 June 1838.
63 K. D. M. Snell, *Annals of the Labouring Poor* (Cambridge 1985), 137.
64 G/F AM1/65.
65 PRO, MH12/5054: 19 Jan. 1838.
66 KAO, G/F Wr m1: Faversham Union Master's Report Book 1837–40.
67 E. A. Wrigley, 'Men on the Land and Men in the Countryside: Employment in Agriculture in Early-Nineteenth-Century England', in L. Bonfield, R. M. Smith, and K. Wrightson (eds.), *The World We Have Gained* (Oxford, 1986), ch. 11.
68 T. L. Richardson, 'The Agricultural Labourer's Standard of Living in Kent 1790–1840', in D. J. Oddy and D. S. Miller (eds.), *The Making of the Modern British Diet* (London, 1976), esp. 110–11. See also his 'The Standard of Living Controversy 1790–1840' (University of Hull Ph.D., 1977).
69 A. Armstrong, *Farmworkers: A Social and Economic History 1770–1980* (London, 1988), 78.
70 KAO, G/F Wr m1; PRO, MH 12/5054: 19 Jan. 1838, 23 March 1838.
71 Liardet, 'State of the Peasantry', 98, 116; *The Times*, 9 June 1838 (for unofficial relief).
72 PRO, MH 12/5054: 19 Jan. 1838.
73 *Kentish Observer*, 18 January 1838.
74 *PP* xxviii (1837–8), 207–8.
75 *PP* xxviii (1837–8), 279, 281; D. Harvey, 'Aspects of Agricultural and Rural Change in Kent 1800–1900' (University of Cambridge Ph.D. thesis, 1961), 99, 188, 228–9.
76 CCDRO, Hernhill Churchwardens' Accounts 1782–1853; CCDRO, Hernhill rate book 1835–8.

Chapter 4

1 CCDRO, Hernhill Tithe Book, 1853: 'The Rev'd C. Handley's Account of the Riot', 7–8.
2 KAO, U 951 C 37/8: Knatchbull Papers.

3 *Kent Herald*, 7 June 1838.
4 See p. 77 above.
5 *Kent Herald*, 7 June 1838; *Kentish Observer*, 7 June 1838.
6 KAO, U 951 C37/3. See also PRO, HO 40/36/365, 381–2: Home Office Correspondence concerning disturbances, 1838: folder, 'Disturbances in Kent 1838'.
7 *The Times*, 6 June 1838; *Canterbury Press and County News*, 30 June 1888 (oral accounts, fifty years after the event).
8 KAO, U 951 C37/3.
9 *The Times*, 17 August 1838.
10 *Kent Herald*, 7 June 1838.
11 *Kentish Express and Ashford News*, 12 February 1910.
12 KAO, U 951 C37/2; *Canterbury Press and County News*, 30 June 1888.
13 KAO, U951 C37/2; PRO, ASSI 36/3: Assizes, South Eastern Circuit, 1838, Depositions on death of H. B. Bennett. I have benefited greatly from discussing the battle with Graham Hudson.
14 *PP* xlii (1837–8), 381; *The Times*, 5 June 1838.
15 *Penny Satirist*, 23 June 1838.
16 *Northern Star*, 9 June 1838, 16 June 1838.
17 PRO, ASSI 36/3.
18 *Morning Herald*, 4 June 1838.
19 *Canterbury Press and County News*, 30 June 1888.
20 *The Times*, 6 June 1838, 9 June 1838.
21 For Newport, see D. J. V. Jones, *The Last Rising: The Newport Insurrection of 1839* (Oxford, 1985).
22 *The Times*, 9 June 1838.
23 KAO, U951 C37/2; PRO, ASSI 36/3.
24 KAO, U951 C37/2.
25 *Morning Herald*, 4 June 1838.
26 *An Account of the Desperate Affray . . . in Blean Wood* (Faversham, [1838]), 20 ff.
27 *Maidstone Journal*, 5 June 1838.
28 F. Liardet, 'State of the Peasantry in the County of Kent', in *Central Society of Education, Third Publication*, 1839 (reprint, London, 1968), 95; *PP* xlii (1837–8), 384–5; *The Times*, 9 June 1838.
29 *PP* xlii (1837–8), 384–5; *The Times*, 4 June 1838.
30 For mobilization, see *PP* xlii (1837–8), 380–6; *Kent Herald*, 7 June 1838; *The Times*, 6 June 1838 (graffiti).
31 See p. 73 above.
32 E. J. Hobsbawm, 'Economic Fluctuations and some Social Movements since 1800', *Economic History Review*, 5 (1952), 6; M. Harrison, 'The Ordering of the Urban Environment: Time, Work and the Occurrence of Crowds 1790–1835', *Past and Present*, 110 (1986), 152–3; A. Howkins, ' "In the Sweat of Thy Face": The Labourer and

Work', in G. E. Mingay (ed.), *The Victorian Countryside* (London, 1981), ii, 511.
33 P. Slack (ed.), *Rebellion, Popular Protest and the Social Order in Early Modern England* (Cambridge, 1984), 11; *The Times*, 10 August 1838.
34 See p. 108 below.
35 *PP* xlii (1837–8), 383; J. Walter, 'A "Rising of the People"? The Oxfordshire Rising of 1596', *Past and Present*, 107 (1985).
36 *Morning Chronicle*, 5 June 1838.
37 CCDRO, 'Rev'd C. Handley's account of the riot', 11, 13.
38 *Kentish Observer*, 7 June 1838; *PP* xlii (1837–8), 384.
39 *The Times*, 10 August 1838.
40 *Northern Liberator*, 9 June 1838; *Kent Herald*, 7 June 1838; *Kentish Observer*, 7 June 1838; *Dover Chronicle*, 2 June 1838, 23 June 1838.
41 *The Times*, 7 June 1838.
42 See p. 161 below; *The Times*, 2 June 1838.
43 PRO, HO 40/36/381–4; *PP* xlii (1837–8), 380.
44 *PP* xlii (1837–8), 385.
45 *The Times*, 9 June 1838; *Kentish Observer*, 7 June 1838.
46 CCDRO, 'Rev'd C. Handley's account of the riot', 13.
47 Liardet, 'State of the Peasantry', 91; *Kent Herald*, 16 August 1838.
48 For an extremely useful history of the term 'jubilee', see M. Chase, 'Jubilee: The History of an Idea', unpublished typescript. (I am very grateful to Dr Chase for letting me see this typescript.) See also M. Chase, *The People's Farm: English Radical Agrarianism 1775–1840* (Oxford, 1988), 55–7.
49 T. R. Knox, 'Thomas Spence: The Trumpet of Jubilee', *Past and Present*, 76 (1977); H. T. Dickinson (ed.), *The Political Works of Thomas Spence* (Newcastle upon Tyne, 1982); Chase, *People's Farm*, 56.
50 I. Prothero, 'William Benbow and the Concept of the "General Strike" ', *Past and Present*, 63 (1974); A. J. C. Rüter, 'William Benbow's Grand National Holiday', *International Review for Social History*, 1 (1936).
51 Most modern accounts of the Courtenay affair mention a Spencean connection. J. F. C. Harrison, for example, writes that Courtenay may have been a member of the Spencean Society. The source for this supposed link is presumably the *Life and Extraordinary Adventures* (see n. 52 below), published in Canterbury in 1838, a turgid, convoluted work, a mixture of fact and fantasy, which attempts to establish other links between Courtenay and various radicalisms and radicals (e.g. William Godwin, Mary Wollstonecraft, and Robert Owen). It does portray Courtenay as a Spencean who anticipated a millennium 'when there would be ... an equal distribution of property throughout the country'. The *Life*, unfortunately, is a totally

unreliable source. The *Penny Satirist*, 9 June 1838, referred to an attempt by Courtenay to publish a pamphlet, *A Plan for the Division of Landed Property in Great Britain, without injury to the existing holders*, but I have been unable to trace any other reference to this work.

52 *Kent Herald*, 4 April 1833; Canterburiensis, *The Life and Extraordinary Adventures of Sir William Courtenay* (Canterbury, 1838), 32–3, 62 ff, 118. For the London Spenceans, see I. Prothero, *Artisans and Politics in Early Nineteenth-Century London* (London, 1981), index: 'Spenceans'; I. McCalman, *Radical Underworld. Prophets, Revolutionaries and Pornographers in London, 1795–1840* (Cambridge, 1988); Chase, *People's Farm*, ch. 3.

53 *The Times*, 9 June 1838.

54 Liardet, 'State of the Peasantry', 94, 97, 109; *Kent Herald*, 7 June 1838; *The Times*, 6 June 1838.

55 *The Times*, 6 June 1838, 9 June 1838, 10 August 1838, Liardet, 'State of the Peasantry', 90–1; *Canterbury Press and County News*, 30 June 1888; *Kent Herald*, 7 June 1838.

56 J. F. C. Harrison, *The Second Coming* (London, 1979); W. H. Oliver, *Prophets and Millennialists: The Uses of Biblical Prophecy in England from the 1790s to the 1840s* (Auckland, 1978).

57 E. Miller, *The History and Doctrine of Irvingism*, 2 vols. (London, 1878); Oliver, *Prophets*, 197–8.

58 KAO, U951 C37/47.

59 KAO, U951 C37/2; PRO, HO 40/36/34; *Kent Herald*, 14 June 1838. I calculated Whitsun from the 'Table of Moveable Feasts' in *The Book of Common Prayer* (1814).

60 Cf. A. J. Peacock, *Bread or Blood* (London, 1965), 87–8, 102; J. L. Hammond and B. Hammond, *The Skilled Labourer 1760–1832* (London, 1936), 361–2; E. J. Hobsbawm and G. Rudé, *Captain Swing* (Harmondsworth, 1973), 174, 178; D. Jones, *Before Rebecca* (London, 1973), 143; Jones, *Last Rising*, ch. 4. For 1835, see pp. 77–8 above.

61 Jones, *Before Rebecca*, 204–5.

62 *The Times*, 4 June 1838, 10 August 1838.

63 Walter, 'Rising of the People', 100.

64 I allude, of course, to the Hammonds' description: see J. L. Hammond and B. Hammond, *The Village Labourer* (London, 1911), chs. 10–11: 'The Last Labourers' Revolt' [1830].

Chapter 5

1 Canterburiensis, *The Life and Extraordinary Adventures of Sir William Courtenay* (Canterbury, 1838).

2 P. G. Rogers, *Battle in Bossenden Wood* (Oxford, 1961).

3 See ibid.; and *Cornwall Royal Gazette*, 15 June 1838.
4 KAO, U951 C37/44–5: Knatchbull Papers.
5 M. Donnelly, *Managing the Mind* (London, 1983), 72; G. E. Berrios, 'Obsessional Disorders during the Nineteenth Century: Terminological and Classificatory Issues', in W. F. Bynum, R. Porter, and M. Shepherd (eds.), *The Anatomy of Madness* (London, 1985), i, ch. 7.
6 KAO, U951 C37/45.
7 KAO, U951 C37/42.
8 *Kent Herald*, 4 April 1833, 14 June 1838.
9 See p. 107 above. For Hunt's activity in London in 1832, see J. Belchem, *'Orator' Hunt: Henry Hunt and English Working-Class Radicalism* (Oxford, 1985), 262.
10 For the above, see Rogers, *Battle in Bossenden Wood*, ch. 2; *Kent Herald*, 7 June 1838; E. Walford, *Tales of Our Great Families* (London, 1877), i, 250–1; and PRO, TS 16/139/503 ff. (for the earldom of Devon).
11 *Morning Chronicle*, 2 June 1838.
12 *The Eccentric and Singular Productions of Sir W. Courtenay* (Canterbury, n.d.), 29–30, 36; CCDRO, Boughton-under-Blean baptisms.
13 *Canterbury Press and County News*, 23 June 1888.
14 F. W. S. Craig (ed.), *British Parliamentary Results 1832–1885* (London, 1977), 78; *Canterbury Press and County News*, 30 June 1888; Rogers, *Battle in Bossenden Wood*, 26.
15 Rogers, *Battle in Bossenden Wood*, 27.
16 CCDRO, Hernhill Tithe Book, 1853: 'The Rev'd C. Handley's Account of the Riot', 4.
17 *Eccentric and Singular Productions* reprints a run of the *Lion*. See also *The British Lion*, 20 April 1833 (British Library, LR 271 b19). Sandys Dawes of Mt. Ephraim, Hernhill, owns several issues, presumably collected originally by Charles Handley.
18 *Kent Herald*, 4 April 1833.
19 *Maidstone Journal*, 30 July 1833; *An Essay on the Character of Sir W. Courtenay* (Canterbury, [1833]).
20 J. Arnould, *Memoir of Thomas, First Lord Denman* (London, 1873), i, 110–12; E. J. Hobsbawm and G. Rudé, *Captain Swing* (Harmondsworth, 1973), 93, 174, 176, 178; *Kentish Gazette*, 9 June 1835; *Kent Herald*, 11 June 1835; D. J. V. Jones, *The Last Rising: The Newport Insurrection of 1839* (Oxford, 1985); D. Thompson, *The Chartists* (London, 1984), 96–9; J. Epstein, *The Lion of Freedom: Feargus O'Connor and the Chartist Movement, 1832–1842* (London, 1982), 90–2.
21 I am thinking here of the work of Epstein, esp. 90–2; Belchem, *'Orator' Hunt*; Thompson, *Chartists*, 96–9.

Notes

22 CCDRO, 'Rev'd C. Handley's Account of the Riot', 2–3; *Kentish Observer*, 13 December 1832; *Morning Chronicle*, 2 June 1838.
23 *Kentish Observer*, 20 December 1832.
24 CCDRO, 'Rev'd C. Handley's Account of the Riot', 1, 2–3.
25 Thompson, *Chartists*, 98–9.
26 K. D. M. Snell, *Annals of the Labouring Poor* (Cambridge, 1985), 330.
27 *The Times*, 4 June 1838.
28 *Eccentric and Singular Productions*, 10–11.
29 P. A. Pickering, 'Class without Words: Symbolic Communication in the Chartist Movement', *Past and Present*, 112 (1986).
30 See M. Brock, *The Great Reform Act* (London, 1973), 295–9, 306–7; D. Fraser, 'The Agitation for Parliamentary Reform', in J. T. Ward (ed.), *Popular Movements c. 1830–1850* (London, 1970), ch. 1.
31 *Eccentric and Singular Productions*, 6, 9. For the ideology of radicalism in the early nineteenth century, see G. Stedman Jones, 'The Language of Chartism', in J. Epstein and D. Thompson (eds.), *The Chartist Experience* (London, 1982), ch. 1.
32 H. Cunningham, 'The Language of Patriotism, 1750–1914', *History Workshop*, 12 (1981).
33 *Essay on the Character*, 21.
34 *Eccentric and Singular Productions*, 29–30.
35 L. Colley, 'Whose Nation? Class and National Consciousness in Britain 1750–1830', *Past and Present*, 113 (1986), 116.
36 *Eccentric and Singular Productions*, 21. It is worth noting that Hunt addressed a rally against military flogging—at Kennington Common in July 1832, when Courtenay was in London (see Belchem, *'Orator' Hunt*, 262).
37 *Eccentric and Singular Productions*, 15, 21.
38 Ibid., 18, 22–3.
39 *The Times*, 6 June 1838.
40 *Canterbury Press and County News*, 23 June 1888.
41 *Kent Herald*, 7 June 1838.
42 *The Times*, 17 August 1838.
43 CCDRO, 'Rev'd C. Handley's Account of the Riot', 10, 12.
44 KAO, U951 C37/47.
45 R. Porter, ' "The Hunger of Imagination": Approaching Samuel Johnson's Melancholy', in Bynum, Porter, and Shepherd, *Anatomy of Madness*, i, ch. 3.
46 A. T. Scull, *Museums of Madness: The Social Organization of Insanity in Nineteenth-Century England* (Harmondsworth, 1982), 238.
47 M. Foucault (ed.), *I, Pierre Rivière* (New York, 1975), x.
48 Ibid., passim.
49 Ibid.

50 KAO, U951, C37/48.
51 KAO, U951 C37/31, 38.
52 *The Times*, 17 August 1838.
53 *Globe*, 4 June 1838; *Kentish Observer*, 14 June 1838.
54 *The Times*, 10 August 1838.
55 C. Dickens, *All the Year Round*, xvii (1867), 441–6.
56 *The Times*, 10 August 1838.
57 J. F. C. Harrison, *The Second Coming* (London, 1979), 215.
58 *Eccentric and Singular Productions*, 6.
59 L. James, *Fiction for the Working Man 1830–1850* (London, 1963), 74–6; 84–5, 88; G. Himmelfarb, *The Idea of Poverty* (London, 1984), chs. 16–17; G. J. Worth, *William Harrison Ainsworth* (New York, 1972).
60 *Kent Herald*, 7 June 1838.
61 W. H. Ainsworth, *Rookwood* (London, 1835, 1836, 1850, 1853).
62 N.Z. Davis, *The Return of Martin Guerre* (Cambridge, Mass., 1983).
63 *Essay on the Character*, 11.
64 KAO, U951 C37/51; *The Times*, 17 August 1838.
65 CCDRO, Hernhill burials, 5 June 1838.
66 *Northern Star*, 9 June 1838.

Chapter 6

1 A detailed list of 'persons concerned in the late Riot' is provided in KAO, U951 C37/40: Knatchbull Papers, and PRO, HO 40/36/435–41: Home Office Correspondence concerning disturbances, 1838. F. Liardet, 'State of the Peasantry in the County of Kent', in *Central Society of Education, Third Publication*, 1839 (reprint, London, 1968), provides further details.
2 *Globe*, 6 June 1838, in *Extracts from Newspapers relating to Courtenay* (1838) (in the British Library).
3 CCDRO, Boughton-under-Blean burials.
4 For these men, see *The Times*, 10 August 1838; *Kent Herald*, 16 August 1838.
5 My figures differ slightly from those of Liardet: cf. Liardet, 'State of the Peasantry', 88.
6 That is, those with Courtenay on 31 May. I have excluded two men from the original list of 46: Thomas Ovenden, a 60-year-old labourer from Whitstable, who was said to be simple-minded and who was just picked up on the road by the rioters: and Edward Newman or Newing, about whom we know nothing, not even his precise name!
7 Most of the details in the pages that follow come from my file on the rioters. It (in turn) is based on my family reconstitution for Dunkirk and Hernhill and the sources in n. 1 above. Additional references are provided in notes. For the Census of 1841, see p. 34 above.

8 Liardet, 'State of the Peasantry', 95.
9 KAO, G/F W1 r 2: Faversham Union Indoor Relief Lists 1838–40, 78.
10 Liardet, 'State of the Peasantry', 95; CCDRO, Hernhill Overseers' Day Book 1821–30; KAO, Fa/JP 7/1: Lathe of Scray Petty Sessions 1832–9: 6 March 1834.
11 He was interviewed for the fiftieth anniversary of the rising: see p. 167 below.
12 Liardet, 'State of the Peasantry', 96; KAO, Q/SBe 146: East Kent Quarter Sessions, Michaelmas 1836; Fa/JP 7/1, 2 July 1836.
13 PRO, IR 29/17/178: Hernhill tithe return, 1840; CCDRO, Hernhill rate book 1835–8.
14 *The Poll for the Knights of the Shire, to Represent the Eastern Division of the County of Kent in Parliament . . . 4th and 5th of August,* 1837 (Canterbury, 1837), 58.
15 Liardet, 'State of the Peasantry', 95.
16 PRO, IR 29/17/178; *The Times*, 11 August 1838.
17 KAO, Q/RPI/174: Land tax 1832; CCDRO, Hernhill rate book 1835–8.
18 KAO, Q/RPI/174.
19 PRO, IR 29/17/178.
20 M. Reed, 'The Peasantry of Nineteenth-Century England: A Neglected Class?' *History Workshop*, 18 (1984), 68–9.
21 CCDRO, Hernhill Overseers' Day Book 1821–30; Hernhill Sacramental Money 1810–61: Christmas relief lists.
22 KAO, PS/US7/315: Settlement Examinations for the Upper Division of the Lathe of Scray 1812–16.
23 KAO, Fa/JP 7/1, 15 August 1836.
24 Most of these details are derived from my family reconstitution files.
25 CCDRO, Hernhill Overseers' Day Book 1821–30.
26 KAO, PS/US19/134: Lathe of Scray Petty Sessions, Bastardy Cases 1825–32.
27 E. J. Hobsbawm and G. Rudé, *Captain Swing* (Harmondsworth, 1973), 209; D. Jones, 'Thomas Campbell Foster and the Rural Labourer: Incendiarism in East Anglia in the 1840s', *Social History*, 1 (1976), 20.
28 The comparisons are based on calculations from the Hernhill census of 1851.
29 For the poverty cycle, see K. D. M. Snell, *Annals of the Labouring Poor* (Cambridge, 1985), 358; M. Anderson, *Family Structure in Nineteenth-Century Lancashire* (Cambridge, 1971), 31–2, 201–2.
30 D. Thomson, 'Provision for the Elderly in England, 1830 to 1908' (University of Cambridge Ph.D. thesis, 1980), 62–3.
31 CCDRO, Hernhill Overseers' Day Book 1821–30; Hernhill Sacramental Money 1810–61: Christmas relief lists.

Notes 211

32 CCDRO, Hernhill Churchwardens' Accounts 1782–1853: assessments on annual rents, 1838.
33 This claim is based on a search of the Petty Sessions and Quarter Sessions records for the 1820s and 1830s (in KAO). I have also used the 'Manuscript Notebook/Account book of John Mears, Constable of Boughton 1825–36', held by the Faversham Society, Faversham. Arthur Percival very kindly arranged for the copying of the notebook and pointed out the names of several future rioters; a pamphlet by Joan White, *Boughton-under-Blean* (Faversham, 1983), first alerted me to the existence of this important source.
34 CCDRO, Hernhill Overseers' Day Book, 1821–30; Hernhill Highway Accounts 1813–27.
35 CCDRO, Hernhill Overseers' Day Book.
36 Ibid.
37 KAO, G/F RA1/51v–52: Faversham Union Outdoor Relief; G/F AM2/115: Minutes of the Board of Faversham Union 1836–8.
38 *The Times*, 10 August 1838.
39 See KAO, Q/SBe 143.
40 For the fates of the Branchetts, see KAO, G/F RAI/18v–19; G/F AM2/185; G/F Wr ml: Faversham Union Master's Report Book 1837–40; G/F W1 a2: Faversham Union Admission and Discharge Book 1835–43; G/F/W1 d1: Register of Deaths in Faversham Union Workhouse 1835–48.
41 Liardet, 'State of the Peasantry', 95.
42 CCDRO, Hernhill Overseers' Day Book.
43 See p. 78 above.
44 Yet again, family reconstitution provides the information, although journalists noted the family links of many of those involved in the events of 1838: *The Times*, 9 June 1838. For a recent reassessment of the role of kinship in English history, which stresses its strength, see D. Cressy, 'Kinship and Kin Interaction in Early Modern England', *Past and Present*, 113 (1986). For the role of kinship in the abortive rising of 1596, see J. Walter, 'A "Rising of the People"? The Oxfordshire Rising of 1596', *Past and Present*, 107 (1985), 105.
45 C. Calhoun, *The Question of Class Struggle. Social Foundations of Popular Radicalism during the Industrial Revolution* (Oxford, 1982), xii.
46 *The Times*, 6 June 1838, 11 August 1838.
47 CCDRO, Hernhill Highway Accounts 1813–27; Hernhill Overseers' Day Book.
48 Liardet, 'State of the Peasantry', 91.
49 Ibid., 92–3.
50 *Kent Herald*, 21 June 1838.
51 *The Times*, 5 June 1838.
52 Liardet, State of the Peasantry', 92–3.

212 Notes

53 Ibid., 91–2.
54 *The Times*, 5 June 1838.
55 Liardet, *State of the Peasantry*, 91, 93.
56 D. M. Valenze, *Prophetic Sons and Daughters. Female Preaching and Popular Religion in Industrial England* (Princeton, 1985).
57 T. C. Smout, 'New Evidence on Popular Religion and Literacy in Eighteenth-Century Scotland', *Past and Present*, 97 (1982), 121–3.
58 These figures are derived from the 1851 Census. For literacy in Hernhill, see pp. 61–3 above.
59 *The Times*, 9 June 1838.
60 Ibid.
61 See pp. 66–7 above.
62 *The Times*, 10 August 1838.
63 *The Times*, 7 June 1838.
64 PRO, HO/40/36/435–41; Liardet, 'State of the Peasantry', 95–6, 113.
65 See p. 159 below.
66 M. Agulhon, 'Working Class and Sociability in France before 1848', in P. Thane, G. Crossick, and R. Floud (eds.), *The Power of the Past* (Cambridge, 1984), 46.
67 Liardet, 'State of the Peasantry', 95–6.
68 Ibid., 96, 112.
69 *The Times*, 9 June 1838.
70 See p. 68 above.
71 D. Vincent, 'Reading in the Working-Class Home', in J. K. Walton and J. Walvin (eds.), *Leisure in Britain 1780–1939* (Manchester, 1983); Liardet, 'State of the Peasantry', 128–9.

Chapter 7

1 The above is based on KAO, U951 C37/5, 6, 9, 15, 31, 46: Knatchbull Papers; *Morning Chronicle*, 6 June 1838; *The Times*, 2 June 1838. See also P. G. Rogers, *Battle in Bossenden Wood* (Oxford, 1961), ch. 8.
2 *Morning Post*, 9 June 1838.
3 F. Liardet, 'State of the Peasantry in the County of Kent', in *Central Society of Education, Third Publication*, 1839 (reprint, London, 1968), 87–139.
4 P.-J. Hélias, *The Horse of Pride* (New Haven, Conn., 1978), xiv.
5 *Morning Post*, 7 June 1838.
6 *Morning Post*, 4 June 1838; *Sun*, 2 June 1838; *Morning Chronicle*, 5 June 1838, 7 June 1838; *The Times*, 7 June 1838. For the press and the battle, see N. Parratt, 'Battle in Bossenden Wood and the press' (University of Birmingham BA thesis, 1974), ch. 3.
7 Quoted in Parratt, 'Battle in Bossenden Wood', 50.
8 *Morning Chronicle*, 8 June 1838.

Notes 213

9 *Northern Star*, 23 June 1838, 30 June 1838, 14 July 1838.
10 KAO, U951 C37/40 and PRO, HO/40/36/435–41 provide a detailed list of 'persons concerned in the late Riot'. See also *The Times*, 5 June 1838.
11 *Canterbury Press and County News*, 23 June 1888; I. Smith, 'The Courtenay Riots in 1838', *Home Counties Magazine*, 5 (1903), 268.
12 *Kent Herald*, 7 June 1838.
13 KAO, U951 C37/3; PRO, MH 32/70: 3 June 1838.
14 *Kentish Observer*, 7 June 1838; KAO, U951 C37/2; PRO, HO 40/36/34.
15 *Kent Herald*, 7 June 1838.
16 Ibid.; *Globe*, 4 June 1838.
17 *Weekly Dispatch*, 10 June 1838; *Kent Herald*, 7 June 1838; *Morning Post*, 9 June 1838; *Canterbury Press and County News*, 23 June 1888.
18 *Kent Herald*, 7 June 1838; *Canterbury Press and County News*, 23 June 1888.
19 KAO, U951 C37/28–9; *The Times*, 6 June 1838.
20 *Morning Chronicle*, 6 June 1838.
21 *The Times*, 6 June 1838.
22 Ibid.; *Morning Chronicle*, 6 June 1838.
23 Oral testimony of Elizabeth Arnold in 1910. Her husband was watching the grave and was told, according to her story, of Courtenay's body's disappearance by one of the Culvers. See *Kentish Express and Ashford News*, 12 February 1910. I am grateful to Sandys Dawes for the clipping.
24 *The Times*, 6 June 1838 (the newspaper accounts got the ages of the dead slightly wrong); KAO, G/F AM3/7–8: Minutes of the Board of Faversham Union 1838–42.
25 CCDRO, Hernhill and Boughton-under-Blean burials, 5 and 6 June 1838.
26 *The Times*, 6 June 1838; *Morning Chronicle*, 6 June 1838; *The Times*, 12 June 1838.
27 PRO, MH 12/5054: Ministry of Health Poor Law Union Papers, Faversham Correspondence, no. 190 (1836–9): 23 June 1838.
28 *Northern Star*, 11 August 1838.
29 *Northern Star*, 14 July 1838.
30 D. Hay, 'Property, Authority and the Criminal Law', in D. Hay and others, *Albion's Fatal Tree* (Harmondsworth, 1977), p. 42.
31 *The Times*, 5 June 1838.
32 For Denman, see J. Arnould, *Memoir of Thomas, First Lord Denman*, 2 vols. (London, 1873).
33 *The Times*, 8 August 1838.
34 *The Times*, 10 August 1838; PRO, ASSI 31/28.
35 See Arnould, *Memoir*, i, 111–12.

214 Notes

36 *The Times*, 8 August 1838.
37 Cf. *The Times*, 8 August 1838, 10 August 1838, 17 August 1838 (report on Parliamentary Select Committee); *Kentish Observer*, 7 June 1838; KAO, U951 C37/2–3; PRO, HO 40/36/366.
38 *The Times*, 11 August 1838.
39 See the accounts of Knatchbull and Poore in KAO, U951 C37/2, 3, 7, 8; and PRO, ASSI 36/3. For the rules governing the use of armed force against civilians, see D. Philips, 'Riots and Public Order in the Black Country, 1835–1860', in J. Stevenson and R. Quinault (eds.), *Popular Protest and Public Order* (London, 1974), ch. 4; W. Nippel, ' "Reading the Riot Act" ', *History and Anthropology*, 1 (1985).
40 PRO, HO 6/23: Circuit Letters, 1838.
41 *The Times*, 11 August 1838.

Chapter 8

1 P. G. Rogers, *Battle in Bossenden Wood* (Oxford, 1961), p. 197.
2 Even in 1988! See *Hernhill News and St Michael's Newsletter*, May 1988: 'John Nichols Tom (alias Sir William Courtenay) by any standards was a mentally unstable character, to put it mildly. A liar, a perjurer, a murderer, a blasphemer—he was all these things, and more. Despite his obvious charisma, he was not a person worthy of our respect; his life could well be ignored. But his actions caused more suffering than we today can easily appreciate. Because of him, men were killed and families rent apart. Hernhill suffered tremendous sadness, and during the next few weeks we shall be remembering those whose lives were made so utterly wretched, not in any sense by way of celebration, but rather commemoration.'
3 KAO, G/F W1 r2/38, 70: Faversham Union Indoor Relief Lists 1838–40; G/FRA1/18v–19: Faversham Union Outdoor Relief; G/F W1 a2: Faversham Union Admission and Discharge Book 1835–43; G/F W1 d1: Register of Deaths in Faversham Union Workhouse 1835–48. Details on ages and births and deaths come from my family reconstitution files.
4 See the Census of 1851 for Seasalter and Faversham (PRO), the Graveney baptisms (CCDRO); KAO, G/F W1 a2; G/FRA1/52v–53.
5 The following, unless otherwise indicated, is based on the PRO census returns 1841–81 and family reconstitution.
6 Somerset House, Will of Noah Miles, 1858.
7 *Faversham Standard Advertiser*, 1 April 1854. I owe this reference to Harold Kay and Arthur Percival.
8 *Canterbury Press and County News*, 30 June 1888.
9 That is in Dunkirk, Hernhill, or Boughton-under-Blean; most stayed in Hernhill.

Notes 215

10 See Hernhill Census, 1841.
11 KAO, PRC 32/71/293: Will of Sarah Spratt, 1849.
12 Collection of Sandys Dawes, Mt. Ephraim (Hernhill): Farming Account Book of Crockham Farm 1837–46.
13 CCDRO, Hernhill Tithe Book, 1853: 'The Rev'd. C. Handley's Account of the Riot', 14.
14 J. W. Horsley, *I Remember* (London, 1912), 4. I owe this reference to the kindness of yet another J. W. Horsley.
15 U. H. Smith, 'Fallow Ground', *Kent Life*, November 1969.
16 KAO, U2394 Z1: Family scrap book of Revd. J. W. Horsley.
17 Ibid.; U. Warren, 'History of the Horsley Family' (unpublished typescript in possession of J. W. Horsley, Steyning, Sussex). J. W. Horsley of Steyning also has a lovely handwritten and watercolour-illustrated nineteenth-century book, 'The History of John William Horsley', which tells of the minister's son's early years in Dunkirk.
18 KAO, U2394 Z1; Warren 'History'.
19 PRO, HO 129/67/19, 30: Religious Census 1851; B. I. Coleman, 'Southern England in the Census of Religious Worship, 1851', *Southern History*, 5 (1983), 183–4. Coleman calculated an Anglican index of attendance of 37.7% of the population for Kent and 39.2% for the census district of Faversham. My calculations for Hernhill and Dunkirk (in the Faversham district) are 43.4 and 48.2% respectively.
20 These figures are arrived at by matching my family reconstitution forms against the Census of 1851 to provide a focal point for generational change; the literacy rates are derived from the marriage registers.
21 Rogers, *Battle in Bossenden Wood*, 202.
22 G. Rudé, *Protest and Punishment* (Oxford, 1978), 212–13.
23 State Library of Tasmania, CON 31/32, 36, 47: Convict Records; CCDRO, 'Rev'd. C. Handley's Account of the Riot', 14 ff.
24 KAO, U2593 B45: Kent Fire Insurance Company Farm Fire Losses, 1830–53.
25 A. Armstrong, *Farmworkers: A Social and Economic History 1770–1980* (London, 1988), chs. 4–5.
26 KAO, PS/US 10: Lathe of Scray Petty Sessions 1839–45: 15 Oct. 1893, 5 Oct. 1843.
27 See KAO, PS/US 10; PS/US 11: Lathe of Scray Petty Sessions 1864–8: 4 Oct. 1866 (for Coachworth).
28 This observation is based on the Quarter Sessions and Assize records for the 1840s and 1850s.
29 *Kent and Sussex Times*, November–December 1878, esp. 16 Nov., 14 Dec., 21 Dec., 28 Dec. 1878. See also F. Carlton, ' "A Substantial and Sterling Friend to the Labouring Man": The Kent and Sussex Labourers' Union 1872–1895' (University of Sussex M.Phil. thesis, 1977), 208 (map); and her 'The Kent and Sussex Labourers' Union

1872–95', in A. Charlesworth (ed.), *An Atlas of Rural Protest in Britain 1548–1900* (London, 1983).

Chapter 9

1 [R. Cobb], 'A Very English Rising', *Times Literary Supplement*, 11 September 1969.
2 R. Wells, 'The Development of the English Rural Proletariat and Social Protest, 1700–1850', *Journal of Peasant Studies*, 6 (1979); A. Charlesworth, 'The Development of the English Rural Proletariat ... A Comment', *Journal of Peasant Studies*, 8 (1980); Wells, 'Social Conflict ... A Rejoinder', *Journal of Peasant Studies*, 8 (1981); M. Reed, 'Social Change and Social Conflict in Nineteenth Century England', *Journal of Peasant Studies*, 12 (1984); D. R. Mills, 'Peasants and Conflict in Nineteenth-Century Rural England', *Journal of Peasant Studies*, 15 (1988).
3 J. Bohstedt, 'Gender, Household and Community Politics: Women in English Riots 1790–1810', *Past and Present*, 120 (1988).
4 J. W. Scott, *Gender and the Politics of History* (New York, 1988), ch. 4.
5 E. J. Hobsbawm and G. Rudé, *Captain Swing* (Harmondsworth, 1973), xxii, 44. But see K. D. M. Snell, *Annals of the Labouring Poor* (Cambridge, 1985), 12.
6 Hobsbawm and Rudé, *Captain Swing*, 251.
7 A. Everitt, *The Pattern of Rural Dissent: The Nineteenth Century* (Leicester, 1972), 25; D. Vincent, 'Reading in the Working-Class Home', in J. Walton and J. Walvin (eds.), *Leisure in Britain 1780–1939* (Manchester, 1983), 212; G. Rudé, *Protest and Punishment* (Oxford, 1978), 120.
8 R. Wells, 'Resistance to the New Poor Law in the Rural South', in M. Chase (ed.), *The New Poor Law* (Middlesborough Centre Occasional Papers, no. 1, 1985), 25, 32.
9 *PP* xviii (1837–8), pt. 3, 196.
10 E. Yeo, 'Christianity in Chartist Struggle 1838–1842', *Past and Present*, 91 (1981).
11 N. Scotland, *Methodism and the Revolt of the Field* (Gloucester, 1981).
12 For the Wells debate, see n. 2 above. For Newby, see C. Bell and H. Newby, 'The Sources of Variation in Agricultural Workers' Images of Society', *Sociological Review*, 21 (1973); I. Carter, 'Agricultural Workers in the Class Structure: A Critical Note', *Sociological Review*, 22 (1974); A. Howkins, 'Structural Conflict and the Farmworker', *Journal of Peasant Studies*, 4 (1977); H. Newby, *The Deferential Worker* (London, 1977).

13 A. Armstrong, *Farmworkers: A Social and Economic History 1770–1980* (London, 1988), 87, 249.
14 J. C. Scott, *Weapons of the Weak: Everyday Forms of Peasant Resistance* (New Haven, Conn., 1985), p. 246. My debt to Scott will be obvious throughout this chapter.
15 Quoted in H. Newby, *Country Life: A Social History of Rural England* (London, 1987), 82.
16 Wells, 'Development of the English Rural Proletariat', 120.
17 *The Times*, 7 June 1838.
18 Newby, *Deferential Worker*, 369.
19 G. Bourne [Sturt], *Change in the Village* (Harmondsworth, 1984), 63 (first published in 1912).
20 *The Times*, 4 June 1838.
21 Bourne [Sturt], *Change in the Village*, 64.
22 K. Wrightson, *English Society 1580–1680* (London, 1982), 58; D. Roberts, *Paternalism in Early Victorian England* (London, 1979).
23 *Kentish Observer*, 7 June 1838; *The Times*, 11 August 1838.
24 F. Liardet, 'State of the Peasantry in the County of Kent', in *Central Society of Education, Third Publication*, 1839 (reprint, London, 1968), 127.
25 Ibid., 134–6.
26 Vincent, 'Reading in the Working-Class Home', 210, 212.
27 Liardet, 'State of the Peasantry', 126–7.
28 See the discussions in J. V. Femia, *Gramsci's Political Thought* (Oxford, 1981), ch. 2; E. P. Thompson, 'Eighteenth-Century English Society: Class Struggle without Class?', *Social History*, 3 (1978); E. P. Thompson, 'Patrician Society, Plebeian Culture', *Journal of Social History*, 7 (1974); Scott, *Weapons of the Weak*, ch. 8.
29 Scott, *Weapons of the Weak*, 325; Newby, *Deferential Worker*, 28.
30 Liardet, 'State of the Peasantry', 98, 133–4.
31 Hobsbawm and Rudé, *Captain Swing*, 34.
32 Ibid., 178.
33 Ibid., 208; J. Stevenson, *Popular Disturbances in England 1700–1870* (London, 1979), 243.
34 See D. Thompson, *The Chartists* (London, 1984), ch. 2.
35 K. Thomas, 'The Meaning of Literacy in Early Modern England', in G. Baumann (ed.), *The Written Word: Literacy in Transition* (Oxford, 1985), 105.
36 J. Scott, 'Everyday Forms of Peasant Resistance', *Journal of Peasant Studies*, 13 (1986).
37 Reed, 'Social Change and Social Conflict', 115.
38 See pp. 75–6, 172 above.
39 See p. 134 above.
40 KAO, Fa/ JP 7/1: Lathe of Scray Petty Sessions 1832–9: 3 April 1833, 19 Sept. 1833, 9 April 1834.

41 See p. 80 above.
42 e.g. C. Tilly, 'Britain Creates the Social Movement', in J. E. Cronin and J. Schneer (eds.), *Social Conflict and the Political Order in Modern Britain* (London, 1982).
43 See n. 2 above.
44 Quoted on p. 102 above.

INDEX

Adams, Peter (rioter) 133, 141
Adams, Thomas (junior) (rioter) 133, 141
Adams, Thomas (senior) 30
Adley, James 69
Adlow, James 52
age structure: of parish 10, 12; of protesters 77, 135–6
agricultural labourers 8, 23, 32, 35–9, 41, 44–68, 78, 81, 92, 93, 106, 108, 109, 115, 118, 121, 130, 131–2, 134, 135, 136, 139–40, 144, 146, 152, 159, 168, 170, 171, 172, 175, 176, 177, 179–89
Ainsworth, William 127
Anderson, M. 36
Anslow, Sarah 35
Anti-Poor Law rioters: (1835) 73, 77–8, 85, 88, 104, 108, 116, 135, 178, 180, 188; (1838) Ch. 4, esp. 88, 104, 137–41, 151, 152, 175
Archer, J. E. 2
Armstrong, A. 49, 172, 179, 188
Armstrong, Major 92, 93, 100
Arnold, Elizabeth 92
Australia 54, 171–2

Badlesmere 72, 153
Baker, Mary 131–2
Baker, Stephen (rioter) 131–2, 141, 144, 158, 166
Baker, Thomas 131–2, 141, 166
Baldock, William 23, 92
Bapchild 67, 77, 88
Barnett, Mary 133
Barnfield Farm 27, 28
Battle in Bosenden Wood 1, 92–100
beershops 15, 34, 44, 49, 54–8, 59, 71, 133, 144, 166–7, 186
Benbow, William 105, 106, 107, 112
Bennett, Lt. Henry Boswell 92, 93, 100, 153, 155, 159, 164
Berkeley Lodge 20
Berry, Thomas 32, 66, 74
Berry, William 66, 170
Bessborough 15, 55, 139, 141, 143, 144, 166, 167; Bessborough Farm 23, 24
Bible Christians 66–7, 106, 146
Birmingham 111, 119

Bishop, George (incendiarist) 75, 77
Bishop, George (rioter) 134, 136, 141, 166
Blake, William 123
Blean: area 23, 72, 175, 181; Forest 8, 72, 88, 170, 172; Parish 18, 55, 66, 71, 74, 75, 77
Bobbing 73
Bodle, Thomas 66
Bohstedt, J. 176
books, see literature
Bosenden Farm 32, 33, 88, 91, 92, 145; Bosenden Wood 92–100
Boughton-under Blean 8, 15, 18, 20, 34, 39, 50, 55, 58, 59, 61, 62, 63, 66, 67, 68, 71, 73, 74, 85, 88, 103, 112–13, 115, 116, 122, 130, 131, 132, 133, 134, 140, 141, 152, 153, 158, 159, 165, 167, 168, 170, 172, 175, 177, 181, 185, 188; Boughton Hill 7, 15, 20, 73, 80, 130, 157; Boughton Street 18, 58, 71, 72, 74, 170
Branchett, Benjamin 165
Branchett, Elizabeth 165
Branchett, George (rioter) 100, 136, 140–1
Branchett, Henry 55
Branchett, John 72
Branchett, Mary 165
Branchett, Sarah, see Gower, Sarah
Branchett, William 130, 136, 146
Brandreth, Jeremiah 116, 163
Bredgar 23
Brenley House 20
bridal pregnancy 12, 135
Bridges, Sir John 23
Bristol riots (1831) 59, 115, 161
British Lion 115, 119–20
Brook Farm 27
Brown, Daniel (rioter) 130
Brown, John 130
Brown, Thomas 130
Browning family 66
Browning, Edward 27
Brunger, John 72
Bullmore, William Henry 111
Burford, Emma 132
Burford, William (rioter) 69, 132, 136, 147, 158

220 Index

burials 42–3, 155–9; see also infant mortality
Butcher, Edward 55
Butcher, Jemima 30, 41
Butcher, John 27, 167
Butcher, Olive 44–5
Butcher, Stephen 27, 41
Butcher, Susannah 58

Calhoun, C. 141
Canterbury 7, 8, 27, 59, 66, 67, 71, 72, 74, 85, 92, 112, 113, 115, 117, 121, 127, 134, 146, 152, 153, 155, 167, 172, 175, 189
Carlile, Richard 161
Carr, Edward 36
Castel, R. 124
Central Society of Education 151–2, 184
Charing 132
Charlesworth, A. 175
Chartham 59, 66, 134, 167, 172
Chartism, Chartists 2, 93, 99, 104, 116, 118, 151, 160, 177, 178, 179, 187
Chase, Malcolm 105
Cherry Orchard Farm 27, 29, 66
children 12–15, 35–6, 39, 43–8, 51–2, 59–61, 64, 68, 80, 136–7, 146, 179
Chilham 66, 135, 172
church 58–9, 64–6, 145, 147, 157–8, 170–1, 178, 179, 188–9
church band 64–5, 147, 186
Church and State (beerhouse) 55, 58
Coachworth, Hannah 166
Coachworth, William (junior) 172
Coachworth, William (rioter) 93, 136, 140, 166
Coatsworth, William, see Coachworth, William
Cobb, John 132
Cobb, R. 175
Cobbett, William 7, 8, 161
Coleman's Land Farm, see Cherry Orchard Farm
Cosway, Sir William 115
Courtenay, Sir William (impostor): and the rising of 1838, Ch. 4; earlier life, Ch. 5 144–5, 151, 152, 155–7, 163, 165, 178–9, 181, 188
Courtenay, William Viscount 112
Cozens, Daniel 167
craftsmen 27, 30, 34–5, 37, 39, 59–60, 64, 66, 73, 79, 81, 110, 112, 121, 127, 131, 133, 134, 177, 187

crime 49, 59, 70–3, 82, 138, 176; see also, woodstealing, poaching, smuggling, social crime
Crockham Farm 27, 30, 32, 39, 51, 168
Culver, Richard 70, 71
Culver, Sarah 88, 107, 145
Culver, William 32, 41, 88, 145
Curling, Charity 132, 167
Curling, Edward Rigden (rioter) 132, 136, 164, 167
Curling, Edward (farmer) 23, 27, 30, 32, 39, 52, 54, 71, 74, 88, 90, 105, 121, 144, 168, 181
Curling, Edward (junior) 168
Curling, George 39
Curling, John (blacksmith) 30, 39
Curling, John (farmer) 32
Curling, Sophia 30
Curling, William (blacksmith) 41
Curling, William (labourer) 30, 32, 36

Dalton, John 71
Dalton, Thomas 136
Dargate 10, 15, 18, 30, 38, 55, 56, 58, 66, 67, 133, 141, 142, 144, 146, 166, 168; Dargate Common 72, 133, 144; Dargate Farm 23, 66; Dargate House 26, 27
Davidoff, L. 39
Davington 71, 88
Davis, N. Z. 127
Dawes family 20, 188
Dean and Chapter of Canterbury 18
demagogues 110, 116–19, 126, 179
Denman, Lord Chief Justice 104, 160–1, 163–4, 184
Denstrode 10, 15, 18, 55, 58, 77
Dering, Sir Edward 18, 20
Dickens, Charles 125, 127, 155
diet 49–50, 80
Doddington 66, 75, 77, 88
Dove (beerhouse) 55, 56, 144, 166–7, 168, 169
Dunkirk, Ville of 7–23, 32–64, 66–74, 77, 79, 81, 85–9, 91–9, 100, 130, 131, 132, 134, 135, 140, 146, 147, 152, 153, 165, 168, 170–1, 172, 175–6, 177, 178, 181, 182, 185, 186, 187, 188
Dyke, John 76

East Anglian riots (1816) 108

Index

Eastling 75, 88
education 60–4, 68, 184; see also schools, literacy
Eldridge, Richard 30
elections: (1832): 85, 115–16, 117–18, 119–20, 132; (1837) 39, 132
electorate 39, 115
Ellenden Wood 72
Elmstead 12
enclosure 10
Epps, George 36
Everitt, A. 7, 177
Eve, Mary 141
Eve, Samuel (rioter) 141
Evington 112
Exton, Lydia 70

Fairbrook Farm 39, 40, 133
family size 12–15, 48–9, 193 n. 22
family structure 12–15
farmers 14, 19, 23–34, 36, 37, 39–41, 51, 55, 59, 64, 66, 71, 72, 74, 76, 79, 80, 81, 88, 92, 104–5, 121, 127, 131, 146, 168, 171, 172, 175, 179, 180, 182, 187, 189
farm servants 35, 42, 50–1, 105, 131, 134, 187
Faversham 8, 23, 59, 66, 67, 72, 74, 75, 76, 80, 81, 88, 116, 131, 135, 147, 153, 157, 159, 160, 165, 167, 172, 182
Fielden, John 152
Fifth of November 59
Foad, Alex (rioter) 30, 32, 99, 132–3, 136, 141, 147, 164, 166, 168
Foad, Mary 166; see also Barnett, Mary
Foad, Mary (junior) 168
Ford, Thomas 23, 74
Fordwich, Viscount 115
Foreman, Elizabeth 66
Foreman, John 27, 66, 105, 139, 144
Foreman, Richard (rioter) 134, 136, 164, 166, 168
Foreman, Sarah 166; see also Longbottom, Sarah
Forester's Lodge Farm 32
Forge Farmhouse 31
Fostall, see Bessborough
Foster, William (rioter) 136, 140, 144, 158, 166
Foucault, M. 123
Francis, George 39, 41, 122, 124, 128–9, 133

Friendly Society 186
Fuller, John 135

Gate Inn 55
gentry 20–3, 88, 92, 103, 106, 115, 121, 160, 180–1, 182
geographic mobility 58–60, 134–5, 186
Gipps, George 23
Goodwin, Edward 166–7
Goodwin, James (rioter) 55, 77, 133–4, 136, 139, 141, 144, 166–7, 168
Goodwin, Mary Ann 167
Gower, Sarah 140
Graveney 88, 167, 168
Gravesend 59, 155
Greenstreet 66, 73
Griggs, Ann 134
Griggs, George (rioter) 99, 134, 147, 158
Griggs, Thomas (rioter) 99, 134, 141, 164, 167, 168
Griggs, William 134
Groves, Col. Percy 20, 88, 189

Hackington 112
Hadlow, Charles (rioter) 78, 133, 136, 139, 141, 144, 147, 167
Hadlow, Henry (rioter) 133, 168
Hadlow, John (senior) (rioter) 30, 41, 92, 133, 136, 144, 167–8
Hadlow, John (junior) (rioter) 133, 168
Hadlow, Lydia (supporter of Courtenay) 92, 107, 133, 144, 145, 167–8
Hadlow, Olive 32
Hadlow, Tamsen 167
Hales, Sir Edward 112
Hall, C. 39
hamlets 15–18, 141–4, 186
Hammond, William 23
Handley, Cassandra 64
Handley, Charles 20, 85, 103, 115, 118, 122, 130, 137, 145, 147, 153, 155, 157, 158, 160, 168, 172
Harbledown 15, 18, 55, 58, 59, 66, 74, 172
Harney, George Julian 118
Harrison, J. F. C. 1, 107, 125
Harvey, John 141, 144, 165
Harvey, Phineas (or Finnis) (rioter) 141, 144, 158, 165
Harvey, William 135
Hasted, E. 8

Index

Hawkins, George 130
Hawkins, James 52
Hay, D. 160
Head, Sir Francis 79
health 50, 78, 79, 179
Hélias, P. J. 152
Hernhill 7, 8, 10–32, 34–74, 77–9, 81, 82, 85–8, 90, 92, 102, 103, 105, 122, 130, 131–48, 152, 153, 155, 157–9, 165–8, 172, 175–8, 181, 185, 186, 188–9
Hernhill rising (1838) Ch. 4, Ch. 6, Ch. 9
High Street 167
Hills, Charles (rioter) 136, 164
Hills, Sarah, see Wraight, Sarah
Hilton family 23
Hilton, Giles 72, 74
Hobsbawm, E. J. 2, 37, 73, 165, 176, 177, 187
Honey Hill 77; Honey Hill Farm 72
Honywood, Sir John Courtenay 112
hops 7, 32, 45, 48, 51, 52, 70, 71, 82
Horsley, John William 170–1
Horsley, J. W. (junior) 168
household: budgets 52–4, 82; literacy 64; structure 12–15, 49, 136–7; violence 68–9
housing 48–9
Howland, George 35, 69
Howland, Jane 35
Hunt, 'Captain' 116
Hunt, Henry 110, 112, 116, 117, 118, 119
Hurst Wood 72
Hyder, William 23, 74

identity 127–9
illegitimacy 12
illiteracy, see literacy
incendiarism, incendiarists 73–7, 102, 104, 135, 172
infant mortality 12
Irving, Edward 107, 112
Irvingites 107

James, George 79
James, Mary 70
Jarman, Edward 20
Jefferies, Richard 54–5
Johncock, Mary 71
Johncock, Susan 71
Johnson, Samuel 123
Jones, D. 2, 108

Journal of Peasant Studies 175
Jubilee 105–6, 109

Kain, R. 10
Kay, William 27, 105, 144, 168
Kean, Edmund 126
Kennett, William 130, 136
Kent and County Hospital 50
Kent County Lunatic Asylum 85, 107, 116, 122, 124, 129, 151
Kent Fire Insurance Company 74, 75, 172
Kent Herald 115, 152, 153
Kentish Observer 81, 125
Kent and Sussex Labourers' Union 172
kin 35, 39, 41, 141, 145, 158–9, 176, 186
King's Arms (public house) 58
Kingsdown 10, 67
Knatchbull, Sir Edward 115, 151
Knatchbull family 20, 23
Knatchbull, Norton 23, 86, 88, 92, 93, 100, 151, 160, 181
Knight, Ann 167; *see also* Millington, Ann
Knight, William (rioter) 134, 136, 139, 140, 141, 144, 167
Knott, J. 2

labourers 37, 41, 61, 66, 70, 71, 72, 73, 77, 82, 85, 86, 92, 100, 103, 104–5, 107, 108, 109, 110, 130, 131, 151, 152, 159, 171, 172, 175; *see also* agricultural labourers
Lade, John Price 20, 74
Lambert family 23
Lambert's Land Farm 32, 50–1
land redistribution 103, 105, 109, 176
landholdings 18–32, 36–7, 103
landownership 18–19, 20–32, 36–7, 103
Laslett, P. 12
Launceston 110
Lavender Farm 23, 25, 39, 66, 92, 133, 167
Lee, Arthur 72
Lenham 75
Liardet, Frederick 7, 8, 20, 36, 55, 60, 61, 62, 63, 64, 72, 73, 130, 132, 137, 138, 140, 145, 147, 148, 152, 178, 182–5, 187
Lion, see *British Lion*
literacy 35, 37, 39, 61–4, 77, 135, 146, 147, 171, 186–7

Index

literature 63–4, 68, 127, 147–8, 187
Liverpool 111, 112, 122
London 59, 67, 81, 106, 107, 112, 119
London Democratic Association 152
Longbottom, Sarah 134
Lower Hardres 175
Lowerson, J. 2
Luddenham 66
Lynsted 77

McCalman, I. 106
machine-breaking 74, 76
madness 111, 122–5
Maidstone 59, 81, 111, 147
Maidstone Journal 100
Manchester 152
marriage: age 12, 193 n. 20; patterns 35, 37, 39, 41, 42
Marx, Karl 179, 185
Mears, John 58, 70, 88
Mears, Nicholas 69, 70, 88, 91, 92, 109, 130, 153
Mears, Thomas, *see* Tyler, Thomas Mears
Merthyr riots (1831) 108
Methodists 64, 146–7, 170; Wesleyan 66, 67, 146–7, 168, 171; Primitive 66–7, 105
Miles, Harriett 41
Miles, James (rioter) 133, 135, 136, 141, 167, 168
Miles, Mary 134, 167
Miles, Noah (rioter) 30, 41, 55, 132, 133, 141, 167
Milgate, Ann 70
millenarianism 85, 92, 105–7, 109, 144–5, 155, 175, 177
Millington, Ann 134
mobility, *see* geographic mobility
mobilization (of protest) 74, 77–8, 85–8, 100–9, 121, Ch. 6 esp. 136–48, Ch. 9.
monomania 111, 124, 125
Morning Chronicle 49, 53, 103, 155, 157
Morning Post 152
Mount Ephraim 20, 21–2
Murton, 'Major' 116
Murton, Thomas 23

Nash Court 20
Nayler, James 125
Neame, Charles 23
Neame family 23

Neame, John 74
neighbourhood 15–18, 54–5, 58, 59, 73, 141–4, 158–9, 176, 186
New Poor Law (1834) 53, 77–82, 85, 88, 104, 108, 137–41, 151, 152, 159, 160, 161, 175, 180, 182
New Zealand 54
Newby, H. 179, 181, 185
Newcastle 152
Newman, Edward (rioter) 88
Newnham 67, 75, 77, 88
Newport rising (1839) 99, 108, 109, 151
Noah's Ark (beerhouse) 55, 57, 144, 167
Northern Liberator 104
Northern Star 93
Nutting, Mary, *see* Eve, Mary
Nutting, William (rioter) 133, 141, 146

Oak Apple Day (29 May) 59, 85, 102–3, 130, 186
Obelkevich, J. 23, 27, 55, 64
O'Brien, Bronterre 93, 152, 159
O'Connor, Feargus 116, 117, 118, 129, 152
Old Poor Law 78–9, 138–41
Oldham 152
Oliver, W. H. 107
'open' and 'close' parishes 18–19
orality, oral culture 63–4, 187
Ospringe 59, 73, 74, 88, 103, 133, 140, 166

Packman, Adman 70
Packman, Eliza 45
Packman, Harriett 166
Packman, William (rioter) 136, 139–40, 141, 144, 166, 168
Packman, William (incendiarist) 75–7
Packman brothers (incendiarists) 75–7, 181
Parren, Mr 75, 76
Past and Present 176

patriotism 120, 121
Payne, Alfred 103
peasantry, *see* small farmers
Peel, Robert 151
Pegden, Christopher 72; *see also* Tong, Christopher
Pell, James 30
Pell, John 134
Penenden Heath 76, 77, 181

Index

Penny Satirist 93, 152
Pentrich rising (1817) 108, 116, 151, 161
Peterloo massacre (1819) 99, 120, 151, 153, 161
Plough Inn 74
poaching 49, 59, 72, 73, 108, 138, 172
poor, poverty 24, 43, 72, 78–82, 85, 102, 104, 106, 109, 112, 118, 121, 134, 136–41, 144, 158, 159, 165, 166, 176, 179
poor-relief 10, 43, 77–82, 132, 134, 137–41, 144, 158, 159, 165
Poore, Revd John 23, 88, 92, 93, 100, 104, 153, 160, 164
population 10–12, 41
Porter, R. 123
poverty cycle 136–7
Prendergast, Lt. 93
prenuptial pregnancy, *see* bridal pregnancy
Preston 23, 67
Price, William (rioter) 136, 161–3, 164, 171
protest 1–3, 73–8, Ch. 4, 172, Ch. 9
public houses 15, 34, 44, 54–8, 59, 153, 155

Queen Caroline Affair (1820) 161

Ralph, Susanna 10
Ralph, Thomas (junior) 10
Ralph, Thomas (senior) 10
Ramsgate 153
recruitment march 85–9, 100, 101–9
Reculver 133
Red Lion (public house) (Dunkirk) 55, 74, 153, 155, 157
Red Lion (public house) (Hernhill) 55, 56
Reed, M. 51, 133, 175, 187
Reform Bill (1832) 112, 115, 119
Reid, Captain 92
religion 61, 64–8, 88, 106–7, 111, 120, 122, 123, 125, 144–8, 177–8, 188; *see also* church, millenarianism
rents 53, 54, 73, 76, 82, 103, 132, 138
Richardson, T. L. 81
Rigden, Edward 39, 66, 74
Rivière, Pierre 123–4
Robin, J. 12
Rochester 116
Rodmersham 67, 77
Rogers, P. G. 1, 85, 130, 165

Rose Inn 74, 112, 115
Rudé, G. 1, 37, 73, 171, 175, 176, 187, 187
Russell, Lord John 104, 151
Rye, Charlotte 165
Rye, Harriett 165
Rye, Jane 139
Rye, Sarah 132, 165
Rye, William (junior) 165
Rye, William (rioter) 78, 132, 136, 139, 140, 144, 158, 165

St Columb 110
St Dunstan's 58, 115
Sand Hole 168
Sandwich 134
Schofield, R. 61
schools, schooling 39, 59–61, 68, 146, 171
Scotland, N. 178
Scott, James 179, 185, 187
Scott, Joan 176
Scull, A. 123
Seasalter 72, 134, 165
selling 72, 88, 131, 134, 172; Selling Court 74
servants 14, 15, 20, 39, 42, 44
settlement examinations 10, 59
Sheerness 67
Sheldwich 72, 88
Shepherd, Julius 23, 30, 92, 133, 144, 155
Sheppey 73
Ship (public house) 55, 58
Simmons, Alfred 53
Sittingbourne 10, 23, 51, 67, 88, 147
small farmers 30–4, 36, 37, 41, 73, 78, 85, 103, 130, 132–3, 168, 188
Smout, T. C. 146
smuggling 8, 72–3, 116, 121, 138
Snell, K. D. M. 45, 80
Snoulton, Osborne (junior) 27, 105, 144
Snoulton, Osborne (senior) 27, 74
social crime 73
Sondes, Lord 20, 58, 72, 74, 88
South Street (Boughton) 58
Southcott, Joanna 125
Spence, Thomas 105–6, 107
Spenceans 105–6, 112, 205–6 n. 51
Spratt, Henry (rioter) 136, 141
Spratt, John (rioter) 37, 38, 136, 139, 141, 168
Spratt, Sarah 37, 38, 168

Spratt, William (rioter) 136, 141
Springett, W. J. 171
Squirrels (public house) 58
Stalisfield 75
standards of living 50–4
Standen, John 35
Standen, William 35
Staple Street 15, 31, 35, 39, 55, 66, 157, 167
Stevens, William 130–1
Stevenson, J. 1, 187
Stone, Edward 20
Sturt, George 181, 182
Sunday school 64, 66, 68, 147
Swalecliffe 67
Swing rising (1830) 3, 55, 73–7, 85, 108, 109, 116, 135, 161, 175, 177, 180, 181, 186, 188

Tappenden, Charles 58
Tasmania 171–2
Teynham 67, 77, 172
Thomas, K. 187
Thompson, E. P. 1, 176
Thomson, D. 79, 137
Thorne, James 67
Three Horse Shoes (public house) 55
Throwley 66, 67, 75, 77, 88
Tilly, C. 2
Times, The 74, 100, 104, 147, 157, 158
Tom, Catherine 111
Tom, Charity 110
Tom, John, *see* Courtenay, Sir William
Tom, William 110
Tong, Christopher, 70; *see also* Pegden, Christopher
trade unionism 172, 177, 178, 179, 188
tradesmen 34, 37, 55, 77, 78, 81, 112, 121, 131, 133–4, 189
trial of the rioters 159–64
Truro 110, 111
Tufnell, E. C. 153
Tyler, Thomas Mears (rioter) 78, 133, 141, 159, 161–3, 164, 171

unemployment 42–3, 53, 80–2, 137–8, 172
Upchurch 73

Valenze, D. 145
vestry 27
Vincent, D. 177, 184

Vincent, D. 177, 184
violence: in parishes 55, 58, 69–70, 179–80; of protesters 77–8, 108–9, 138, 175–6, 186

Wadebridge 110
wages 51, 52–4, 74, 76, 81, 108, 131, 132, 172, 179
Walter, J. 103, 109
Ward, Ann 39
Waterham 15, 92, 132, 167; Waterham Farm 15, 23, 26
Watson, Richard 115
Way Street 15; Way Street Farm 23
Wellbrook 20
Wells, R. 2, 175, 179, 180
Westgate 10; *see also* Dunkirk
Westwell 132
White Horse (public house) 58, 153
white witch, witches 50, 107
Whitstable 59, 66, 71, 72, 114, 131, 166, 167
Whitsun 103, 108
Wildish, Mary 55
Wilks, John 23
Williams, R. 179
Wills, Edward 30
Wills family 30
Wills, Helen Courtenay 167
Wills, Lucy 133, 167, 172
Wills, Lydia, *see* Hadlow, Lydia
Wills, William (junior) 167, 172
Wills, William (rioter) 64, 88, 107, 133, 136, 141, 144, 147, 151, 164, 167, 172
Wills–Cozens family 167
Wilson's Wonderful Characters 152
Winterbourne 15
women: and Courtenay 88, 127, 144–6, 176; literacy 145–6, 187; mourning 159; protest 88, 144–6, 176; reproduction 12, 48–9, 176; socialization 58; violence against 69–70, 132; and work 30, 36, 43–8, 49, 51, 52, 58, 78, 136, 179
Woodman's Hall (public house) 55
woodland 7–8, 32, 36, 48, 52, 54
woodstealers, wood-theft 8, 44, 54, 58, 71–2, 73, 138, 172
Woolright, Henry 20
work 42–8, 51–2, 144, 186
work gangs 144, 186
workhouse 59, 80, 81, 104, 131–2, 140, 159, 165, 166, 167, 182

226 Index

Wraight, Edward (junior) (rioter) 133–4, 136, 141, 144, 164, 166, 168
Wraight, Edward (senior) (rioter) 30, 132, 133, 141, 147, 158
Wraight, Elias 166
Wraight, Hannah 41
Wraight, James (junior), farmer 27, 41
Wraight, James (rioter) 136, 140, 141, 144, 166
Wraight, James (senior), farmer 27
Wraight, Mary (of Boughton) 69
Wraight, Mary (wife of Edward sr., rioter) 30
Wraight, Mary (wife of Noah Miles) 41, 132
Wraight, Sarah 134, 144, 145, 166
Wraight, Susanna 41
Wraight, William (senior) 41, 74, 75, 76, 77, 144
Wrightson, K. 182
Wrigley, E. A. 80

Yeo, Eileen 178
Yocketts (or Yorkletts) Farm 23, 32